Socialism: A Reader

Socialism: A Reader

Introduced by

Sanil M. Neelakandan

AAKAR

Socialism: A Reader

First Aakar Edition 2019

ISBN 978-93-5002-620-5

Published by
AAKAR BOOKS
28 E Pocket IV, Mayur Vihar Phase I
Delhi 110 091
www.aakarbooks.com

Designed by
Limited Colors, Delhi 110 092

Printed at
D.K. Fine Art Press, Delhi

Contents

Introduction

The neoliberal phase of capitalism is relentlessly unleashing its disastrous effect across the globe, where political articulations are being complicated by the protean character of capitalism; religion is being revived through the vicious nexus of neoliberal ideologues and detrimental clergy; knowledge that possesses a radical edge has succumbed to the charming, albeit reactionary, ideas of the self-consumed oligarchy, resulting in depoliticised democracy; the global right is acquiring its unique space through skewed economism; and, a repressive state is busy chanting the mantra of ethical capitalism.

One may wonder that the popular understanding of 'business ethics' as well as 'capitalism with a human face' is being circulated as synonyms of praxis in the space of political inertia. The neoliberal state also represses the struggles of people in a ruthless manner. The key questions that come up at such a political juncture are: how does the working class react to this pernicious onslaught of neoliberalism? What are the political moves that can enable them to challenge the capitalistic vicissitudes? Questions of class are being highly re-read in the context of a post-linguistic-driven social theory. For instance, Gary Browning has challenged the claims of the global theory that projects itself as different from the classical theories related to capitalism, class and so on (Browning, 2011).

The consciousness of the working class is usually analysed in the backdrop of the struggle against capitalism. Socialist consciousness and its readings by the diverse leftist traditions have undergone major changes across the world. One of the central questions that is usually asked is: how does class antagonism get rearticulated in the contemporary world? The postmodern tirade against diverse forms of social and political critiques has raised major theoretical challenges as well as inactions. Theorists and activists are conscious of the capitalist ideology that neutralises radical struggles against exploitative social and political systems. At the same time, the fall of socialism was celebrated by the remorseless global right and corporate lobbies. However, complex global conditions force us to revisit the larger questions of socialism. Marxism, for Geoffrey Pilling, understands its character of struggle in the direction of socialist consciousness (Pilling, 2010: 135). Rudolf Schlesinger emphasised the future of socialism within the frameworks of a socialist formation of state and a revolutionary socialist state (Schlesinger, 2010: 253). Scepticism is also prevalent in reducing socialism to particular parts of the world, such as the former Eastern Soviet Block. Soviet ethics are also compared with that of socialist internationalism (Kubalkova and Cruickshank, 2018: 227). Simultaneously, we are being bombarded with multiple tropes of socialism in the matrix of an eclectic social media. Such proliferation of constructions of socialism is being questioned, as well. Most of such theorizations have created an ambiguous understanding related to socialism and communism. Karl Marx's understanding of socialism, for Paresh Chattopadhyay, is different from the broader, popular theoretical understanding of socialism (Chattopadhyay, 2018: 37). According to Marx, 'Socialism is neither the transition to communism nor the lower phase of communism. It is communism *tout court*' (Chattopadhyay, 2018: 37). It is further analysed that 'the only human and humane alternative to the inhuman reign of capital is socialism–the association of free individuals, as Marx envisaged it' (Chattopadhyay, 2018: 56).

For Jacques Bidet, Marx's discourse on socialism is, in reality, prescriptive: it affirms the unity of theoretical and practical reasons—the rationality of production and equality of participation, respectively (Bidet, 2015: 286). Leon Trotsky, however, departed from the Menshevik reduction related to socialism and freedom. It is observed that 'the road to socialism lies through the highest concentration of state power...like a light bulb, which, before extinguishing itself, flashes brightly, so as the state, prior to its disappearance, takes the form of the dictatorship of the proletariat, i.e. of the pitiless state, which coercively...controls the life of the citizens in all aspects' (Trotsky, cited in Nove, 2018: 13). On the other hand, Daniel Guerin, the anarchist, fiercely discards the illusory, bourgeois democracy than the totalitarian socialist (Guerin, 2010: 17). Adolf Fischer opined that 'every anarchist is a socialist but not every socialist is necessarily an anarchist (Fischer, cited in Chomsky, 2010: xii).

The category of socialism is contested. B.R. Ambedkar raised pertinent enquiries related to socialism and caste in India. He suspected whether one can have economic reform without first bringing about a reform of the social order (Ambedkar, 1989: 46). Socialism in India is also theorised through critical Buddhist realism such as *Sauntrantikavada* (Patil, 2005: 298). Direct socialism for an Asiatic mode of production is conceptualised through 'a direct jump of skipping the entire capitalist mode of production' (Jal, 2017: xxix). Indian socialism is criticised for having a particular approach that 'has not been able to draw a fine line between its national vision and that of the Indian right' (Prashad, 2015: 111) Ideological differences within the socialist camp were delineated through categorizations, such as 'socialist capitalism of Scandinavia' and the 'capitalist socialism of Yugoslavia' (Boulding, 1965: 167). Still, socialism is much reflected in the history of the working class and unions. A moral critique of capitalism via socialism is analysed as central to the labour movement. For instance, Harold Gibbons argued that socialism 'gave me a picture of the nature of the society we live in' (Gibbons, cited in Bussel, 2015: 19). Leftist traditions are also reflexive about the genealogy of socialist debates. Hugo Chavez deployed the category of '21st century socialism' as a departure from the prior connotations related to the socialism of the Eastern Soviet Block and foregrounded it as one that assures a new vision without 'resorting to state capitalism' (Chavez, cited in Harnecker, 2015: 58–9). Socialism is facing ideological, fastidious critiques from social democrats.

There are critiques on the ways in which socialism is being interpreted. For instance, Alexandria Ocasio-Cortez argued that 'what it (democratic socialism) means to me is healthcare as a social right, it means that every child no matter where you are born should have access to a college or trade school education, if they so choose it. I think that no person should be homeless if we have public structures or public policy to allow for people to have homes and food and lead a dignified life in the United States' (Alexandria, cited in Desan and Michael, 2018). According to Mathieu Desan and Michael A. McCarthy, 'while these reforms are crucial to countering the misery we face under capitalism, it runs the risk of equating socialism with welfare liberalism or social democracy. But these things are not the same' (Desan and Michael, 2018). Socialism in the European context is facing major theoretical and political challenges. The question of leaving the traditional baggage of Marxism in the context of the French electoral discourse is analysed as the complex character of the contemporary French left (Andrieu, 2007). The aforementioned perspectives may be helpful to have a meaningful return to the fundamental debate on socialism.

Essays in this Reader attempt to revisit the rudimentary debates that reflect on the multiple dimensions of socialism. These essays by renowned thinkers will enable us to map the spirit of socialism. Robert Owen, in his introductory essay, looks at the emergence of ideas from across the globe. Owen delineated the contradictions between theory and practice. He emphasised the necessity to carve out universal space. Rationality was one of the core words in his approach. Owen underlined the intricacies of socialism and its impact on human civilization. He argued for the collectivism that is grounded in reading, writing and knowledge. Marxism provided a distinct twist to this debate. Friedrich Engels analysed the nature of communism and the origin of the proletariat as the core background to the principles of communism. Engels also described the emergence of the big capitalist class and the property-less classes. The historical transformation of the working class is narrated to understand the differences between slaves and the proletariat. The abolition of private property is discussed as a precondition for the emancipation of slaves, as well as of the proletariat. Democracy and the sustenance of the working class are analysed as a means to envisage the direction of the proletariat. Communists are also differentiated from socialists through their world views and practices. The hagiographies of socialism are questioned through a candid portrayal of the reactionary socialists as traitors to the revolution. Bourgeois socialists are examined as groups within socialists who are obsessed with welfare reform measures and anti-communist approaches. Karl Marx and Friedrich Engels explicated the ways in which diverse forms of power suppress the labour through appropriation. Socialism is also analysed as appropriated by Christian asceticism. Petty bourgeois socialism is also evaluated as status-quoist, orthodox and utopian. True and German socialism is analysed as an ideological project that aimed to destroy the industrial and political supremacy of the bourgeois. It is critiqued as a stream within socialism that challenged the concentration of capital. Conservative or bourgeois socialism is analysed as one that requires all benefits of modern social change without any struggle. It is criticised as systemic without engaging with revolution. It is also shown as an ideological articulation that desires a bourgeois society without the working class. The paternalistic tendencies of the bourgeois towards the working class are also criticised as part of a critical understanding of socialism. They also reflect on the possibilities of a critical utopian socialism. It is viewed as one that lacks in the clear articulation of class distinctions. At the same time, Marx and Engels vehemently questioned the socialist tendencies that rejected political and revolutionary action. An experimental recognition of social utopianism appeared in their perspectives. Marx in his works analysed the alienation of labour, and the product of the labour and its relationship with the estranged labour and private property. He also emphasised equal rights and labour beyond the means of life. One of the central facets that was stressed was the revolutionary dictatorship of the proletariat. On the other hand, Eduard Bernstein in his essay analysed the transition from revolutionary socialism to evolutionary socialism via revisionism. These debates are analysed in the context of the *Communist Manifesto* and the evolution of modern society. Bernstein was also sceptical whether the appropriation of political power by the working class would lead to social democracy or not. The struggle of the German social democracy for the political and economic rights of the German working class is also analysed to map the growth of socialism. An essay by Alexandre Millerand articulated the consequence of socialism on the reformists. At the same time, the socialist impact on the reformists was probed through the nuances of French socialist reformism. Millerand also demonstrated how truncated versions of socialism according to political transformations diverted themselves from the quintessential nature of socialism. The core arguments on socialism, for Millerand, have to move beyond the rhetoric related to socialism. Sidney Webb shared a different approach related to socialism. The formulation of socialism is not reduced to the replacement of one political machinery by the other. Socialism is viewed as one project that accelerates democracy. The end of the privileged is considered as the consequence of the progress in democracy. Socialism is largely read in the context of economic realities. Webb also emphasised the economic and social protection as well as the political power of the worker. On the perspectives related to socialism and anarchism, G.V. Plekhanov shared the commonalities between the French materialists and socialists in relation to their pursuit of social organization. A comparative approach to legislation was carried out to arrive at the understandings on social organizations. While analysing socialism and political struggles, Plekhanov, in another essay, initiated the discussion with the potential of Narodism, and his departure from it due to its political limitations. This pamphlet is deployed as an ideological ground to spell out his differences with Narodism. The archetypal nature of socialism is analysed through his rigorous critique of the anarchist perceptions about the state. Thus, the Bakunian anarchism based on political non-interference is also explained to show the ideological differences between socialism and anarchism. The political movement of the working class and the scientific socialism's materialistic conception of history are central to this essay. The coexistence of economic and political revolution and the socialist understanding of Marxism are regarded as integral parts to the development of the socialist approach. One of the germane questions that is discussed in this context is that whether the bourgeois leadership should organise the working class to fight against the bourgeois. It is further emphasised that the working class has to overthrow capitalism in order to regain science. The Russian social reality is also evaluated through the internal differences that exist across the Russian left. The objective conditions for production are pointed out as the essential basis for the blooming of socialism. Rosa Luxemburg, in her essay, delineated the background to the facile distinctions between religion and socialism. The attempt is to map the historical anchorages of the Marxist treatment of socialism. Conflicts between the socialist democrats and the church are explored to challenge the usual, exiguous frame related to religion and socialism. The Church is critiqued as the religious force that pacifies the pro-poor, anti-capitalist assertions of the socialist democrats. Luxemburg also delineated how the privilege was being defended through the gaps between the principles and practices of the Church. The egalitarian dimensions of Christianity and its limits are analysed as incompetent to subvert the power structure. It is further explored as to how Christianity acquired the form of a religious establishment and departed from the revolutionary nature of the first apostles. A historical overview of the schisms within Christianity and its gradual surrender to capitalism is captured in order to rethink about the possibilities of socialism. Religion is being forcefully articulated in the heyday of the capitalistic phase of neoliberalism and postmodern, non-committal, academic capitalistic cultures. The politicization of religion has encompassed all spheres of human life. The political interventions of Lenin contributed to unique frameworks on socialism. Religious indoctrination was critiqued by Lenin as an ideological obstacle that deterred the working class from their struggle against capitalism. Lenin's perspective foregrounds the revolutionary working class which embraced socialism and discarded religion. One of the central facets of Lenin's writings is that it articulates how religion should be treated as a private affair and how it should be differentiated from the state. It is further argued that the Party should consider religion as a private affair. It is further argued that the Party should declare religion as a private affair. The states that defend religion as a sound premise to establish socialism are also criticised. Lenin attempted to debunk the historical and economic roots of 'religious fog' (in his own words). At the same time, he invoked a return to the Enlightenment, thus making us aware about the entrenched nuances of religion and its calamitous impact on the political consciousness of workers. Broadly, this Reader is an attempt to rethink about the wilderness and the possibilities of socialism. Such an endeavour is essential in a political conjuncture determined by the nostalgia for Enlightenment and the spectacles of counter-enlightenment. A return to reason may thus prevail through big explorations related to socialism, communism and new political imaginations.

References

Ambedkar, B.R. 1989. *Caste in India: Their Mechanism, Genesis and Development. BAWS* 1, Edited by Vasant Moon. Education Department, Government of India, pp. 32–80.

Andrieu, Hector. 2007. *A Lost Left: The Soul of French Socialism.* Available at https://www.opendemocracy.net/globalization-institutions_government/lost_left_4672.jsp (accessed December 2018).

Bidet, Jacques. 2015. *Exploring Marx's Capital: Philosophical, Economic and Political Dimensions.* Translated by David Fernbach. Delhi: Aakar Books.

Boulding, Kenneth. 1965. *The Meaning of the Twentieth Century: The Great Transition.* London: George Allen and Unwin Ltd.

Browning, Gary. 2011. *Global Theory from Kant to Hardt and Negri.* Palgrave Macmillan.

Bussel, Robert. 2015. *Fighting for Total Person Unionism: Harold Gibbons, Ernest Galloway and Working-Class Citizenship*. Urbana, Chicago and Springfield: University of Illinois Press.

Chattopadhyay, Paresh. 2018. *The Myth of Twentieth Century Socialism and the Continuing Relevance of Karl Marx'*, in Marcello Musto (Ed), *Marx for Today*. Delhi: Aakar Books, pp. 36–58.

Chomsky, Noam. 2010. Introduction, in Daniel Guerin, *Anarchism: From Theory to Practice*. Delhi: Aakar Books, pp. vii–xx.

Desan, Mathieu and Michael A. McCarthy. 2018. *A Time to Be Bold*. Available at https://jacobinmag.com/2018/07/socialism-democrats-alexandria-ocasio-cortez (accessed December 2018).

Engels, Friedrich. 1978. *Socialism: Utopian and Scientific*. Moscow: Progress Publishers.

Guerin, Daniel. 2010. *Anarchism: From Theory to Practice*. Delhi: Aakar Books.

Harnecker, Marta. 2015. *A World to Build: New Paths Toward Twenty-First Century Socialism*. Delhi: Aakar Books.

Jal, Murzban. 2017. Introduction: 'In the Name of Marx', in Murzban Jal (ed.), *Challenges for the Indian Left*. Delhi: Aakar Books, pp. xi–xcii.

Kubalkova, V., and Cruickshank, A. 2018. *Marxism-Leninism and the Theory of International Relations*. London and New York: Routledge.

Nove, A. 2018. *Marxism and 'Really Existing Socialism'*. London and New York: Routledge.

Patil, Sharad. 2005. *Caste-Ending Bourgeois Democratic Revolution and Its Socialist Consummation*. Pune: Mavalai Prakashan.

Pilling, Geoffrey. 2010. *Marx's 'Capital' Philosophy and Political Economy*. London and New York: Routledge.

Prashad, Vijay. 2015. *No Free Left: The Futures of Indian Communism*. New Delhi: LeftWord.

Schlesinger, Rudolf. 2010. *Marx His Times and Ours*. London and New York: Routledge.

1

A New View of Society, or, Essays on the Principles of the Formation of the Human Character, and the Application of the Principles to Practice

Robert Owen

Any general character, from the best to the worst, from the most ignorant to the most enlightened, may be given to any community, even to the world at large, by the application of proper means; which means are to a great extent at the command and under the control of those who have influence in the affairs of men.

According to the last returns under the Population Act, the poor and working classes of Great Britain and Ireland have been found to exceed fifteen millions of persons, or nearly three-fourths of the population of the British Islands. The characters of these persons are now permitted to be very generally formed without proper guidance or direction, and, in many cases, under circumstances which directly impel them to a course of extreme vice and misery; thus rendering them the worst and most dangerous subjects in the empire; while the far greater part of the remainder of the community are educated upon the most mistaken principles of human nature, such, indeed, as cannot fail to produce a general conduct throughout society, totally unworthy of the character of rational beings.

The first thus unhappily situated are the poor and the uneducated profligate among the working classes, who are now trained to commit crimes, for the commission of which they are afterwards punished.

The second is the remaining mass of the population, who are now instructed to believe, or at least to acknowledge, that certain principles are unerringly true, and to act as though they were grossly false; thus filling the world with folly and inconsistency, and making society, throughout all its ramifications, a scene of insincerity and counteraction.

In this state the world has continued to the present time; its evils have been and are continually increasing; they cry aloud for efficient corrective measures, which if we longer delay, general disorder must ensue. 'But,' say those who have not deeply investigated the subject, 'attempts to apply remedies have been often made, yet all of them have failed. The evil is now of a magnitude not to be controlled; the torrent is already too strong to be stemmed; and we can only wait with fear or calm resignation to see it carry destruction in its course, by confounding all distinctions of right and wrong.'

Such is the language now held, and such are the general feelings on this most important subject. These, however, if longer suffered to continue, must lead to the most lamentable consequences. Rather than pursue such a course, the character of legislators would be infinitely raised, if, forgetting the petty and humiliating contentions of sects and parties, they would thoroughly investigate the subject, and endeavour to arrest and overcome these mighty evils. The chief object of these essays is to assist and forward investigations of such vital importance to the well-being of this country, and of society in general. The view of the subject which is about to be given has arisen from extensive experience for upwards of twenty years, during which period its truth and importance have been proved by multiplied experiments. That the writer may not be charged with precipitation or presumption, he has had the principle and its consequences examined, scrutinized, and fully canvassed, by some of the most learned, intelligent, and competent characters of the present day: who, on every principle of duty as well as of interest, if they had discovered error in either, would have exposed it—but who, on the contrary, have fairly acknowledged their incontrovertible truth and practical importance.

Assured, therefore, that his principles are true, he proceeds with confidence, and courts the most ample and free discussion of the subject; courts it for the sake of humanity—for the sake of his fellow creatures millions of whom experience sufferings which, were they to be unfolded, would compel those who govern the world to exclaim —'Can these things exist and we have no knowledge of them?' but they do exist and even the heart-rending statements which are made known to the public during the discussions upon negro-slavery, do not exhibit more afflicting scenes than those which, in various parts of the world, daily arise from the injustice of society towards itself; from the inattention of mankind to the circumstances which incessantly surround them; and from the want of a correct knowledge of human nature in those who govern and control the affairs of men.

If these circumstances did not exist to an extent almost incredible, it would be unnecessary now to contend for a principle regarding Man, which scarcely requires more than to be fairly stated to make it self-evident.

This principle is, that 'Any general character, from the best to the worst, from the most ignorant to the most enlightened, may be given to any community, even to the world at large, by the application of proper means,' which means are to a great extent at the command and under the control of those who have influence in the affairs of men,' The principle as now stated is a broad one, and, if it should be found to be true, cannot fail to find a new character to legislative proceedings, and such a character as will be most favourable to the well-being of society. That this principle is true to the utmost limit of the terms, is evident from the experience of all past ages, and from every existing fact.

Shall misery, then, most complicated and extensive, be experienced, from the prince to the peasant, throughout all the nations of the world, and shall its cause and the means of its prevention be known, and yet these means withheld? The undertaking is replete with difficulties which can only be overcome by those who have influence in society: who, by foreseeing its important practical benefits, may be induced to contend against those difficulties; and who, when its advantages are clearly seen and strongly felt, will not suffer individual considerations to be put in competition with their attainment. It is true their ease and comfort may be for a time sacrificed to those prejudices; but, if they persevere, the principles on which this knowledge is founded must ultimately universally prevail. In preparing the way for the introduction of these principles, it cannot now be necessary to enter into the detail of acts to prove that children can be trained to acquire 'any language, sentiments, belief, or any bodily habits and manners, not contrary to human nature'.

For that this has been done, the history of every nation of which we have records, abundantly confirms; and that this is, and may be again done, the facts which exist around us and throughout all the countries in the world, prove to demonstration. Possessing, then, the knowledge of a power so important, which when understood is capable of being wielded with the certainty of a law of nature, and which would gradually remove the evils which now chiefly afflict mankind, shall we permit it to remain dormant and useless, and suffer the plagues of society perpetually to exist and increase?

No: the time is now arrived when the public mind of this country, and the general state of the world, call imperatively for the introduction of this all-pervading principle, not only in theory, but into practice.

Nor can any human power now impede its rapid progress. Silence will not retard its course, and opposition will give increased celerity to its movements. The commencement of the work will, in fact, ensure its accomplishment; henceforth all the irritating angry passions, arising from ignorance of the true cause of bodily and mental character, will gradually subside, and be replaced by the most frank and conciliating confidence and goodwill.

Nor will it be possible hereafter for comparatively a few individuals unintentionally to occasion the rest of mankind to be surrounded by circumstances which inevitably form such characters as they afterwards deem it a duty and a right to punish even to death; and that, too, while they themselves have been the instruments of forming those characters. Such proceedings not only create innumerable evils to the directing few, but essentially retard them and the great mass of society from attaining the enjoyment of a high degree of positive happiness.

Instead of punishing crimes after they have permitted the human character to be formed so as to commit them, they will adopt the only means which can be adopted to prevent the existence of those crimes; means by which they may be most easily prevented. Happily for poor traduced and degraded human nature, the principle for which we now contend will speedily divest it of all the ridiculous and absurd mystery with which it has been hitherto enveloped by the ignorance of preceding times: and all the complicated and counteracting motives for good conduct; which have been multiplied almost to infinity, will be reduced to one single principle of action, which, by its evident operation and sufficiency, shall render this intricate system unnecessary: and ultimately supersede it in all parts of the earth. That principle is the happiness of self, clearly understood and uniformly practised; which can only be attained by conduct that must promote the happiness of the community. For that power which governs and pervades the universe has, evidently so formed man, that he must progressively pass from a state of ignorance to intelligence, the limits of which it is not for man himself to define; and in that progress to discover, that his individual happiness can be increased and extended only in proportion as he actively endeavours to increase and extend the happiness of all around him. The principle admits neither of exclusion nor of limitation; and such appears evidently the state of the public mind, that it will now seize and cherish this principle as the most precious boon which it has yet been allowed to attain. The errors of all opposing motives will appear in their true light, and the ignorance whence they arose will become so glaring, that even the most unenlightened will speedily reject them.

For this state of matters, and for all the gradual changes contemplated, the extraordinary events of the present times have essentially contributed to prepare the way. Even the late Ruler of France, although immediately influenced by the most mistaken principles of ambition, has contributed to this happy result, by shaking to its foundation that mass of superstition and bigotry, which on the continent of Europe had been accumulating for ages, until it had so overpowered and depressed the human intellect, that to attempt improvement without its removal would have been most unavailing. And in the next place, by carrying the mistaken selfish principles in which mankind have been hitherto educated to the extreme in practice, he has rendered their error manifest, and left no doubt of the fallacy of the source whence they originated.

These transactions, in which millions have been immolated, or consigned to poverty and bereft of friends, will be preserved in the records of time, and impress future ages with a just estimation of the principles now about to be introduced into practice; and will thus prove perpetually useful to all succeeding generations.

For the direful effects of Napoleon's government have created the most deep-rooted disgust at notions which could produce a belief that such conduct was glorious, or calculated to increase the happiness of even the individual by whom it was pursued. And the late discoveries and proceedings of the Rev Dr Bell and Mr Joseph Lancaster have also been preparing the way, in a manner the most opposite, but yet not less effectual, by directing the public attention to the beneficial effects, on the young and unresisting mind, of even the limited education which their systems embrace.

They have already effected enough to prove that all which is now in contemplation respecting the training of youth may be accomplished without fear of disappointment. And by so doing, as the consequences of their improvements cannot be confined within the British Isles, they will for ever be ranked among the most important benefactors of the human race, but henceforward to contend for any new exclusive system will be in vain: the public mind is already too well informed, and has too far passed the possibility of retrogression, much longer to permit the continuance of any such evil. For it is now obvious that such a system must be destructive of the happiness of the excluded, by their seeing others enjoy what they are not permitted to possess; and also that it tends, by creating opposition from the justly injured feelings of the excluded, in proportion to the extent of the exclusion, to diminish the happiness even of the privileged: the former therefore can have no rational motive for its continuance. If, however, owing to the irrational principles by which the world has been hitherto governed, individuals, or sects, or parties, shall yet by their plans of exclusion attempt to retard the amelioration of society, and prevent the introduction into practice of that truly just spirit which knows no exclusion, such facts shall yet be brought forward as cannot fail to render all their efforts vain.

It will therefore be the essence of wisdom in the privileged class to cooperate sincerely and cordially with those who desire not to touch one iota of the supposed advantages which they now possess; and whose first and last wish is to increase the particular happiness of those classes, as well as the general happiness of society. A very little reflection on the part of the privileged will ensure this line of conduct; whence, without domestic revolution without war or bloodshed nay, without prematurely disturbing any thing which exists, the world will be prepared to receive principles which are alone calculated to build up a system of happiness, and to destroy those irritable feelings which have so long afflicted society solely because society has hitherto been ignorant of the true means by which the most useful and valuable character may be formed.

This ignorance being removed, experience will soon teach us how to form character, individually and generally, so as to give the greatest sum of happiness to the individual and to mankind. These principles require only to be known in order to establish themselves; the outline of our future proceedings then becomes clear and defined, nor will they permit us henceforth to wander from the right path. They direct that the governing powers of all countries should establish rational plans for the education and general formation of the characters of their subjects. These plans must be devised to train children from their earliest infancy in good habits of every description which will of course prevent them from acquiring those of falsehood and deception. They must afterwards be rationally educated, and their labour be usefully directed. Such habits and education will impress them with an active and ardent desire to promote the happiness of every individual, and that without the shadow of exceptions for sect, or party, or country, or climate. They will also ensure, with the fewest possible exceptions, health, strength, and vigour of body; for the happiness of man can be erected only on the foundations of health of body and peace of mind.

And that health of body and peace of mind may be preserved sound and entire, through youth and manhood, to old age, it becomes equally necessary that the irresistible propensities which form a part of his nature, and which now produce the endless and ever multiplying evils with which humanity is afflicted, should be so directed as to increase and not to counteract his happiness.

The knowledge however thus introduced will make it evident to the understanding, that by far the greater part of the misery with which man is encircled may be easily dissipated and removed; and that with mathematical precision he may be surrounded with those circumstances which must gradually increase his happiness. Hereafter, when the public at large shall be satisfied that these principles can and will withstand the ordeal through which they must inevitably pass; when they shall prove themselves true to the clear comprehension and certain conviction of the unenlightened as well as the learned; and when, by the irresistible power of truth, detached from falsehood, they shall establish themselves in the mind, no more to be removed but by the entire annihilation of human intellect; then the consequent practice which they direct shall be explained, and rendered easy of adoption.

In the meantime, let no one anticipate evil, even in the slightest degree, from these principles; they are not innoxious only, but pregnant with consequences to be wished and desired beyond all others by every individual in society. Some of the best intentioned among the various classes in society may still say, 'All this is very delightful and very beautiful in theory, but visionaries alone expect to see it realized.' To this remark only one reply can or ought to be made; that these principles have been carried most successfully into practice. (The beneficial effects of this practice have been experienced for, many years among a population of between two and three thousand at New Lanark, in Scotland; at Munich, in Bavaria; and in the Pauper Colonies, at Fredericks-oord.)

The present essays, therefore, are not brought forward as a mere matter of speculation, to amuse the idle visionary who thinks in his closet, and never acts in the world; but to create universal activity, pervade society with a knowledge of its true interests, and direct the public mind to the most important object to which it can be directed to a national proceeding for rationally forming the character of that immense mass of population which is now allowed to be so formed as to fill the world with crimes.

Shall questions of merely local and temporary interest, whose ultimate results are calculated only to withdraw pecuniary profits from one set of individuals and give them to others, engage day after day the attention of politicians and ministers; call forth petitions and delegates from the widely spread agricultural and commercial interests of the empire and shall the well-being of millions of the poor, half-naked, half-famished, untaught, and untrained, hourly increasing to a most alarming extent in these islands, not call forth one petition, one delegate, or one rational effective legislative measure? No! for such has been our education, that we hesitate not to devote years and expend millions in the detection and punishment of crimes, and in the attainment of objects whose ultimate results are, in comparison with this, insignificancy itself: and yet we have not moved one step in the true path to prevent crimes, and to diminish the innumerable evils with which mankind are now afflicted.

Are these false principles of conduct in those who govern the world to influence mankind permanently? And if not, how, and when is the change to commence? These important considerations shall form the subject of the next essay.

* * *

> The Principles of the Former Essay continued, and applied in part to practice. It is not unreasonable to hope that hostility may cease, even where perfect agreement cannot be established. If we cannot reconcile all opinions, let us endeavour to unite all hearts.

General principles only were developed in the First Essay. In this an attempt will be made to show the advantages which may be derived from the adoption of those principles into practice, and to explain the mode by which the practice may, without inconvenience, be generally introduced. Some of the most important benefits to be derived from the introduction of those principles into practice are, that they will create the most cogent reasons to induce each man 'to have charity for all men'. No feeling short of this can indeed find place in any mind which has been taught clearly to understand that children in all parts of the earth have been, are, and everlastingly will be, impressed with habits and sentiments similar to those of their parents and instructors; modified, however, by the circumstances in which they have been, are, or may be placed, and by the peculiar organizations of each individual. Yet not one of these causes of character is at the command, or in any manner under the control of infants, who (whatever absurdity we may have been taught to the contrary), cannot possibly be accountable for the sentiments and manners which may be given to them. And here lies the fundamental error of society; and from hence have proceeded, and do proceed, most of the miseries of mankind.

Children are, without exception, passive and wonderfully contrived compounds; which, by an accurate previous and subsequent attention, founded on a correct knowledge of the subject, may be formed collectively to have any human character. And although these compounds, like all the other works of nature, possess endless varieties, yet they partake of that plastic quality, which, by perseverance under judicious management, may be ultimately moulded into the very image of rational wishes and desires.

In the next place these principles cannot fail to create feelings which, without force or the production of any counteracting motive, will irresistibly lead those who possess them to make due allowance for the difference of sentiments and manners, not only among their friends and countrymen, but also among the inhabitants of every region of the earth, even including their enemies. With this insight into the formation of character, there is no conceivable foundation for private displeasure or public enmity. Say, if it be within the sphere of possibility that children can be trained to attain that knowledge, and at the same time to acquire feelings of enmity towards a single human creature? The child who from infancy has been rationally instructed in these principles, will readily discover and trace whence the opinions and habits of his associates have arisen, and why they possess them. At the same age he will have acquired reason sufficient to exhibit to him forcibly the irrationality of being angry with an individual for possessing qualities which, as a passive being during the formation of those qualities, he had not the means of preventing.

Such are the impressions these principles will make on the mind of every child so taught; and, instead of generating anger or displeasure, they will produce commiseration and pity for those individuals who possess either habits or sentiments which appear to him to be destructive of their own comfort, pleasure, or happiness; and will produce on his part a desire to remove those causes of distress, and his own feelings of commiseration and pity may be also removed. The pleasure which he cannot avoid experiencing by this mode of conduct will likewise stimulate him to the most active endeavours to withdraw those circumstances which surround any part of mankind with causes of misery, and to replace them with others which have a tendency to increase happiness. He will then also strongly entertain the desire 'to do good to all men', and even to those who think themselves his enemies.

Thus shortly, directly, and certainly may mankind be taught the essence, and to attain the ultimate object, of all former moral and religious instruction. These essays, however, are intended to explain that which is true, and not to attack that which is false. For to explain that which is true may permanently improve, without creating even temporary evil; whereas to attack that which is false, is often productive of very fatal consequences. The former convinces the judgement when the mind possesses full and deliberate powers of judging; the latter instantly arouses irritation, and renders the judgement unfit for its office, and useless. But why should we ever irritate? Do not these principles make it so obvious as to place it beyond any doubt, that even the present irrational ideas and practices prevalent throughout the world are not to be charged as either a fault or a culpable error of the existing generation? The immediate cause of them was the partial ignorance of our forefathers, who, although they acquire some vague disjointed knowledge of the principles on which character is formed, could not discover the connected chain of those principles, and consequently knew not how to apply them to practice. They taught their children that which they had themselves been taught, that which they had acquired, and in so doing they acted like their forefathers; who retained the established customs of former generations until better and superior were discovered and made evident to them.

The present race of men have also instructed their children as they had been previously instructed, and are equally unblameable for any defects which their systems contain. And however erroneous or injurious that instruction and those systems may now be proved to be, the principles on which these essays are founded will be misunderstood, and their spirit will be wholly misconceived, if either irritation or the slightest degree of ill will shall be generated against those who even tenaciously adhere to the worst parts of that instruction, and support the most pernicious of those systems. For such individuals, sects, or parties have been trained from infancy to consider it their duty and interest so to act, and in so acting they merely continue the customs of their predecessors. Let truth unaccompanied with error be placed before them; give them time to examine it and to see that it is in unison with all previously ascertained truths; and conviction and acknowledgement of it will follow of course. It is weakness itself to require assent before conviction; and afterwards it will not be withheld. To endeavour to force conclusions without making the subject clear to the understanding, is most unjustifiable and irrational, and must prove useless or injurious to the mental faculties.

In the spirit thus described we therefore proceed in the investigation of the subject. The facts which by the invention of printing have gradually accumulated now show the errors of the systems of our forefathers so distinctly, that they must be, when pointed out, evident to all classes of the community, and render it absolutely necessary that new legislative measures be immediately adopted to prevent the confusion which must arise from even the most ignorant being competent to detect the absurdity and glaring injustice of many of those laws by which they are now governed.

Such are those laws which enact punishments for a very great variety of actions designated crimes; while those from whom such actions proceed are regularly trained to acquire no other knowledge than that which compels them to conclude that those actions are the best they could perform.

How much longer shall we continue to allow generation after generation to be taught crime from their infancy, and, when so taught, hunt them like beasts of the forest, until they are entangled beyond escape in the toils and nets of the law? When, if the circumstances of those poor unpitied sufferers had been reversed with those who are even surrounded with the pomp and dignity of justice, these latter would have been at the bar of the culprit, and the former would have been in the judgement seat.

Had the present judges of these realms been born and educated among the poor and profligate of St Giles's or some similar situation, it is not certain, inasmuch as they possess native energies and abilities, that ere this they would have been at the head of their then profession, and, in consequence of that superiority and proficiency, would have already suffered imprisonment, transportation, or death? Can we for a moment hesitate to decide, that if some of those men whom the laws dispensed by the present judges have doomed to suffer capital punishments, had been born, trained, and circumstanced, as these judges were born, trained, and circumstanced, that some of those who had so suffered would have been the identical individuals who would have passed the same awful sentences on the present highly esteemed dignitaries of the law.

If we open our eyes and attentively notice events, we shall observe these facts to multiply before us. Is the evil then of so small magnitude as to be totally disregarded and passed by as the ordinary occurrences of the day, and as not deserving of one reflection? And shall we be longer told, that the convenient time to attend to inquiries of this nature is not yet come: that other matters of far weightier import engage our attention, and it must remain over till a season of more leisure?'

To those who may be inclined to think and speak thus, I would say 'Let feelings of humanity or strict justice induce you to devote a few hours to visit some of the public prisons of the metropolis, and patiently inquire, with kind commiserating solicitude, of their various inhabitants, the events of their lives and the lives of their various connections. Then will tales unfold that must arrest attention, that will disclose sufferings, misery, and injustice, upon which, for obvious reasons, will not now dwell, but which previously, I am persuaded, you could not suppose it possible to exist in any civilized state, far less that they should be permitted for centuries to increase around the very fountain of British jurisprudence.' The true cause, however, of this conduct, so contrary to the general humanity of the natives of these Islands, is, that a practical remedy for the evil, on clearly defined and sound principles, had not yet been suggested. But the principles developed in this 'New View of Society', will point out a remedy which is almost simplicity itself, possessing no more practical difficulties than many of the common employments of life,; and such as are readily overcome by men of very ordinary practical talents. That such a remedy is easily practicable, may be collected from the account of the following very partial experiment. In the year 1784 the late Mr Dale, of Glasgow, founded a manufactory for spinning of cotton, near the falls of the Clyde, in the county of Lanark, in Scotland; and about that period cotton mills were first introduced into the northern part of the kingdom.

It was the power which could be obtained from the falls of water that induced Mr Dale to erect his mills in this situation; for in other respects it was not well chosen. The country around was uncultivated; the inhabitants were poor and few in number; and the roads in the neighbourhood were so bad, that the Falls, now so celebrated, were then unknown to strangers. It was therefore necessary to collect a new population to supply, the infant establishment with labourers. This, however, was no light task; for all the regularly trained Scotch peasantry disdained the idea of working early and late, day after day, within cotton mills. Two modes then only remained of obtaining these labourers; the one, to procure children from the various public charities of the country; and the other, to induce families to settle around the works.

To accommodate the first, a large house was erected, which ultimately contained about 500 children, who were procured chiefly from workhouses and charities in Edinburgh. These children were to be fed, clothed, and educated; and these duties Mr Dale performed with the unwearied benevolence which it is well known he possessed.

To obtain the second, a village was built; and the houses were lėt at a low rent to such families as could be induced to accept employment in the mills; but such was the general dislike of that occupation at the time, that, with a few exceptions, only those destitute of friends, employment, and character, were found willing to try the experiment; and of these a sufficient number to supply a constant increase of the manufactory could not be obtained. It was therefore deemed a favour on the part even of such individuals to reside at the village, and, when taught the business, they grew so valuable to the establishment, that they became agents not to be governed contrary to their own inclinations.

Mr Dale's principal avocations were at a distance from the works, which he seldom visited more than once for a few hours in three or four months; he was therefore under the necessity of committing the management of the establishment to various servants with more or less power.

Those who have a practical knowledge of mankind will readily anticipate the character which a population so collected and constituted would acquire. It is therefore scarcely necessary to state, that the community by degrees was formed under these circumstances into a very wretched society... every man did that which was right in his own eyes, and vice and immorality prevailed to a monstrous extent. The population lived in idleness, in poverty, in almost every kind of crime; consequently, in debt, out of health, and in misery. Yet to make matters still worse although the cause proceeded from the best possible motive, a conscientious adherence to principle the whole was under a strong sectarian influence, which gave a marked and decided preference to one set of religious opinions over all others, and the professors of the favoured opinions were the privileged of the community.

The boarding-house containing the children presented a very different scene. The benevolent proprietor spared no expense to give comfort to the poor children. The rooms provided for them were spacious, always clean, and well ventilated; the food was abundant, and of the best quality; the clothes were neat and useful; a surgeon was kept in constant pay, to direct how to prevent or cure disease; and the best instructors which the country afforded were appointed to teach such branches of education as were deemed likely to be useful to children in their situation. Kind and well-disposed people were appointed to superintend all their proceedings. Nothing, in short, at first sight seemed wanting to render it a most complete charity.

But to defray the expense of these well-devised arrangements, and to support the establishment generally, it was absolutely necessary that the children should be employed within the mills from six o'clock in the morning till seven in the evening, summer and winter; and after these hours their education commenced. The directors of the public charities, from mistaken economy, would not consent to send the children under their care to cotton mills, unless the children were received by the proprietors at the ages of six, seven and eight. And Mr Dale was under the necessity of accepting them at those ages, or of stopping the manufactory which he had commenced.

It is not to be supposed that children so young could remain, with the intervals of meals only, from six in the morning until seven in the evening, in constant employment, on their feet, within cotton mills, and afterwards acquire much proficiency in education. And so it proved; for many of them became dwarfs in body and mind, and some of them were deformed. Their labour through the day and their education at night became so irksome, that numbers of them continually ran away, and almost all looked forward with impatience and anxiety to the expiration of their apprenticeship of seven, eight, and nine years, which generally expired when they were from thirteen to fifteen years old. At this period of life, unaccustomed to provide for themselves, and unacquainted with the world, they usually went to Edinburgh or Glasgow, where boys and girls were soon assailed by the innumerable temptations which all large towns present, and to which many of them fell sacrifices.Thus Mr Dale's arrangements, and his kind solicitude for the comfort and happiness of these children, were rendered in their ultimate effect almost nugatory. They were hired by him and sent to be employed, and without their labour he could not support them; but, while under his care, he did all that any individual, circumstanced as he was, could do for his fellow creatures. The error proceeded from the children being sent from the workhouses at an age much too young for employment. They ought to have been detained four years longer, and educated; and then some of the evils which followed would have been prevented. If such be a true picture, not overcharged, of parish apprentices to our manufacturing system, under the best and most humane regulations, in what colours must it be exhibited under the worst?

Mr Dale was advancing in years: he had no son to succeed him; and, finding the consequences just described to be the result of all his strenuous exertions for the improvement and happiness of his fellow creatures, it is not surprising that he became disposed to retire from the cares of the establishment. He accordingly sold it to some English merchants and manufacturers; one of whom, under the circumstances just narrated, undertook the management of the concern, and fixed his residence in the midst of the population. This individual had been previously in the management of large establishments, employing a number of workpeople, in the neighbourhood of Manchester, and, in every case, by the steady application of certain general principles, he succeeded in reforming the habits of those under his care, and who always, among their associates in similar employment, appeared conspicuous for their good conduct. With this previous success in remodelling English character, but ignorant of the local ideas, manners, and customs, of those now committed to his management, the stranger commenced his task.

At that time the lower classes of Scotland, like those of other countries, had strong prejudices against strangers having any authority over them, and particularly against the English, few of whom had then settled in Scotland, and not one in the neighbourhood of the scenes under description. It is also well known that even the Scotch peasantry and working classes possess the habit of making observations and reasoning thereon with great acuteness; and in the present case those employed naturally concluded that the new purchasers intended merely to make the utmost profit by the establishment, from the abuses of which many of themselves were then deriving support. The persons employed at these works were therefore strongly prejudiced against the new director of the establishment prejudiced, because he was a stranger, and from England—because he succeeded Mr Dale, under whose proprietorship they acted almost as they liked because his religious creed was not theirs—and because they concluded that the works would be governed by new laws and regulations, calculated to squeeze, as they often termed it, the greatest sum of gain out of their labour.

In consequence, from the day he arrived amongst them every means which ingenuity could devise was set to work to counteract the plan which he attempted to introduce; and for two years it was a regular attack and defence of prejudices and malpractices between the manager and the population of the place, without the former being able to make much progress, or to convince the latter of the sincerity of his good intentions for their welfare. He, however, did not lose his patience, his temper, or his confidence in the certain success of the principles on which he founded his conduct.

These principles ultimately prevailed: the population could not continue to resist a firm well-directed kindness, administering justice to all. They therefore slowly and cautiously began to give him some portion of their confidence; and as this increased, he was enabled more and more to develop his plans for their amelioration. It may with truth be said, that at this period they possessed almost all the vices and very few of the virtues of a social community. Theft and the receipt of stolen goods was their trade, idleness and drunkenness their habit, falsehood and deception their garb, dissensions, civil and religious, their daily practice; they united only in a zealous systematic opposition to their employers. Here then was a fair field on which to try the efficacy in practice of principles supposed capable of altering any characters. The manager formed his plans accordingly. He spent some time in finding out the full extent of the evil against which he had to contend, and in tracing the true causes which had produced and were continuing those effects. He found that all was distrust, disorder, and disunion; and he wished to introduce confidence, regularity, and harmony. He therefore began to bring forward his various expedients to withdraw the unfavourable circumstances by which they had hitherto been surrounded, and to replace them by others calculated to produce a more happy result. He soon discovered that theft was extended through almost all the ramifications of the community, and the receipt of stolen goods through all the country around. To remedy this evil, not one legal punishment was inflicted, not one individual imprisoned, even for an hour; but checks and other regulations of prevention were introduced; a short plain explanation of the immediate benefits they would derive from a different conduct was inculcated by those instructed for the purpose, who had the best powers of reasoning among themselves. They were at the same time instructed how to direct their industry in legal and useful occupations, by which, without danger or disgrace, they could really earn more than they had previously obtained by dishonest practices. Thus the difficulty of committing the crime was increased, the detection afterwards rendered more easy, the habit of honest industry formed, and the pleasure of good conduct experienced.

Drunkenness was attacked in the same manner; it was discountenanced on every occasion by those who had charge of any department: its destructive and pernicious effects were frequently stated by his own more prudent comrades, at the proper moment when the individual was soberly suffering from the effects of his previous excess; pot- and public-houses were gradually removed from the immediate vicinity of their dwellings; the health and comfort of temperance were made familiar to them; by degrees drunkenness disappeared, and many who were habitual bacchanalians are now conspicuous for undeviating sobriety. Falsehood and deception met with a similar fate: they were held in disgrace; their practical evils were shortly explained; and every countenance was given to truth and open conduct. The pleasure and substantial advantages derived from the latter soon overcame the impolicy, error, and consequent misery, which the former mode of acting had created. Dissensions and quarrels were undermined by analagous expedients. When they could not be readily adjusted between the parties themselves, they were stated to the manager; and as in such cases both disputants were usually more or less in the wrong, that wrong was in as few words as possible explained, forgiveness and friendship recommended, and one simple and easily remembered precept inculcated, as the most valuable rule for their whole conduct, and the advantages of which they would experience every moment of their lives; viz. —'That in future they should endeavour to use the same active exertions to make each other happy and comfortable, as they had hitherto done to make each other miserable; and by carrying this short memorandum in their mind, and applying it on all occasions, they would soon render that place a paradise, which, from the most mistaken principle of action, they now made the abode of misery.' The experiment was tried: the parties enjoyed the gratification of this new mode of conduct; references rapidly subsided; and now serious differences are scarcely known. Considerable jealousies also existed on account of one religious sect possessing a decided preference over the others.

This was corrected by discontinuing that preference, and by giving a uniform encouragement to those who conducted themselves well among all the various religious persuasions; by recommending the same consideration to be shown to the conscientious opinions of each sect, on the ground that all must believe the particular doctrines which they had been taught, and consequently that all were in that respect on an equal footing, nor was it possible yet to say which was right or wrong. It was likewise inculcated that all should attend to the essence of religion, and not act as the world was now taught and trained to do; that is, to overlook the substance and essence of religion, and devote their talents, time, and money, to that which is far worse than its shadow, sectarianism; another term for something very injurious to society, and very absurd, which one or other well-meaning enthusiast has added to true religion, which, without these defects, would soon form those characters which every wise and good man is anxious to see.

Such statements and conduct arrested sectarian animosity and ignorant intolerance; each retains full liberty of conscience, and in consequence each partakes of the sincere friendship of many sects instead of one. They act with cordiality together in the same departments and pursuits, and associate as though the whole community were not of different sectarian persuasions; and not one evil ensues.

The same principles were applied to correct the irregular intercourse of the sexes: such conduct was discountenanced and held in disgrace; fines were levied upon both parties for the use of the support fund of the community. (This fund arose from each individual contributing one sixtieth part of their wages, which, under their management, was applied to support the sick, and injured by accident, and the aged.) But because they had once unfortunately offended against the established laws and customs of society, they were not forced to become vicious, abandoned, and miserable; the door was left open for them to return to the comforts of kind friends and respected acquaintances; and, beyond any previous expectation, the evil became greatly diminished.

The system of receiving apprentices from public charities was abolished; permanent settlers with large families were encouraged, and comfortable houses were built for their accommodation.

The practice of employing children in the mills, of six, seven and eight years of age, was discontinued, and their parents advised to allow them to acquire health and education until they were ten years old. (It may be remarked, that even this age is too early to keep them at constant employment in manufactories, from six in the morning to seven in the evening. Far better would it be for the children, their parents, and for society, that the first should not commence employment until they attain the age of twelve, when their education might be finished, and their bodies would be more competent to undergo the fatigue and exertions required of them. When parents can be trained to afford this additional time to their children without inconvenience, they will, of course, adopt the practice now recommended.) The children were taught reading, writing, and arithmetic, during five years, that is, from five to ten, in the village school, without expense to their parents. All the modern improvements in education have been adopted, or are in process of adoption. (To avoid the inconveniences which must ever arise from the introduction of a particular creed into a school, the children are taught to read in such books as inculcate those precepts of the Christian religion, which are common to all denominations.) They may therefore be taught and well-trained before they engage in any regular employment. Another important consideration is, that all their instruction is rendered a pleasure and delight to them; they are much more anxious for the hour of school-time to arrive than to end; they therefore make a rapid progress; and it may be safely asserted, that if they shall not be trained to form such characters as may be most desired, the fault will not proceed from the children; the cause will be in the want of a true knowledge of human nature in those who have the management of them and their parents. During the period that these changes were going forward, attention was given to the domestic arrangements of the community.

Their houses were rendered more comfortable, their streets were improved, the best provisions were purchased, and sold to them at low rates, yet covering the original expense, and under such regulations as taught them how to proportion their expenditure to their income. Fuel and clothes were obtained for them in the same manner; and no advantage was attempted to be taken of them, or means used to deceive them. In consequence, their animosity and opposition to the stranger subsided, their full confidence was obtained, and they became satisfied that no evil was intended them; they were convinced that a real desire existed to increase their happiness upon those grounds alone on which it could be permanently increased. All difficulties in the way of future improvement vanished. They were taught to be rational, and they acted rationally. Thus both parties experienced the incalculable advantages of the system which had been adopted. Those employed became industrious, temperate, healthy, faithful to their employers, and kind to each other, while the proprietors were deriving services from their attachment, almost without inspection, far beyond those which could be obtained by any other means than those of mutual confidence and kindness. Such was the effect of these principles on the adults; on those whose previous habits had been as ill-formed as habits could be; and certainly the application of the principles to practice was made under the most unfavourable circumstances. (It may be supposed that this community was separated from other society; but the supposition would be erroneous, for it had daily and hourly communication with a population exceeding its own number. The royal borough of Lanark is only one mile distant from the works; many individuals came daily from the former to be employed at the latter, and a general intercourse is constantly maintained between the old and new towns.)

I have thus given a detailed account of this experiment, although a partial application of the principles is of far less importance than a clear and accurate account of the principles themselves, in order that they may be so well understood as to be easily rendered applicable to practice in any community and under any circumstances. Without this, particular facts may indeed amuse or astonish, but they would not contain that substantial value which the principles will be found to possess. But if the relation of the narrative shall forward this object, the experiment cannot fail to prove the certain means of renovating the moral and religious principles of the world, by showing whence arise the various opinions, manners, vices, and virtues of mankind, and how the best or the worst of them may, with mathematical precision, be taught to the rising generation. Let it not, therefore, be longer said that evil or injurious actions cannot be prevented, or that the most rational habits in the rising generation cannot be universally formed. In those characters which now exhibit crime, the fault is obviously not in the individual, but the defects proceed from the system in which the individual was trained. Withdraw those circumstances which tend to create crime in the human character, and crime will not be created.

Replace them with such as are calculated to form habits of order, regularity, temperance, industry; and these qualities will be formed. Adopt measures of fair equity and justice, and you will readily acquire the full and complete confidence of the lower orders. Proceed systematically on principles of undeviating persevering kindness, yet retaining and using, with the least possible severity, the means of restraining crime from immediately injuring society', and by degrees even the crimes now existing in the adults will also gradually disappear: for the worst formed disposition, short of incurable insanity, will not long resist a firm, determined, well-directed, persevering kindness. Such a proceeding, whenever practised, will be found the most powerful and effective corrector of crime, and of all injurious and improper habits.

The experiment narrated shows that this is not hypothesis and theory. The principles may be with confidence stated to be universal, and applicable to all times, persons, and circumstances. And the most obvious application of them would be to adopt rational means to remove the temptation to commit crimes, and increase the difficulties of committing them; while, at the same time, a proper direction should be given to the active powers of the individual; and a due share provided of uninjurious amusements and recreation. Care must also be taken to remove the causes of jealousy, dissensions, and irritation; to introduce sentiments calculated to create union and confidence among all the members of the community; and the whole should be directed by a persevering kindness, sufficiently evident to prove that a sincere desire exists to increase, and not to diminish, happiness.

These principles, applied to the community at New Lanark, at first under many of the most discouraging circumstances, but persevered in for sixteen years, effected a complete change in the general character of the village, containing upwards of 2,000 inhabitants, and into which, also, there was a constant influx of newcomers. But as the promulgation of new miracles is not for present times, it is not pretended that under such circumstances one and all are become wise and good; or, that they are free from error. But it may be truly stated, that they now constitute a very improved society; that their worst habits are gone, and that their minor ones will soon disappear under a continuance of the application of the same principles; that during the period mentioned, scarcely a legal punishment has been inflicted, or an application been made for parish funds by any individual among them. Drunkenness is not seen in their streets; and the children are taught and trained in the institution for forming their character without any punishment. The community exhibits the general appearance of industry, temperance, comfort, health, and happiness. These are and ever will be the sure and certain effects of the adoption of the principles explained; and these principles, applied with judgement, will effectually reform the most vicious community existing, and train the younger part of it to any character which may be desired; and that, too, much more easily on an extended than on a limited scale. To apply these principles, however, successfully to practice, both a comprehensive and a minute view must be taken of the existing state of the society on which they are intended to operate. The causes of the most prevalent evils must be accurately traced, and those means which appear the most easy and simple should be immediately applied to remove them.

In this progress the smallest alteration, adequate to produce any good effect, should be made at one time; indeed, if possible, the change should be so gradual as to be almost imperceptible, yet always making a permanent advance in the desired improvements. By this procedure the most rapid practical progress will be obtained, because the inclination to resistance will be removed, and time will be given for reason to weaken the force of long-established injurious prejudices. The removal of the first evil will prepare the way for the removal of the second; and this facility will increase, not in an arithmetical, but in a geometrical proportion; until the directors of the system will themselves be gratified beyond expression with the beneficial magnitude of their own proceedings.

Nor while these principles shall be acted upon can there be any retrogression in this good work; for the permanence of the amelioration will be equal to its extent. What then remains to prevent such a system from being immediately adopted into national practice? Nothing, surely, but a general destitution of the knowledge of the practice. For with the certain means of preventing crimes, can it be supposed that British legislators, as soon as these means shall be made evident, will longer withhold them from their fellow subjects? No: I am persuaded that neither prince, ministers, parliament, nor any party in church or state, will avow inclination to act on principles of such flagrant injustice. Have they not on many occasions evinced a sincere and ardent desire to ameliorate the condition of the subjects of the empire, when practicable means of amelioration were explained to them, which could be adopted without risking the safety of the state? For some time to come there can be but one practicable, and therefore one rational reform, which without danger can be attempted in these realms; a reform in which all men and all parties may join that is, a reform in the training and in the management of the poor, the ignorant, the untaught and untrained, or ill-taught and ill-trained, among the whole mass of British population; and a plain, simple, practicable plan which would not contain the least danger to any individual, or to any part of society, may be devised for that purpose.

That plan is a national, well-digested, unexclusive system for the formation of character and general amelioration of the lower orders. On the experience of a life devoted to the subject, I hesitate not to say, that the members of any community may by degrees be trained to live without idleness, without poverty, without crime, and without punishment; for each of these is the effect of error in the various systems prevalent throughout the world. They are all necessary consequences of ignorance. Train any population rationally, and they will be rational. Furnish honest and useful employments to those so trained, and such employments they will greatly prefer to dishonest or injurious occupations. It is beyond all calculation the interest of every government to provide that training and that employment; and to provide both is easily practicable. The first, as before stated, is to be obtained by a national system for the formation of character; the second, by governments preparing a reserve of employment for the surplus working classes, when the general demand for labour throughout the country, is not equal to the full occupation of the whole: that employment to be on useful national objects from which the public may derive advantage equal to the expense which those works may require.

The national plan for the formation of character should include all the modern improvements of education, without regard to the system of any one individual; and should not exclude the child of any one subject in the empire. Anything short of this would be an act of intolerance and injustice to the excluded, and of injury to society, so glaring and manifest, that I shall be deceived in the character of my countrymen if any of those who have influence in church and state should now be found willing to attempt it. Is it not indeed strikingly evident even to common observers, that any further effort to enforce religious exclusion would involve the certain and speedy destruction of the present church establishment, and would even endanger our civil institutions?

It may be said, however, that ministers and parliament have many other important subjects under discussion. This is evidently true; but will they not have high national concerns always to engage their attention? And can any question be brought forward of deeper interest to the community than that which affects the formation of character and the well-being of every individual within the empire? A question, too, which, when understood, will be found to offer the means of amelioration to the revenues of these kingdoms, far beyond any practical plan now likely to be devised. Yet, important as are considerations of revenue, they must appear secondary when put in competition with the lives, liberty, and comfort of our fellow subjects, which are now hourly sacrificed for want of an effective legislative measure to prevent crime. And is an act of such vital importance to the well-being of all to be longer delayed? Shall yet another year pass in which crime shall be forced on the infant, who in ten, twenty, or thirty years hence shall suffer death for being taught that crime? Surely it is impossible. Should it be so delayed, the individuals of the present parliament, the legislators of this day, ought in strict and impartial justice to be amenable to the laws for not adopting the means in their power to prevent the crime; rather than the poor, untrained, and unprotected culprit, whose previous years, if he had language to describe them, would exhibit a life of unceasing wretchedness, arising solely from the errors of society.

Much might be added on these momentous subjects, even to make them evident to the capacities of children: but for obvious reasons the outlines are merely sketched; and it is hoped these outlines will be sufficient to induce the well-disposed of all parties cordially to unite in this vital measure for the preservation of everything dear to society.

In the next essay an account will be given of the plans which are in progress at New Lanark for the further comfort and improvement of its inhabitants; and a general practical system be described, by which the same advantages may be gradually introduced among the poor and working classes throughout the United Kingdom.

* * *

The Principles of the Former Essays applied to a Particular Situation Truth must ultimately prevail over error. At the conclusion of the Second Essay, a promise was made that an account should be given of the plans which were in progress at New Lanark for the further improvement of its inhabitants; and that a practical system should be sketched, by which equal advantages might be generally introduced among the poor and working classes throughout the United Kingdom.

This account became necessary, in order to exhibit even a limited view of the principles on which the plans of the author are founded, and to recommend them generally to practice.

That which has been hitherto done for the community at New Lanark, as described in the Second Essay, has chiefly consisted in withdrawing some of those circumstances which tended to generate, continue, or increase early bad habits, that is to say, undoing that which society had from ignorance permitted to be done.

To effect this, however, was a far more difficult task than to train up a child from infancy in the way he should go; for that is the most easy process for the formation of character; while to unlearn and to change long acquired habits is a proceeding directly opposed to the most tenacious feelings of human nature.

Nevertheless, the proper application steadily pursued did effect beneficial changes on these old habits, even beyond the most sanguine expectations of the party by whom the task was undertaken.

The principles were driven from the study of human nature itself and they could not fail to succeed. Still, however, very little, comparatively speaking, had been done for them. They had not been taught the most valuable domestic and social habits: such as the most economical method of preparing food; how to arrange their dwellings with neatness, and to keep them always clean and in order; but, what was of infinitely more importance, they had not been instructed how to train their children to form them into valuable members of the community, or to know that principles existed, which, when properly applied to practice from infancy, would ensure from man to man, without chance of failure, a just, open, sincere, and benevolent conduct.

It was in this stage of the progress of improvement, that it became necessary to form arrangements for surrounding them with circumstances which should gradually prepare the individuals to receive and firmly retain those domestic and social acquirements and habits. For this purpose a building, which may be termed the 'new institution', was erected in the centre of the establishment, with an enclosed area before it. The area is intended for a playground for the children of the villagers, from the time they can walk alone until they enter the school. It must be evident to those who have been in the practice of observing children with attention, that much of good or evil is taught to or acquired by a child at a very early period of its life; that much of temper or disposition is correctly or incorrectly formed before he attains his second year and that many durable impressions are made at the termination of the first twelve or even six months of his existence. The children, therefore, of the uninstructed and ill-instructed, suffer material injury in the formation of their characters during these and the subsequent years of childhood and of youth. It was to prevent, or as much as possible to counteract, these primary evils, to which the poor and working classes are exposed when infants, that the area became part of the New Institution.

Into this playground the children are to be received as soon as they can freely walk alone; to be superintended by persons instructed to take charge of them. As the happiness of man chiefly, if not altogether, depends on his own sentiments and habits, as well as those of the individuals around him; and as any sentiments and habits may be given to all infants, it becomes of primary importance that those alone should be given to them which can contribute to their happiness. Each child, therefore, on his entrance into the playground, is to be told in language which he can understand, that 'he is never to injure his playfellows; but that, on the contrary, he is to contribute all in his power to make them happy. This simple precept, when comprehended in all its bearings, and the habits which will arise from its early adoption into practice, if no counteracting principle be forced upon the young mind, will effectually supersede all the errors which have hitherto kept the world in ignorance and misery. So simple a precept, too, will be easily taught, and as easily acquired; or the chief employment of the superintendents will be to prevent any deviation from it in practice. The older children, when they shall have experienced the endless advantages from acting on this principle, will, by their example, soon enforce the practice of it on the young strangers: and the happiness, which the little groups will enjoy from this rational conduct, will ensure its speedy and general and willing adoption. The habit also which they will acquire at this early period of life by continually acting on the principle, will fix it firmly; it will become easy and familiar to them, or, as it is often termed, natural.

Thus, by merely attending to the evidence of our senses respecting human nature, and disregarding the wild, inconsistent, and absurd theories in which man has been hitherto trained in all parts of the earth, we shall accomplish with ease and certainty the supposed Herculean labour of forming a rational character in man, and that, too, chiefly before the child commences the ordinary course of education.

The character thus early formed will be as durable as it will be advantageous to the individual and to the community, for by the constitution of our nature, when once the mind fully understands that which is true, the impression of that truth cannot be erased except by mental disease or death; while error must be relinquished at every period of life, whenever it can be made manifest to the mind in which; it has been received. This part of the arrangement, therefore, will effect the following purposes:

The child will be removed, so far as is at present practicable, from the erroneous treatment of the yet untrained and untaught parents. The parents will be relieved from the loss of time and from the care and anxiety which are now occasioned by attendance on their children from the period when they can go alone to that at which they enter the school. The child will be placed in a situation of safety, where, with its future schoolfellows and companions, it will acquire the best habits and principles, while at mealtimes and at night it will return to the caresses of its parents; and the affections of each are likely to be increased by the separation. The area is also to be a place of meeting for the children from five to ten years of age, previous to and after school-hours, and to serve for a drill-ground, the object of which will be hereafter explained; and a shade will be formed, under which in stormy weather the children may retire for shelter.

These are the important purposes to which a playground attached to a school may be applied. Those who have derived a knowledge of human nature from observation know that man in every situation requires relaxation from his constant and regular occupations, whatever they be: and that if he shall not be provided with or permitted to enjoy innocent and uninjurious amusements, he must and will partake of those which he can obtain, to give him temporary relief from his exertions, although the means of gaining that relief should be most pernicious. For man, irrationally instructed, is ever influenced far more by immediate feelings than by remote considerations.

Those, then, who desire to give mankind the character which it would be for the happiness of all that they should possess, will not fail to make careful provision for their amusement and recreation.

The Sabbath was originally so intended. It was instituted to be a day of universal enjoyment and happiness to the human race. It is frequently made, however, from the opposite extremes of error, either a day of superstitious gloom and tyranny over the mind, or of the most destructive intemperance and licentiousness. The one of these has been the cause of the other; the latter the certain and natural consequence of the former. Relieve the human mind from useless and superstitious restraints; train it on those principles which facts, ascertained from the first knowledge of time to this day, demonstrate to be the only principles which are true; and intemperance and licentiousness will not exist; for such conduct in itself is neither the immediate nor the future interest of man; and he is ever governed by one or other of these considerations, according to the habits which have been given to him from infancy.

The Sabbath, in many parts of Scotland, is not a day of innocent and cheerful recreation to the labouring man; nor can those who are confined all the week to sedentary occupations, freely partake, without censure, of the air and exercise to which nature invites them, and which their health demands. The errors of the times of superstition and bigotry still hold some sway, and compel those who wish to preserve a regard to their respectability in society, to an overstrained demeanour; and this demeanour sometimes degenerates into hypocrisy, and is often the cause of great inconsistency. It is destructive of every open, honest, generous, and manly feeling. It disgusts many, and drives them to the opposite extreme. It is sometimes the cause of insanity. It is founded on ignorance, and defeats its own object. While erroneous customs prevail in any country, it would evince an ignorance of human nature in any individual to offend against them, until he has convinced the community of their error.

To counteract, in some degree, the inconvenience which arose from the misapplication of the Sabbath, it became necessary to introduce on the other days of the week some innocent amusement and recreation for those whose labours were unceasing, and in winter almost uniform. In summer, the inhabitants of the village of New Lanark have their gardens and potato grounds to cultivate; they have walks laid out to give them health and the habit of being gratified with the ever-changing scenes of nature—for those scenes afford not only the most economical, but also the most innocent pleasures which man can enjoy; and all men may be easily trained to enjoy them. In winter the community are deprived of these healthy occupations and amusements; they are employed ten hours and three-quarters every day in the week, except Sunday, and generally every individual continues during that time at the same work: and experience has shown that the average health and spirits of the community are several degrees lower in winter than in summer; and this in part may be fairly attributed to that cause.

These considerations suggested the necessity of rooms for innocent amusements and rational recreation. Many well-intentioned individuals, unaccustomed to witness the conduct of those among the lower orders who have been rationally treated and trained, may fancy such an assemblage will necessarily become a scene of confusion and disorder; instead of which, however, it proceeds with uniform propriety, it is highly favourable to the health, spirits, and dispositions of the individuals so engaged; and if any irregularity should arise, the cause will be solely owing to the parties who attempt to direct the proceedings being deficient in a practical knowledge of human nature.

It has been and ever will be found far more easy to lead mankind to virtue, or to rational conduct, by providing them with well-regulated innocent amusements and recreations, than by forcing them to submit to useless restraints, which tend only to create disgust, and often to connect such feelings even with that which is excellent in itself, merely because it has been judiciously associated.

Hitherto, indeed, in all ages and in all countries, man seems to have blindly conspired against the happiness of man, and to have remained as ignorant of himself as he was of the solar system prior to the days of Copernicus and Galileo. Many of the learned and wise among our ancestors were conscious of this ignorance, and deeply lamented its effects; and some of them recommended the partial adoption of those principles which can alone relieve the world from the miserable effects of ignorance.

The time, however, for the emancipation of the human mind had not then arrived: the world was not prepared to receive it. The history of humanity shows it to be an undeviating law of nature, that man shall not prematurely break the shell of ignorance; that he must patiently wait until the principle of knowledge has pervaded the whole mass of the light of day. Those who have duly reflected on the nature and extent of the mental movements of the world for the last half-century, must be conscious that great changes are in progress; that man is about to advance another important step towards that degree of intelligence which his natural powers seem capable of attaining. Observe the transactions of the passing hours; see the whole mass of mind in full motion; behold it momentarily increasing in vigour, and preparing ere long to burst its confinement. But what is to be the nature of this change? A due attention to the facts around us, and to those transmitted by the invention of printing from former ages, will afford a satisfactory reply.

From the earliest ages it has been the practice of the world to act on the supposition that each individual man forms his own character, and that therefore he is accountable for all his sentiments and habits, and consequently merits reward for some and punishment for others. Every system which has been established among men has been founded on these erroneous principles. When, however, they shall be brought to the test of fair examination, they will be found not only unsupported, but in direct opposition to all experience, and to the evidence of our senses.

This is not a slight mistake, which involves only trivial consequences; it is a fundamental error of the highest possible magnitude; it enters into all our proceedings regarding man from his infancy; and it will be found to be the true and sole origin of evil. It generates and perpetuates ignorance, hatred, and revenge, where, without such error, only intelligence, confidence, and kindness, would exist. It has hitherto been the Evil Genius of the world. It severs man from man throughout the various regions of the earth; and makes enemies of those who, but for this gross error, would have enjoyed each other's kind offices and sincere friendship. It is, in short, an error which carries misery in all its consequences.

This error cannot much longer exist; for every day will make it more and more evident that the character of man is, without a single exception, always formed for him; that it may be, and is, chiefly created by his predecessors; that they give him, or may give him, his ideas and habits, which are the powers that govern and direct his conduct. Man, therefore, never did, nor is it possible he ever can, form his own character.

The knowledge of this important fact has not been derived from any of the wild and heated speculations of an ardent and ungoverned imagination; on the contrary, it proceeds from a long and patient study of the theory and practice of human nature, under many varied circumstances; it will be found to be a deduction drawn from such a multiplicity of facts, as to afford the most complete demonstration.

Had not mankind been misinstructed from infancy on this subject, making it necessary that they should unlearn what they have been taught, the simple statement of this truth would render it instantly obvious to every rational mind. Men would know that their predecessors might have given them the habits of ferocious cannibalism, or of the highest known benevolence and intelligence; and by the acquirement of this knowledge they would soon learn that, as parents, preceptors, and legislators united, they possess the means of training the rising generations to either of those extremes; that they may with the greatest certainty make them the conscientious worshippers of Juggernaut, or of the most pure spirit, possessing the essence of every excellence which the human imagination can conceive; that they may train the young to become effeminate, deceitful, ignorantly selfish, intemperate, revengeful, murderous of course ignorant, irrational, and miserable; or to be manly, just, generous, temperate, active, kind, and benevolent that is intelligent, rational, and happy. The knowledge of these principles having been derived from facts which perpetually exist, they defy ingenuity itself to confute them; nay, the most severe scrutiny will make it evident that they are utterly unassailable.

Is it then wisdom to think and to act in opposition to the facts which hourly exhibit themselves around us, and in direct contradiction to the evidence of our senses? Inquire of the most learned and wise of the present day, ask them to speak with sincerity, and they will tell you that they have long known the principles on which society has been found to be false. Hitherto, however, the tide of public opinion, in all countries, has been directed by a combination of prejudice, bigotry, and fanaticism, derived from the wildest imaginations of ignorance; and the most enlightened men have not dared to expose those errors which to them were offensive, prominent, and glaring.

Happily for man this reign of ignorance rapidly approaches to dissolution; its terrors are already on the wing, and soon they will be compelled to take their flight, never more to return. For now the knowledge of the existing errors is not only possessed by the learned and reflecting, but it is spreading far and wide throughout society; and before long it will be fully comprehended even by the most ignorant.

Attempts may indeed be made by individuals, who through ignorance mistake their real interests, to retard the progress of this knowledge; but as it will prove itself to be in unison with the evidence of our senses, and therefore true beyond the possibility of disproof, it cannot be impeded, and in its course will overwhelm all opposition.

These principles, however, are not more true in theory than beneficial in practice, whenever they are properly applied. Why, then, should all their substantial advantages be longer withheld from the mass of mankind? Can it, by possibility, be a crime to pursue the only practical means which a rational being can adopt to diminish the misery of man, and increase his happiness?

These questions, of the deepest interest to society, are now brought to the fair test of public experiment. It remains to be proved, whether the character of man shall continue to be formed under the guidance of the most inconsistent notions, the errors of which for centuries past have been manifest to every reflecting rational mind; or whether it shall be moulded under the direction of uniformly consistent principles, derived from the unvarying facts of the creation; principles, the truth of which no sane man will now attempt to deny.

It is then by the full and complete disclosure of these principles, that the destruction of ignorance and misery is to be effected, and the reign of reason, intelligence, and happiness, is to be firmly established. It was necessary to give this development of the principles advocated, that the remaining parts of the New Institution, yet to be described, may be clearly understood. We now proceed to explain the several purposes intended to be accomplished by the School, Lecture Room, and Church.

It must be evident to those who have any powers of reason yet undestroyed, that man is now taught and trained in a theory and practice directly opposed to each other. Hence the perpetual inconsistencies, follies, and absurdities, which everyone can readily discover in his neighbour, without being conscious that he also possesses similar incongruities. The instruction to be given in the School, Lecture Room, and Church, is intended to counteract and remedy this evil; and to prove the incalculable advantages which society would derive from the introduction of a theory and practice consistent with each other. The uppermost storey of the New Institution is arranged to serve for a School, Lecture Room, and Church. And these are intended to have a direct influence in forming the character of the villagers.

It is comparatively, of little avail to give to either young or old 'precept upon precept, and line upon line', except the means shall be also prepared to train them in good practical habits. Hence an education for the untaught and ill-taught becomes of the first importance to the welfare of society and it is this which has influenced all the arrangements connected with the New Institution. The time the children will remain under the discipline of the playground and school, will afford all the opportunity that can be desired to create, cultivate, and establish, those habits and sentiments which tend to the welfare of the individual and of the community. And in conformity to this plan of proceeding, the precept which was given to the child of two years old, on coming into the playground, 'that he must endeavour to make his companions happy', is to be renewed and enforced on his entrance into the school: and the first duty of the schoolmaster will be to train his pupils to acquire the practice of always acting on this principle. It is a simple rule, the plain and obvious reasons for which children at an early age may be readily taught to comprehend, and as they advance in years, become familiarized with its practice, and experience the beneficial effects to themselves, they will better feel and understand all its important consequences to society.

Such then being the foundation on which the practical habits of the children are to be formed, we proceed to explain the superstructure.

In addition to the knowledge of the principle and practice of the above-mentioned precept, the boys and girls are to be taught in the school to read well, and to understand what they read; to write expeditiously a good legible hand; and to learn correctly, so that they may comprehend and use with facility the fundamental rules of arithmetic. The girls are also to be taught to sew, cut out, and make up useful family garments; and, after acquiring a sufficient knowledge of these, they are to attend in rotation in the public kitchen and eating rooms, to learn to prepare wholesome food in an economical manner, and to keep a house neat and well arranged.

It was said that the children are to be taught to read well, and to understand what they read. In many schools, the children of the poor and labouring classes are never taught to understand what they read; the time therefore which is occupied in the mockery of the instruction is lost. In other schools, the children, through the ignorance of their instructors, are taught to believe without reasoning, and thus never to think or to reason correctly. These truly lamentable practices cannot fail to indispose, the young mind for plain, simple, and rational instruction.

The books by which it is now the common custom to teach children to read, inform them of anything except that which, at their age, they ought to be taught; hence the inconsistencies and follies of adults. It is full time that this system should be changed. Can man, when possessing the full vigour of his faculties, form a rational judgement on any subject, until he has first collected all the facts respecting it which are known? Has not this been, and will not this ever remain, the only path by which human knowledge can be obtained? Then children ought to be instructed on the same principles. They should first be taught the knowledge of facts, commencing with those which are most familiar to the young mind, and gradually proceeding to the most useful and necessary to be known by the respective individuals in the rank of life in which they are likely to be placed; and in all cases the children should have as clear an explanation of each fact as their minds can comprehend, rendering those explanations more detailed as the child acquires strength and capacity of intellect.

As soon as the young mind shall be duly prepared for such instruction, the master should not allow any opportunity to escape, that would enable him to enforce the clear and inseparable connection which exists between the interest and happiness of each individual and the interest and happiness of every other individual. This should be the beginning and end of all instruction; and by degrees it will be so well understood by his pupils, that they will receive the same conviction of its truth, that those familiar with mathematics now entertain of the demonstrations of Euclid. And when thus comprehended, the all prevailing principle of known life, the desire of happiness, will compel them without deviation to pursue it in practice. It is much to be regretted that the strength and capacity of the minds of children are yet unknown; their faculties have been hitherto estimated by the folly of instruction which has been given to them; while, if they were never taught to acquire error, they would speedily exhibit such powers of mind, as would convince the most incredulous how much the human intellect has been injured by the ignorance of former and present treatment. It is therefore indeed important that the mind from its birth should receive those ideas only which are consistent with each other, which are in unison with all the known facts of the creation, and which are therefore true. Now, however, from the day they are born, the minds of children are impressed with false notions of themselves and of mankind; and in lieu of being conducted into the plain path leading to health and happiness, the utmost pains are taken to compel them to pursue an opposite direction, in which they can attain only inconsistency and error.

Let the plan which has now been recommended be steadily put in practice from infancy, without counteraction from the systems of education which now exist, and characters, even in youth, may be formed, that in true knowledge, and in every good and valuable quality, will not only greatly surpass the wise and learned of the present and preceding times, but will appear, as they really will be, a race of rational or superior beings. It is true, this change cannot be instantaneously established; it cannot be created by magic, or by a miracle; it must be effected gradually and to accomplish it finally will prove a work of labour and of years. For those who have been misinstructed from infancy, who have now influence and are active in the world, and whose activity is directed by the false notions of their forefathers, will of course endeavour to obstruct the change. Those who have been systematically impressed with early errors, and conscientiously think them to be truths, will of necessity, while such errors remain, endeavour to perpetuate them in their children. Some simple but general method, therefore, becomes necessary to counteract as speedily as possible an evil of so formidable a magnitude.

It was this view of the subject which suggested the utility of preparing the means to admit of evening lectures in the New Institution; and it is intended they should be given, during winter, three nights in the week, alternately with dancing. To the ill-trained and ill-taught these lectures may be made invaluable; and these are now numerous; for the far greater part of the population of the world has been permitted to pass the proper season for instruction without being trained to be rational; and they have acquired only the ideas and habits which proceed from ignorant association and erroneous instruction. It is intended that the lectures should be familiar discourses, delivered in plain impressive language, to instruct the adult part of the community in the most useful practical parts of knowledge in which they are deficient, particularly in the proper method of training their children to become rational creatures; how to expend the earnings of their own labour to advantage; and how to appropriate the surplus gains which will be left to them, in order to create a fund which will relieve them from the anxious fear of future want, and thus give them, under the many errors of the present system, that rational confidence in their own exertions and good conduct, without which, consistency of character or domestic comfort cannot be obtained, and ought not to be expected. The young people may be also questioned relative to their progress in useful knowledge, and allowed to ask for explanations. In short, these lectures may be made to convey, in an amusing and agreeable manner, highly valuable and substantial information to those who are now the most ignorant in the community; and by similar means, which at a trifling expense may be put into action over the whole kingdom, the most important benefits may be given to the labouring classes, and through them, to the whole mass of society.

For it should be considered that the far greater part of the population belong to or have risen from the labouring classes, and by them the happiness and comfort of all ranks, not excluding the highest, are very essentially influenced: because even much more of the character of children in all families is formed by the servants, than is ever supposed by those unaccustomed to trace with attention the human mind from earliest infancy. It is indeed impossible that children in any situation can be correctly trained, until those who surround them from infancy shall be previously well instructed; and the value of good servants may be duly appreciated by those who have experienced the difference between the very good and very bad.

The last part of the intended arrangement of the New Institution remains yet to be described. This is the Church and its doctrines; and they involve considerations of the highest interest and importance; inasmuch as a knowledge of truth on the subject of religion would permanently establish the happiness of man; for it is the inconsistencies alone, proceeding from the want of this knowledge, which have created, and still create, a great proportion of the miseries which exist in the world.

The only certain criterion of truth is, that it is always consistent with itself; it remains one and the same under every view and comparison of it which can be made; while error will not stand the test of this investigation and comparison, because it ever leads to absurd conclusions.

Those whose minds are equal to the subject will, ere this, have discovered, that the principles in which mankind have been hitherto instructed, and by which they have been governed, will not bear the test of this criterion. Investigate and compare them; they betray absurdity, folly, and weakness; hence the infinity of jarring opinions, dissensions, and miseries, which have hitherto prevailed.

Had any one of the various opposing systems which have governed the world and disunited man from man, been true, without any mixture of error—that system, very speedily after its public promulgation, would have pervaded society, and compelled all men to have acknowledged its truth.

The criterion, however, which has been stated, shows, that they are all, without an exception, in part inconsistent with the works of nature; that is, with the facts which exist around us.

Those systems therefore must have contained some fundamental errors; and it is utterly impossible for man to become rational, or enjoy the happiness he is capable of attaining, until those errors are exposed and annihilated.

Each of those systems contains some truth with more error; hence it is that no one of them has gained, or is likely to gain, universality.

The truth which the several systems possess, serves to cover and perpetuate the errors which they contain; but those errors are most obvious to all who have not from infancy been taught to receive them.

Is proof demanded? Ask, in succession, those who are esteemed the most intelligent and enlightened of every sect and party, what is their opinion of every other sect and party throughout the world. Is it not evident that, without one exception, the answer will be, that they all contain errors so clearly in opposition to reason and equity, that he can only feel pity and deep commiseration for the individuals whose minds have been thus perverted and rendered irrational? And this reply they will all make, unconscious that they themselves are of the number whom they commiserate.

The doctrines which have been taught to every known sect, combined with the external circumstances by which they have been surrounded, have been directly calculated, and could not fail, to produce the characters which have existed. And the doctrines in which the inhabitants of the world are now instructed, combined with the external circumstances by which they are surrounded, form the characters which at present pervade society.

The doctrines which have been and now are taught throughout the world, must necessarily create and perpetuate, and they do create and perpetuate, a total want of mental charity among men. They also generate superstitions, bigotry, hypocrisy, hatred, revenge, wars, and all their evil consequences. For it has been and is a fundamental principle in every system hitherto taught, with exceptions more nominal than real, 'That man will possess merit, and receive eternal reward, by believing the doctrines of that peculiar system; that he will be eternally punished if he disbelieves them; that all those innumerable individuals also, who, through time, have been taught to believe other than the tenets of this system, must be doomed to eternal misery.' Yet nature itself, in all its works, is perpetually operating to convince man of such gross absurdities.

Yes, my deluded fellow men, believe me, for your future happiness, that the facts around us, when you shall observe them aright, will make it evident, even to demonstration, that all such doctrines must he erroneous, because THE WILL OF MAN HAS NO POWER WHATEVER OVER HIS OPINIONS; HE MUST, AND EVER DID, AND EVER WILL BELIEVE WHAT HAS BEEN, IS, OR MAY BE IMPRESSED ON HIS MIND BY HIS PREDECESSORS AND THE CIRCUMSTANCES WHICH SURROUND HIM. It becomes therefore the essence of irrationality to suppose that any human being, from the creation to this day, could deserve praise or blame, reward or punishment, for the prepossessions of early education.

It is from these fundamental errors, in all systems which have been hitherto taught to the mass of mankind, that the misery of the human race has to so great an extent proceeded;

for, in consequence of them, man has been always instructed from infancy to believe impossibilities he is still taught to pursue the same insane course, and the result still is misery. Let this source of wretchedness, this most lamentable of all errors, this scourge of the human race, be publicly exposed; and let those just principles be introduced, which prove themselves true by their uniform consistency and the evidence of our senses; hence insincerity, hatred, revenge, and even a wish to injure a fellow creature, will ere long be unknown; and mental charity, heartfelt benevolence, and acts of kindness to one another, will be the distinguished characters of human nature.

Shall then misery most complicated and extensive be experienced, from the prince to the peasant, in all nations throughout the world, and shall its cause and prevention be known, and yet withheld? The knowledge of this cause, however, cannot be communicated to mankind without offending against the deep-rooted prejudices of all. The work is therefore replete with difficulties, which can alone be overcome by those who, foreseeing all its important practical advantages, may be induced to contend against them.

Yet, difficult as it may be to establish this grand truth generally throughout society, on account of the dark and gross errors in which the world to this period has been instructed, it will be found, whenever the subject shall undergo a full investigation, that the principles now brought forward cannot, by possibility, injure any class of men, or even a single individual. On the contrary, there is not one member of the great family of the world, from the highest to the lowest, that will not derive the most important benefits from its public promulgation. And when such incalculable, substantial, and permanent advantages are clearly seen and strongly felt, shall individual considerations be for a moment put in competition with its attainment? No! Ease, comfort, the good opinion of part of society, and even life itself, may be sacrificed to those prejudices; and yet the principles on which this knowledge is founded must ultimately and universally prevail.

This high event, of unequalled magnitude in the history of humanity, is thus confidently predicted, because the knowledge whence that confidence proceeds is not derived from any of the uncertain legends of the days of dark and gross ignorance, but from the plain and obvious facts which now exist throughout the world. Due attention to these facts, to these truly revealed works of nature, will soon instruct, or rather compel mankind to discover the universal errors in which they have been trained.

The principle, then, on which the doctrines taught in the New Institution are proposed to be founded, is, that they shall be in unison with universally revealed facts, which cannot but be true. The following are some of the facts, which, with a view to this part of the undertaking, may be deemed fundamental:

That man is born with a desire to obtain happiness, which desire is the primary cause of all his actions, continues through life, and, in popular language, is called self-interest.

That he is also born with the germs of animal propensities, or the desire to sustain, enjoy, and propagate life; and which desires, as they grow and develop themselves, are termed his natural inclinations.

That he is born likewise with faculties which, in their growth, receive, convey, compare, and become conscious of receiving and comparing ideas.

That the ideas so received, conveyed, compared, and understood, constitute human knowledge, or mind, which acquires strength and maturity with the growth of the individual. That the desire of happiness in man, the germs of his natural inclinations, and the faculties by which he acquires knowledge, are formed unknown to himself in the womb; and whether perfect or imperfect, they are alone the immediate work of the Creator, and over which the infant and future man have no control.

That these inclinations and faculties are not formed exactly alike in any two individuals; hence the diversity of talents, and the varied impressions called liking and disliking which the same external objects make on different persons, and the lesser varieties which exist among men whose characters have been formed apparently under similar circumstances.

That the knowledge which man receives is derived from the objects around him, and chiefly from the example and instruction of his immediate predecessors.

That this knowledge may be limited or extended, erroneous or true; limited, when the individual receives few, and extended when he receives many ideas; erroneous, when those ideas are inconsistent with the facts which exist around him, and true when they are uniformly consistent with them. That the misery which he experiences, and the happiness which he enjoys, depend on the kind and degree of knowledge which he receives, and on that which is possessed by those around him. That when the knowledge which he receives is true and unmixed with error, although it be limited, if the community in which he lives possesses the same kind and degree of knowledge, he will enjoy happiness in proportion to the extent of that knowledge. On the contrary, when the opinions which he receives are erroneous, and the opinions possessed by the community in which he resides are equally erroneous, his misery will be in proportion to the extent of those erroneous opinions.

That when the knowledge which man receives shall be extended to its utmost limit, and true without any mixture of error, then he may and will enjoy all the happiness of which his nature will be capable.

That it consequently becomes of the first and highest importance that man should be taught to distinguish truth from error.

That man has no other means of discovering what is false, except by his faculty of reason, or the power of acquiring and comparing the ideas which he receives.

That when this faculty is properly cultivated or trained from infancy, and the child is rationally instructed to retain no impressions or ideas which by his powers of comparing them appear to be inconsistent, then the individual will acquire real knowledge, or those ideas only which will leave an impression of their consistency or truth on all minds which have not been rendered irrational by an opposite procedure.

That the reasoning faculty may be injured and destroyed during its growth, by reiterated impressions being made upon it of notions not derived from realities, and which it therefore cannot compare with the ideas previously received from the objects around it. And when the mind receives these notions which it cannot comprehend, along with those ideas which it is conscious are true and which yet are inconsistent with such notions, then the reasoning faculties become injured, the individual is taught or forced to believe, and not to think or reason, and partial insanity or defective powers of judging ensue.

That all men are thus erroneously trained at present, and hence the inconsistencies and misery of the world. That the fundamental errors now impressed from infancy on the minds of all men, and from whence all their other errors proceed, are, that they form their own individual characters, and possess merit or demerit for the peculiar notions impressed on the mind during its early growth, before they have acquired strength and experience to judge of or resist the impression of those notions or opinions, which, on investigation, appear contradictions to facts existing around them, and which are therefore false.

That these false notions have ever produced evil and misery in the world; and that they still disseminate them in every direction. That the sole cause of their existence hitherto has been man's ignorance of human nature: while their consequences have been all the evil and misery, except those of accidents, disease, and death, with which man has been and is afflicted: and that the evil and misery which arise from accidents, disease, and death, are also greatly increased and extended by man's ignorance of himself.

That, in proportion as man's desire of self-happiness, or his self-love, is directed by true knowledge, those actions will abound which are virtuous and beneficial to man; that in proportion as it is influenced by false notions, or the absence of true knowledge, those actions will prevail which generate crimes, from whence arises an endless variety of misery, and, consequently, that every rational means should be now adopted to detect error, and to increase true knowledge among men. That when these truths are made evident, every individual will necessarily endeavour to promote the happiness of every other individual within his sphere of action; because he must clearly, and without any doubt, comprehend such conduct to be the essence of self-interest, or the true cause of self-happiness. Here, then, is a firm foundation on which to erect vital religion, pure and undefiled, and the only one which, without any counteracting evil, can give peace and happiness to man. It is to bring into practical operation, in forming the character of men, these most important of all truths, that the religious part of the Institution at New Lanark will be chiefly directed, and such are the fundamental principles upon which the Instructor will proceed. They are thus publicly avowed before all men, that they may undergo discussion and the most severe scrutiny and investigation.

Let those, therefore, who are esteemed the most learned and wise, throughout the various states and empires in the world, examine them to their foundation, compare them with every fact which exists, and if the shadow of inconsistency and falsehood be discovered, let it be publicly exposed, that error may not more abound.

But should they withstand this extended ordeal, and prove themselves uniformly consistent with every known fact, and therefore true, then let it be declared, that man may be permitted by man to become rational, and that the misery of the world may be speedily removed.

Having alluded to the chief uses of the playground and exercise rooms, with the School, Lecture Room, and Church, it remains, to complete the account of the New Institution, that the object of the drill exercises mentioned when stating the purposes of the playground, should be explained; and to this we now proceed.

Were all men trained to be rational, the art of war would be rendered useless. While, however, any part of mankind shall be taught that they form their own characters, and shall continue to be trained from infancy to think and act irrationally that is, to acquire feelings of enmity, and to deem it a duty to engage in war against those who have been instructed to differ from them in sentiments and habits—even the most rational must, for their personal security, learn the means of defence; and every community of such characters, while surrounded by men who have been thus improperly taught, should acquire a knowledge of this destructive art, that they may be enabled to overrule the actions of irrational beings, and maintain peace.

To accomplish these objects to the utmost practical limit, and with the least inconvenience, every male should be instructed how best to defend, when attacked, the community to which he belongs. And these advantages are, only to be obtained by providing proper means for the instruction of all boys in the use of arms and the arts of war.

As an example how easily and effectually this might be accomplished over the British Isles, it is intended that the boys trained and educated at the Institution at New Lanark shall be thus instructed; that the person appointed to attend the children in the playground shall be qualified to drill and teach the boys the manual exercise, and that he shall be frequently so employed; that afterwards, firearms, of proportionate weight and size to the age and strength of the boys, shall be provided for them, when also they might be taught to practise and understand the more complicated military movements.

This exercise, properly administered, will greatly contribute to the health and spirits of the boys, give them an erect and proper form, and habits of attention, celerity, and order. They will, however, be taught to consider this exercise, an art, rendered absolutely necessary by the partial insanity of some of their fellow creatures who by the errors of their predecessors, transmitted through preceding generations, have been taught to acquire feelings of enmity, increasing to madness, against those who could not avoid differing from them in sentiments and habits; that this art should never be brought into practice except to restrain the violence of such madmen; and, in these cases, that it should be administered with the least possible severity, and solely to prevent the evil consequences of those rash acts of the insane, and, if possible, to cure them of their disease.

Thus, in a few years, by foresight and arrangement, may almost the whole expense and inconvenience attending the local military be superseded, and a permanent force created, which in numbers, discipline, and principles, would be superior, beyond all comparison, for the purposes of defence; always ready in case of need, yet without the loss which is now sustained by the community of efficient and valuable labour. The expenditure which would be saved by this simple expedient, would be far more than competent to educate the whole of the poor and labouring classes of these kingdoms.

There is still another arrangement in contemplation for the community at New Lanark, and without which the establishment will remain incomplete.

It is an expedient to enable the individuals, by their own foresight, prudence, and industry, to secure to themselves in old age a comfortable provision and asylum. Those now employed at the establishment contribute to a fund which supports them when too ill to work, or superannuated. This fund, however, is not calculated to give them more than a bare existence; and it is surely desirable that, after they have spent nearly half a century in unremitting industry, they should, if possible, enjoy a comfortable independence.

To effect this object, it is intended that in the most pleasant situation near the present village, neat and convenient dwellings should be erected, with gardens attached; that they should be surrounded and sheltered by plantations, through which public walks should be formed; and the whole arranged to give the occupiers the most substantial comforts.

That these dwellings, with the privileges of the public walks, etc., shall become the property of those individuals who, without compulsion, shall subscribe each equitable sums monthly, as, in a given number of years will be equal to the purchase, and to create a fund from which, when these individuals become occupiers of their new residences they may receive weekly, monthly, or quarterly payments, sufficient for their support; the expenses of which may be reduced to a very low rate individually, by arrangements which may be easily formed to supply all their wants with little trouble to themselves; and by their previous instruction they will be enabled to afford the small additional subscription which will be required for these purposes.

This part of the arrangement would always present a prospect of rest, comfort, and happiness to those employed; in consequence, their daily occupations would be performed with more spirit and cheerfulness, and their labour would appear comparatively light and easy. Those still engaged in active operations would, of course, frequently visit their former companions and friends, who, after having spent their years of toil, were in the actual enjoyment of this simple retreat; and from this intercourse each party would naturally derive pleasure.

The reflections of each would be most gratifying. The old would rejoice that they had been trained in habits of industry, temperance, and foresight, to enable them to receive and enjoy in their declining years every reasonable comfort which the present state of society will admit; the young and middle-aged, that they were pursuing the same course, and that they had not been trained to waste their, money, time, and health, in idleness and intemperance. These and many similar reflections could not fail often to arise in their minds; and those who could look forward with confident hopes to such certain comfort and independence would, in part, enjoy by anticipation these advantages. In short, when this part of the arrangement is well considered, it will be found to be the most important to the community and to the proprietors; indeed, the extensively good effects of it will be experienced in such a variety of ways, that to describe them even below the truth would appear an extravagant exaggeration. They will not, however, prove the less true because mankind are yet ignorant of the practice, and of the principles on which it has been founded.

These, then, are the plans which are in progress or intended for the further improvement of the inhabitants of New Lanark. They have uniformly proceeded from the principles which have been developed through these Essays, restrained, however, hitherto, in their operations, by the local sentiments and unfounded notions of the community and neighbourhood, and by the peculiar circumstances of the establishment.

In every measure to be introduced at the place in question, for the comfort and happiness of man, the existing errors of the country were always to be considered; and as the establishment belonged to parties whose views were various, it became also necessary to devise means to create pecuniary gains from each improvement, sufficient to satisfy the spirit of commerce. All, therefore, which has been done for the happiness of this community, which consists of between two and three thousand individuals, is far short of what might have been easily effected in practice had not mankind been previously trained in error. Hence, in devising these plans, the sole consideration was not, what were the measures dictated by these principles, which would produce the greatest happiness to man; but what could be effected in practice under the present irrational systems by which these proceedings were surrounded?

Imperfect, however, as these proceedings must yet be, in consequence of the formidable obstructions enumerated, they will yet appear, upon a full minute investigation by minds equal to the comprehension of such a system, to combine a greater degree of substantial comfort to the individuals employed in the manufactory, and of pecuniary profit to the proprietors, than has hitherto been found attainable.

But to whom can such arrangements be submitted? Not to the mere commercial character, in whose estimation to forsake the path of immediate individual gain would be to show symptoms of a disordered imagination; for the children of commerce have been trained to direct all their faculties to buy cheap and sell dear; and consequently, those who are the most expert and successful in this wise and noble art, are, in the commercial world, deemed to possess foresight and superior acquirements; while such as attempt to improve the moral habits and increase the comforts of those whom they employ, are termed wild enthusiasts.

Nor yet are they to be submitted to the mere men of the law; for these are necessarily trained to endeavour to make wrong appear right, or to involve both in a maze of intricacies, and to legalize injustice. Nor to mere political leaders or their partisans; for they are embarrassed by the trammels of party, which mislead their judgement, and often constrain them to sacrifice the real well-being of the community and of themselves, to an apparent but most mistaken self-interest.

Nor to those termed heroes and conquerors, or to their followers; for their minds have been trained to consider the infliction of human misery, and the commission of military murders, a glorious duty, almost beyond reward. Nor yet to the fashionable or splendid in their appearance; for these are from infancy trained to deceive and to be deceived, to accept shadows for substances, and to live a life of insincerity, and of consequent discontent and misery. Still less are they to be exclusively submitted to the official expounders and defenders of the various opposing religious systems throughout the world; for many of these are actively engaged in propagating imaginary notions, which cannot fail to vitiate the rational powers of man, and to perpetuate his misery.

These principles, therefore, and the practical systems which they recommend, are not to be submitted to the judgement of those who have been trained under, and continue in, any of these unhappy combinations of circumstances. But they are to be submitted to the dispassionate and patient investigation and decision of those individuals of every rank and class and denomination of society, who have become in some degree conscious of the errors in which they exist; who have felt the thick mental darkness by which they are surrounded; who are ardently desirous of discovering and following truth wherever it may lead; and who can perceive the inseparable connection which exists between individual and general, between private and public good! It has been said, and it is now repeated, that these principles, thus combined, will prove themselves unerringly true against the most insidious or open attack; and, ere long, they will, by their irresistible truth, pervade society to the utmost bounds of the earth; for 'silence will not retard their progress, and opposition will give increased celerity to their movements'.

When they shall have dissipated in some degree, as they speedily will dissipate, the thick darkness in which the human mind has been and is still enveloped, the endless beneficial consequences which must follow the general introduction of them into practice may then be explained in greater detail, and urged upon minds to which they will then appear less questionable.

In the meantime we shall proceed to state, in a Fourth Essay, of what improvements the present state of the British population is susceptible in practice.

The Principles of the Former Essays applied to Government. It is beyond all comparison better to prevent than to punish crime. A system of government therefore which shall prevent ignorance, and consequently crime, will be infinitely superior to one, which, by encouraging the first, creates a necessity for the last, and afterwards inflicts punishment on both.

The end of government is to make the governed and the governors happy. That government, then, is the best, which in practice produces the greatest happiness to the greatest number; including those who govern, and those who obey. In a former Essay we said, and it admits of practical demonstration, that by adopting the proper means, man may by degrees be trained to live in any part of the world without poverty, without crime, and without punishment; for all these are the effects of error in the various systems of training and governing error proceeding from very gross ignorance of human nature.

It is of primary importance to make this ignorance manifest, and to show what are the means which are endowed with that transcendent efficacy.

We have also said that man may be trained to acquire any sentiments and habits, or any character; and no one now, possessing pretensions to the knowledge of human nature, will deny that the government of any independent community may form the individuals of that community into the best, or into the worst characters.

If there be one duty therefore more imperative than another, on the government of every country, it is, that it should adopt, without delay, the proper means to form those sentiments and habits in the people, which shall give the most permanent and substantial advantages to the individuals and to the community.

Survey the acquirements of the earliest ages; trace the progress of those acquirements, through all the subsequent periods, to the present hour; and say if there be anything of real value in them, except that which contributes in practice to increase the happiness of the world.

And yet, with all the parade of learning contained in the myriads of volumes which have been written, and which still daily pour from the press, the knowledge of the first step of the progress which leads to human happiness remains yet unknown or disregarded by the mass of mankind.

The important knowledge to which we allude is, 'That the old collectively may train the young collectively, to be ignorant and miserable, or to be intelligent and happy, And, on investigation, this will be found to be one of those simple yet grand laws of the universe, which experience discovers and confirms, and which, as soon as men become familiar with it, will no longer admit of denial or dispute. Fortunate will be that government which shall first acquire this knowledge in theory, and adopt it in practice. To obtain its introduction into our own country first, a mode of procedure is now submitted to the immediate governing powers of the British Empire; and it is so submitted, with an ardent desire that it may undergo the most full and ample discussion, that if it shall, as on investigation it will, be found to be the only consistent and therefore rational, system of conducting human beings, it may be temperately and progressively introduced, instead of those defective national practices by which the state is now governed.

We therefore proceed to explain how this principle may now be introduced into practice, without injury to any part of society. For it, is the time and manner of introducing this principle and its consequent practice, which alone constitute any difficulty. This will appear evident when it is considered that although, from a plain statement of the most simple facts, the truth of the principle cannot fail to prove so obvious that no one will ever attempt openly to attack it; and although its adoption into practice will speedily accumulate benefits of which the world can now form no adequate conception; yet both theory and practice are to be introduced into a society trained and matured under principles that have impressed upon the individuals who compose it the most opposite habits and sentiments: which have been so entwined from infancy in their bodily and mental growth, that the simplicity and irresistible power of truth alone can disentangle them and expose their fallacy. It becomes then necessary, to prevent the evils of a too sudden change, that those who have been thus nursed in ignorance may be progressively removed from the abodes of mental darkness to the intellectual light which this principle cannot fail to produce. The light of true knowledge, therefore, must be first made to dawn on those dwellings of darkness, and afterwards gradually to increase, as it can be borne, by the opening faculties of their inhabitants. To proceed on this plan it becomes necessary to direct our attention to the actual state of the British population, to disclose the cause of those great and leading evils of which all now complain.

It will then be seen that the foundation on which these evils have been erected is ignorance, proceeding from the errors which have been impressed on the minds of the present generation by its predecessors; and chiefly by that greatest of all errors, the notion that individuals form their own characters. For while this most inconsistent, and therefore most absurd, of all human conceptions shall continue to be forced upon the young mind, there will remain no foundation whatever on which to build a sincere love and extended charity for man to his fellow creatures.

But destroy this hydra of human calamity, this immolator of every principle of rationality, this monster, which hitherto has effectually guarded every avenue that can lead to true benevolence and active kindness, and human happiness will be speedily established on a rock from whence it shall never more be removed.

This enemy of humanity may now be most easily destroyed. Let it be dragged forth from beneath the dark mysterious veil by which till now it has been hid from the eyes of the world; expose it but for an instant to the clear light of intellectual day; and, as though conscious of its own deformity, it will instantaneously vanish, never to reappear.

As a groundwork, then, of a rational system, let this absurd doctrine, and all the chain of consequences which follow from it, be withdrawn; and let that only be taught as sacred, which can be demonstrated by its never-failing consistency to be true. This essential object being accomplished (and accomplished it must be before another step can be taken to form man into a rational being), the next is to withdraw those national laws which chiefly emanate from that erroneous doctrine, and which now exist in full vigour, training the population to almost every kind of crime. For these laws are, without chance of failure, adapted to produce a long train of crimes; which crimes are accordingly produced.

Some of the most prominent to which allusion is made, are such as encourage the consumption of ardent spirits, by fostering and extending those receptacles to seduce the ignorant and wretched, called gin-shops and pot-houses; those laws which sanction and legalize gambling among the poor, under the name of a state lottery; those which are insidiously destroying the real strength of the country, under the name of providing for the poor; and those of punishment, which, under the present irrational system of legislation, are supposed to be absolutely necessary to hold society together.

To prove the accuracy of this deduction, millions of facts exist around us, speaking in a language so clearly connected and audible, that it is scarcely credible any man can misunderstand it. These facts proclaim aloud to the universe, that ignorance generates, fosters, and multiplies sentiments and actions which must produce private and public misery; and that when evils are experienced, instead of withdrawing the cause which created them, it invents and applies punishments, which, to a superficial observer, may appear to lessen the evils which afflict society, while, in reality, they greatly increase them. Intelligence, on the contrary, traces to its source the cause of every evil which exists; adopts the proper measures to remove the cause; and then, with the most unerring confidence, rests satisfied that its object will be accomplished. Thus then intelligence, or in other words plain unsophisticated reason, will consider the various sentiments and actions which now create misery in society, will patiently trace the cause whence those sentiments and actions proceed, and immediately apply the proper remedies to remove them. And attention, thus directed, discovers that the cause of such sentiments and actions in the British population is the laws which have been enumerated, and others which shall be hereafter noticed.

To withdraw, therefore, the existing evils which afflict society, these unwise laws must be progressively repealed or modified. The British constitution, in its present outline, is admirably adapted to effect these changes, without the evils which always accompany a coerced or ill-prepared change. As a preliminary step, however, to the commence-ment of national improvements, it should be declared with a sincerity which shall not admit of any after deviation, that no individual of the present generation should be deprived of the emolument which he now receives, or of that which has been officially or legally promised.

The next step in national reform is to withdraw from the national church those tenets which constitute its weakness and create its danger. Yet still, to prevent the evils of any premature change, let the church in other respects remain as it is; because under the old established forms it may effect the most valuable purposes.

To render it truly a national church, all tests, as they are called, that is, declarations of belief in which all cannot conscientiously join, should be withdrawn: this alteration would tend more perhaps than any other which can be devised, to give stability both to the national church and to the state; and a conduct thus rational would at once terminate all the theological differences which now confound the intellects of men and disseminate universal discord.

The next measure of national improvement should be to repeal or modify those laws which leave the lower orders in ignorance, train them to become intemperate, and produce idleness, gambling, poverty, disease, and murder. The production and consumption of ardent spirits are now legally encouraged; licences to keepers of gin-shops and unnecessary pot-houses are by thousands annually distributed; the laws of the state now direct those licences to be distributed; and yet, perhaps, not one of the authors or guardians of these laws has once reflected how much each of those houses daily contributes to public crime, disease, and weakness, or how much they add to the stock of private misery. Shall we then continue to surround our fellow creatures with a temptation which, as many of them are now trained, we know they are unable to resist with a temptation, too, which predisposes its victims to proceed gradually from a state of temporary insanity, into which they had been led by the example and instruction of those around them, to one of madness and bodily disease, creating more than infantile weakness, which again produces mental torments and horrors, that silently, yet most effectually, undermine every faculty in man which can contribute to private or public happiness?

Can the British government longer preserve such laws, or countenance a system which trains man to devise and enforce such laws?

In the year 1736, an act of parliament—stat. 9, Geo, II., c. 23— was passed, of which the preamble is as follows: 'Whereas the drinking of spirituous liquors or strong waters is become very common, especially among the people of lower and inferior rank, the constant and excessive use of which tends greatly to the destruction, of their health, rendering them unfit for useful labour and business, debauching their morals, and inciting them to perpetrate all manner of vices; and the ill consequences of the excessive use of such liquors are not confined to the present generation, but extend to future ages, and tend to the devastation and ruin of this kingdom.' It was therefore enacted, that no person should retail spirits without a licence, for which £50 was to be paid annually, with other provisions to restrain the sale of spirits.

By a report of His Majesty's Justices of the Peace for the county of Middlesex, made in January, 1736, it appeared that there were then within Westminster, Holborn, the Tower, and Finsbury division exclusive of London and Southwark 7,044 houses and shops wherein spirituous liquors were publicly sold by retail, of which they had got an account, and that they believed it was far short of the true number. Enough surely has been said to exhibit the evil consequences of these laws in their true colours. Let the duties therefore on the production of ardent spirits be gradually increased, until the price shall exceed the means of ordinary consumption. Let the licences be progressively withdrawn from the present occupiers of gin-shops and unnecessary pot-houses; and let the duties on the production and consumption of malt liquor be diminished, that the poor and working classes may be the more readily induced to abandon their destructive habits of dram-drinking, and by degrees to withdraw altogether from this incentive to crime and sure source of misery.

The next improvement should be to discontinue the state lottery. The law which creates this measure is neither more nor less than a law to legalize gambling, entrap the unwary, and rob the ignorant. How great must be the error of that system which can induce a state to deceive and injure its subjects, and yet expect that those subjects shall not be necessarily trained to injure and to deceive. These measures may be thought detrimental to the national revenues.

Those who have reflected on the nature of public revenue, and who possess minds capable of comprehending the subject, know that revenue has but one legitimate source that it is derived directly or indirectly from the labour of man, and that it may be more or less from any given number of men (other circumstances being similar), in proportion to their strength, industry, and capacity.

The efficient strength of a state governed by laws founded on an accurate knowledge of human nature, in which the whole population are well trained, will greatly exceed one of equal extent of numbers, in which a large part of the population are improperly trained, and governed by laws founded in ignorance. Thus were the small states of Greece, while governed by laws comparatively wise, superior in national strength to the extended empire of Persia.

On this plain and obvious principle will the effective power and resources of the British empire be largely increased, by withdrawing those laws which, under the plausible appearance of adding a few, and but a few, millions to the annual revenues of this kingdom, in reality feed on the very vitals of the state. For such laws destroy the energies and capacities of its population, which, so weakened and trained to crime, requires a far greater expenditure to protect and govern it.

Confidently may it be said, that a short experience in practice is alone necessary to make the truth of these positions self-evident even to the most common understandings. The next measure for the general improvement of the British population should be to revise the laws relative to the poor. For pure and benevolent as, no doubt, were the motives which actuated those with whom the Poor Laws originated, the direct and certain effects of these laws are to injure the poor, and through them, the state, as much almost as they can be injured. They exhibit the appearance of affording aid to the distressed, while, in reality, they prepare the poor to acquire the worst habits, and to practise every kind of crime. They thus increase the number of the poor and add to their distress. It becomes, therefore, necessary that decisive and effectual measures should be adopted to remove those evils which the existing laws have created.

Benevolence says, that the destitute must not starve; and to this declaration political wisdom readily assents. Yet can that system be right, which compels the industrious, temperate, and comparatively virtuous, to support the ignorant, the idle, and comparatively vicious? Such, however, is the effect of the present British Poor Laws; for they publicly proclaim greater encouragement to idleness, ignorance, extravagance, and intemperance, than to industry and good conduct: and the evils which arise from a system so irrational are hourly experienced, and hourly increasing.

It thus becomes necessary that some counteracting remedy be immediately devised and applied: for, injurious as these laws are, it is obviously impracticable, in the present state of the British population, to annul at once a system to which so large a portion of the people has been taught to look for support. These laws should be progressively undermined by a system of an opposite nature, and ultimately rendered altogether nugatory. The proper system to supersede these laws has been in part already explained, but we proceed to unfold it still more. It may be called 'A System for the Prevention of Crime, and the Formation of Human Character' and, under an established and well-intentioned government it will be found more efficacious in producing public benefit than any of the laws now in existence. The fundamental principle on which all these Essays proceed is, that 'children collectively may be taught any sentiments and habits' or, in other words, 'trained to acquire any character'. It is of importance that this principle should be for ever present in the mind, and that its truth should be established beyond even the shadow of doubt. To the superficial observer it may appear to be an abstract truth of little value; but to the reflecting and accurate reasoner, it will speedily discover itself to be a power which ultimately must destroy the ignorance and consequent prejudices that have accumulated through all preceding ages. For, as it is a deduction from all the leading facts in the past history of the world, so it will be found, on the most extensive investigation, to be consistent with every fact which now exists. It is calculated, therefore, to become the foundation of a new system, which, because true and of unparalleled importance, must prove irresistible, will speedily, supersede all those which exist, and itself become permanent.

It is necessary, however, prior to the introduction of this system in all its bearings and consequences, that the public mind should be impressed with the deepest conviction of its truth. For this purpose, let us in imagination survey the various states and empires of the world, and attentively observe man as in these arbitrary divisions of the earth he is known to exist. Compare the national character of each community with the laws and customs by which they are respectively governed, and, without an exception, the one will be found the archetype of the other.

Where, in former ages, the laws and customs established by Lycurgus formed man into a model for martial exploits, and a perfect instrument for war, he is now trained, by other laws and customs, to be the instrument of a despotism which renders him almost, or altogether, unfit for war. And where the law and custom of Athens trained the young mind to acquire as high a degree of partial rationality as the history of preceding times records, man is now reduced, by a total change of laws and customs, to the lowest state of mental degradation. Also, where, formerly, the superior native American tribes roamed fearlessly through their trackless forests, uniformly exhibiting the hardy, penetrating, elevated, and sincere character, which was at a loss to comprehend how a rational being could desire to possess more than his nature could enjoy; now, on the very same soil, in the same climate, characters are formed under laws and customs so opposite, that all their bodily and mental faculties are individually exerted to obtain, if possible, ten thousand times more than any man can enjoy.

But why proceed to enumerate such endless results as these, of the never-failing influence of training over human nature, when it may be easily rendered self-evident even to the most illiterate, by daily examples around their own dwellings? No one, it may be supposed, can now be so defective in knowledge as to imagine it is a different human nature, which by its own powers forms itself into a child of ignorance, of poverty, and of habits leading to crime and to punishment; or into a votary of fashion, claiming distinction from its folly and inconsistency; or, to fancy, that it is some undefined, blind, unconscious process of human nature itself, distinct from instruction, that forms the sentiments and habits of the man of commerce, of agriculture, the law, the church, the army, the navy, or of the private and illegal depredator on society...or that it is a different human nature which constitutes the societies of the Jews, of Friends, and of all the various religious denominations which have existed or which now exist.

No! Human nature, save the minute differences which are ever found in all the compounds of the creation, is one and the same in all; it is without exception universally plastic, and by judicious training the infants of any one class in the world may be readily formed into men of any other class, even to believe and declare that conduct to be right and virtuous, and to die in its defence, which their parents had been taught to believe and say was wrong and vicious, and to oppose which, those parents would also have willingly sacrificed their lives.

Whence then the foundation of your claim, ye advocates for the superiority of the early prepossessions of your sect or party, in opposition to those taught to other men? Ignorance itself, at this day, might almost make it evident that one particle of merit is not due to you, for not possessing those notions and habits which you now the most contemn. Ought you not, and will you not, then, have charity for those who have been taught different sentiments and habits from yourselves? Let all men fairly investigate this subject for themselves; it well merits their most attentive examination. They will then discover that it is from the errors of education, misinstructing the young mind relative to the true cause of early prepossessions, that almost all the evils of life proceed.

Whence then, ye advocates for the merit and demerit of early prepossessions of opinion, do you derive your principles? Let this system of misery be seen in all its naked deformity! It ought to be exposed; for the instruction which it inculcates at the outset of forming human character is destructive of the genuine charity which can alone train man to be truly benevolent to all other men. The ideas of exclusive right and consequent superiority which men have hitherto been taught to attach to the early sentiments and habits in which they have been instructed, are the chief cause of disunion throughout society; such notions are, indeed, in direct opposition to pure and undefiled religion; nor can they ever exist together. The extent of the misery which they generate cannot, however, be much longer concealed. They are already hastening fast to meet the fate of all errors; for the gross ignorance on which this system of misery has been raised, is exposed to the world on its proper foundation, and, so exposed, its supporters will shrink from the task of defence, and no rational mind will be found to give it support.

Having exhibited the error on which ignorance has erected the systems by which man has been governed, or compelled to become irrational and miserable; and having laid an immovable foundation for a system devoid of that error, which, when fully comprehended and adopted into practice, must train mankind 'to think of and act to others as they would wish others to think of and act to them', we proceed further to explain this system without error, and which may be termed a system without mystery. As then children collectively may be formed into any characters, by whom ought their characters to be formed? The kind and degree of misery or happiness experienced by the members of any community, depend on the characters which have been formed in the individuals which constitute the community.

It becomes, then, the highest interest, and consequently the first and most important duty, of every state, to form the individual characters of which the state is composed. And if any characters, from the most ignorant and miserable to the most rational and happy, can be formed, it surely merits the deepest attention of every state to adopt those means by which the formation of the latter may be secured, and that of the former prevented.

It follows that every state, to be well governed, ought to direct its chief attention to the formation of character; and thus the best governed state will be that which shall possess the best national system of education.

Under the guidance of minds competent to its direction, a national system of training and education may be formed, to become the most safe, easy, effectual, and economical instrument of government that can be devised. And it may be made to possess a power equal to the accomplishment of the most grand and beneficial purposes.

It is, however, by instruction only, that the population of the world can be made conscious of the irrational state in which they now exist; and, until that instruction is given, it is premature to introduce a national system of education.

But the time is now arrived when the British Government may with safety adopt a national system of training and education for the poor and uninstructed; and this measure alone, if the plan shall be well devised and executed, will effect the most importantly beneficial changes.

As a preliminary step, however, it is necessary to observe, that to create a well-trained, united, and happy people, this national system should be uniform over the United Kingdom; it should be also founded in the spirit of peace and of rationality, and, for the most obvious reasons, the thought of exclusion to one child in the empire should not for a moment be entertained.

Several plans have been lately proposed for the national education of the poor, but these have not been calculated to effect all that a national system of education of the poor ought to accomplish.

For the authors and supporters of these systems we feel those sentiments which the principles developed throughout these essays must create in any minds on which they have been early and effectually impressed; and we are desirous of rendering their labours for the community as extensively beneficial as they can be made. To fulfil, however, a great and important public duty, the plans which they have devised must be considered as though they had been produced and published in the days of antiquity. The plans alluded to are those of the Rev. Dr Bell, Mr Joseph Lancaster, and Mr Whitbread.

The systems of Dr Bell and Mr Lancaster, for instructing the poor in reading, writing, and arithmetic, prove the extreme ignorance which previously existed in the manner of training the young; for it is in the manner alone of giving instruction that these new systems are an improvement on the modes of instruction which were formerly practised.

The arrangement of the room and many of the details in Mr Lancaster's plan, are, in some respects, better calculated to give instruction in the elements enumerated, than those recommended by Dr Bell, although some of the details introduced by the latter are very superior, and highly deserving of adoption.

The essence, however, of national training and education is to impress on the young, ideas and habits which shall contribute to the future happiness of the individuals and of the state; and this can be accomplished only by instructing them to become rational beings.

It must be evident to common observers, that children may be taught, by either Dr Bell's or Mr Lancaster's system, to read, write, account, and sew, and yet acquire the worst habits, and have their minds rendered irrational for life.

Reading and writing are merely instruments by which knowledge either true or false, may be imparted; and, when given to children, are of little comparative value, unless they are also taught how to make a proper use of them. When a child receives a full and fair explanation of the objects and characters around him, and when he is also taught to reason correctly, so that he may learn to discover general truths from falsehood, he will be much better instructed, although without the knowledge of one letter or figure, than those are who have been compelled to believe, and whose reasoning faculties have been confounded or destroyed by what is most erroneously termed learning.

It is readily acknowledged that the manner of instructing children is of importance and deserves all the attention it has lately received; that those who discover or introduce improvements which facilitate the acquirement of knowledge are important benefactors of their fellow creatures. Yet the manner of giving instruction is one thing, the instruction itself another; and no two objects can be more distinct. The worst manner may be applied to give the best instruction, and the best manner to give the worst instruction. Were the real importance of both to be estimated by numbers, the manner of instruction may be compared to one, and the matter of instruction to millions: the first is the means only; the last, the end to be accomplished by those means. If, therefore, in a national system of education for the poor, it be desirable to adopt the best manner, it is surely so much the more desirable to adopt also the best matter, of instruction.

Either give the poor a rational and useful training, or mock not their ignorance, their poverty, and their misery, by merely instructing them to become conscious of the extent of the degradation under which they exist. And, therefore, in pity to suffering humanity, either keep the poor, if you now can, in the state of the most abject ignorance, as near as possible to animal life, or at once determine to form them into rational beings, into useful and effective members of the state. Were it possible, without national prejudice, to examine into the matter of instruction which is now given in some of our boasted new systems for the instruction of the poor, it would be found to be almost as wretched as any which can be devised. In proof of this statement, enter any one of the schools denominated national, and request the master to show the acquirements of the children. These are called out, and he asks them theological questions to which men of the most profound erudition cannot make a rational reply; the children, however, readily answer as they had been previously instructed; for memory, in this mockery of learning, is all that is required.

Thus the child whose natural faculty of comparing ideas, or whose rational powers, shall be the soonest destroyed, if, at the same time, he possess a memory to retain incongruities without connection, will become what is termed the first scholar in the class; and three-fourths of the time which ought to be devoted to the acquirement of useful instruction, will be really occupied in destroying the mental powers of the children. To those accustomed attentively to notice the human countenance from infancy to age, in the various classes and religious denominations of the British population, it is truly an instructive although melancholy employment, to observe in the countenances of the poor children in these schools the evident expression of mental injury derived from the well-intentioned, but most mistaken, plan of their instruction. It is an important lesson, because it affords another recent and striking example to the millions which previously existed, of the ease with which children may be taught to receive any sectarian notions, and thence acquire any habits, however contrary to their real happiness.

To those trained to become truly conscientious in any of the present sectarian errors which distract the world, this free exposure of the weakness of the peculiar tenets in which such individuals have been instructed, will, at first, excite feelings of high displeasure and horror, and these feelings will be acute and poignant in proportion to the obvious and irresistible evidence on which the disclosure of their errors is founded. Let them, however, begin to think calmly on these subjects, to examine their own minds and the minds of all around them, and they will become conscious of the absurdities and inconsistencies in which their forefathers have trained them; they will then abhor the errors by which they have been so long abused; and, with an earnestness not to be resisted, they will exert their utmost faculties to remove the cause of so much misery to man. Enough surely has now been said of the manner and matter of instruction in these new systems, to exhibit them in a just and true light.

The improvements in the manner of teaching children whatever may be deemed proper for them to learn—improvements which, we may easily predict, will soon receive great additions and amendments have proceeded from the Rev. Dr Bell and Mr Lancaster; while the errors which their respective systems assist to engrave on the ductile mind of infancy and childhood, are derived from times when ignorance gave countenance to every kind of absurdity. Mr Whitbread's scheme for the education of the poor was evidently the production of an ardent mind possessing considerable abilities; his mind, however, had been irregularly formed by the errors of his early education; and this was most conspicuous in the speech which introduced the plan he had devised to the House of Commons, and in the plan itself.

The first was a clear exposition of all the reasons for the education of the poor which could be expected from a human being trained from infancy under the systems in which Mr Whitbread had been instructed.

The plan itself evinced the fallacy of the principles which he had imbibed, and showed that he had not acquired a practical knowledge of the feelings and habits of the poor, or of the only effectual means by which they could be trained to be useful to themselves and to the community.

Had Mr Whitbread not been trained, as almost all the Members of both Houses of Parliament have been, in delusive theories, devoid of rational foundation, which prevent them from acquiring any extensive practical knowledge of human nature, he would not have committed a plan for the national education of the poor to the sole management and direction of the ministers, churchwardens, and overseers of parishes, whose present interests must have appeared to be opposed to the measure. He would surely, first, have devised a plan to make it the evident interest of the ministers, churchwardens, and overseers, to co-operate in giving efficacy to the system which he wished to introduce to their superintendence; and also to render them, by previous training, competent to that superintendence for which now they are in general unprepared.

For, trained as these individuals have hitherto been, they must be deficient in the practical knowledge necessary to enable them successfully to direct the instruction of others; and had an attempt been made to carry Mr Whitbread's plan into execution, it would have created a scene of confusion over the whole kingdom. Attention to the subject will make it evident that it never was, and that it never can be, the interest of any sect claiming exclusive privileges on account of professing high and mysterious doctrines, about which the best and most conscientious men may differ in opinion, that the mass of the people should be otherwise instructed than in those doctrines which were and are in unison with its peculiar tenets; and that at this hour a national system of education for the lower orders, on sound political principles, is really dreaded, even by some of the most learned and intelligent members of the Church of England. Such feelings in the members of the national church are those only which ought to be expected; for most men so trained and circumstanced must of necessity acquire these feelings. Why, therefore, should any class of men endeavour to rouse the indignation of the public against them? Their conduct and their motives are equally correct, and therefore, equally good, with those who raise the cry against and oppose the errors of the church. And let it ever be remembered, that an establishment which possesses the power of propagating principles, may be rendered truly valuable when directed to inculcate a system of self-evident truth, unobstructed by inconsistencies and counteractions.

The dignitaries of the church, and their adherents, foresaw that a national system for the education of the poor, unless it were placed under the immediate influence and management of individuals belonging to the church, would effectually and rapidly undermine the errors, not only of their own, but of every other ecclesiastical establishment. In this foresight they evinced the superiority of their penetration over the sectaries by whom the unexclusive system is supported. The heads of the church have wisely discovered that reason and inconsistency cannot long exist together; that the one must inevitably destroy the other, and reign paramount. They have witnessed the regular, and latterly the rapid progress which reason has made; they know that its accumulating strength cannot be much longer resisted; and, as they now see the contest is hopeless, the unsuccessful attempt to destroy the Lancastrian system of education is the last effort they will ever make to counteract the dissemination of knowledge which is now widely extending itself in every direction.

The establishment of the Rev. Dr Bell's system of initiating the children of the poor in all the tenets of the Church of England, is an attempt to ward off a little longer the yet dreaded period of a change from ignorance to reason, from misery to happiness.

Let us, however, not attempt impossibilities; the task is vain and hopeless; the Church, while it adheres to the defective and injurious parts of its system, cannot be induced to act cordially in opposition to its apparent interests.

The principles here advocated will not admit the application of any deception to any class of men; they countenance no proceedings in practice, but of unlimited sincerity and candour. They give rise to no one sentiment which is not in unison with the happiness of the human race; and they impart knowledge, which renders it evident that such happiness can never be acquired until every particle of falsehood and deception shall be eradicated from the instructions which the old force upon the young.

Let us then in this spirit openly declare to the Church, that a national unexclusive plan of education for the poor will, without the shadow of doubt, destroy all the errors which are attached to the various systems; and that, when this plan shall be fully established, not one of the tenets which is in opposition to facts can long be upheld.

This unexclusive system for the education of the poor has gone forth, and, having found a resting place in the minds of its supporters, it will never more return even to the control of its projectors; but it will be speedily so improved, that by rapidly increasing strides it will firmly establish the reign of reason and happiness.

Seeing and knowing this, let us also make it equally evident to the Church warn it of its actual state—cordially and sincerely assist its members quietly to withdraw those inconsistencies from the system, which now create its weakness and its danger; that it may retain those rational principles alone which can be successfully defended against attack, or which rather will prevent any attack from being attempted, or even meditated.

The wise and prudent, then, of all parties, instead of wishing to destroy national establishments, will use their utmost exertions to render them so consistent and reasonable in all their parts, that every well-disposed mind may be induced to give them their hearty and willing support.

For the first grand step towards effecting any substantial improvement in these realms, without injury to any part of the community, is to make it the clear an decided interest of the Church to cooperate cordially in all the projected ameliorations. Once found a national church on the true, unlimited, and genuine principles of mental charity, and all the members of the state will soon improve in every truly valuable quality. If the temperate and discerning of all parties will not now lend their aid to effect this change by peaceable means (which may with the greatest ease and with unerring certainty be done), it is evident to every calm observer, that the struggle by those who now exist in unnecessary misery, to attain that degree of happiness which they may attain in practice, cannot long be deferred. It will therefore prove true political wisdom to anticipate and guide these feelings.

To those who can reflect and will attend to the passing scenes before them, the times are indeed awfully interesting; some change of high import, scarcely yet perhaps to be scanned by the present ill-taught race of men, is evidently in progress: in consequence, well-founded, prompt, and decisive measures are now required in the British councils, to direct this change, and to relieve the nation from the errors of its present systems. It must surely then be the desire of every rational man, of every true friend to humanity, that a cordial cooperation and unity of action should be effected between the British Executive, the

Parliament, the Church, and the People, to lay a broad and firm foundation for the future happiness of themselves and the world.

Say not, my countrymen, that such an event is impracticable; for, by adopting the evident means to form a rational character in man, there is a plain and direct road opened, which, if pursued, will render its accomplishment not only possible but certain. That road, too, will be found the most safe and pleasant that human beings have ever yet travelled. It leads direct to intelligence and true knowledge, and will show the boasted acquirements of Greece, of Rome, and of all antiquity, to be the mere weakness of mental infancy. Those who travel this road will find it so straight and well defined, that no one will be in danger of wandering from the right course. Nor is it yet a narrow or exclusive path; it admits of no exclusion: every colour of body and diversity of mind are freely and alike admitted. It is open to the human race, and it is broad and spacious enough to receive the whole, were they increased a thousandfold. We well know that a declaration like the one now made must sound chimerical in the ears of those who have hitherto wandered in the dark mazes of ignorance, error, and exclusion, and who have been taught folly and inconsistencies only from their cradle.

But if every known fact connected with the subject proves that, from the day in which man first saw light to that in which the sun now shines, the old collectively have taught the young collectively the sentiments and habits which the young have acquired; and that the present generation and every following generation must in like manner instruct their successors; then do we say, with a confidence founded on certainty itself, that even much more shall come to pass than has yet been foretold or promised. When these principles, derived from the unchangeable laws of nature, and equally revealed to all men, shall, as soon as they will, be publicly established in the world, no conceivable obstacle can remain to prevent a sincere and cordial union and cooperation for every wise and good purpose, not only among all the members of the same state, but also among the rulers of those kingdoms and empires whose enmity and rancour against each other have been carried to the utmost stretch of melancholy folly, and even occasionally to a high degree of madness.

Such, my fellow men, are some, and yet but a few, of the mighty consequences which must result from the public acknowledgement of these plain, simple, and irresistible truths. They will not prove a delusive promise of mockery, but will in reality speedily and effectively establish peace, goodwill, and an ever-active benevolence throughout the whole human race. The public avowal of these principles, and their general introduction into practice, will constitute the invaluable secret, for which the human mind, from its birth, has been in perpetual search; its future beneficial consequences no man can yet foresee.

We will now show how these principles may be immediately and most advantageously introduced into general practice. It has been said that 'the state which shall possess the best national, system of education, will be the best governed'; and if the principle on which the reasoning of these essays is founded be true, then is that sentiment also true. Yet (will future ages credit the fact?) to this day the British Government is without any national system of training and education even for its millions of poor and uninstructed!! The formation of the mind and habits of its subjects is permitted to go on at random, often in the hands of those who are the most incompetent in the empire; and the result is, the gross ignorance and disunion which now everywhere abound!! (Even the recent attempts which have been made are conducted on the narrow principle of debasing man to a mere irrational military machine which is to be rapidly moved by animal force.) Instead of continuing such unwise proceedings, a national system for the training and education of the labouring classes ought to be immediately arranged; and, if judiciously devised, it may be rendered the most valuable improvement ever yet introduced into practice.

For this purpose an act should be passed for the instruction of all the poor and labouring classes in the three kingdoms. In this act, provision should be made:

1. For the appointment of proper persons to direct this new department of government, which will be found ultimately to prove the most important of all its departments; consequently, those individuals who possess the highest integrity, abilities, and influence in the state, should be appointed to its direction.
2. For the establishment of seminaries in which those individuals who shall be destined to form the minds and bodies of the future subjects of these realms should be well initiated in the art and matter of instruction.

This is, and ought to be considered, an office of the greatest practical trust and confidence in the empire; for let this duty be well performed, and the government must proceed with ease to the people and with high gratification to those who govern.

At present there are not any individuals in the kingdom who have been trained to instruct the rising generation as it is for the interest and happiness of all that it should be instructed. The training of those who are to form the future man, becomes a consideration of the utmost magnitude; for, on due reflection, it will appear, that instruction to the young must be, of necessity, the only foundation upon which the superstructure of society can be raised. Let this instruction continue to be left, as heretofore, to chance, and often to the most inefficient members of the community, and society must still experience the endless miseries which still arise from such weak and puerile conduct. On the contrary, let the instruction to the young be well devised and well executed, and no subsequent proceedings in the state can be materially injurious. For it may truly be said to be a wonder-working power; one that merits the deepest attention of the legislature; with ease it may be used to train man into a demon of mischief to himself and to all around him, or into an agent of unlimited benevolence.

3. For the establishment of seminaries over the United Kingdoms; to be conveniently placed, and of sufficient extent to receive all those who require instruction.
4. For supplying the requisite expenditure for the building and support of those seminaries.
5. For the arrangement of the plan which, for the manner of instruction, upon a due comparison of the various modes now in practice, or which may be devised, shall appear to be the best.
6. For the appointment of proper masters to each of the schools. And,
7. The matter of instruction, both for body and mind, in these seminaries, should be substantially beneficial to the individuals and to the state. For this is, or ought to be, the sole motive for the establishment of national seminaries.

These are the outlines of the provisions necessary to prepare the most powerful instrument of good that has ever yet been placed in the hands of man.

The last national improvement which remains to be proposed in the present state of the public mind, is, that another legislative act should be passed, for the purpose of obtaining regular and accurate information relative to the value of and demand for labour over the United Kingdom. This information is necessary, preparatory to the adoption of measures which will be proposed, to provide labour for those who may be occasionally unable to procure other employment. In this act provision should be made, to obtain accurate quarterly returns of the state of labour in each country or smaller district; the returns to be made either by the clergy, justices of the peace, or other more competent persons. These returns should contain,

1. The average price of manual labour within the district for the period included in the return.
2. The number, of those in each district who depend on their daily labour or on the parish for their support; and

who may be at the period of these returns unemployed, and yet able to labour.

3. The number of those who, at the period of each return, are but partially employed; and the extent of that partial employment. Provision should also be made to obtain a statement of the general occupations in which the individuals had been formerly employed, with the best conjectures as to the kind and quantity of work which each may be supposed still capable of performing.

The want of due attention to this highly necessary branch of government, occasions thousands of our fellow subjects to be made wretched; while, from the same cause, the revenues of the empire are annually deteriorated to an enormous amount.

We have stated, because it is easy of proof, that the revenues of all countries are derived directly or indirectly, from the labour of man; and yet the British Government, which, with all its errors, is among the best devised and most enlightened that has hitherto been established, makes extravagant and unnecessary waste of that labour. It makes this waste, too, in the midst of its greatest pecuniary difficulties, and when the utmost efforts of every individual in the state are requisite! This waste of human labour, as it is highly unjust to all, is not only impolitic in a national view, but is most cruel to the individuals who, in consequence of this waste, are the immediate sufferers.

It would be an Herculean task to trace through all their ramifications the various injurious effects which result from the fundamental errors by which man has been, and is governed; nor is the world yet fully prepared for such development. We shall, therefore, now merely sketch some of the most direct and palpable of these effects, relative to the oversight of governments in regard to the non-application or misapplication of the labour of the poor and unoccupied.

It has been shown that the governing powers of any country may easily and economically give the subjects just sentiments and the best habits; and so long as this shall remain unattempted, governments will continue to neglect their most important duties as well as interests. Such neglect now exists in Britain, where, in lieu of the governing powers making any effort to attain these inestimable benefits for the individuals belonging to the empire, they must content themselves with the existence of laws which must create sentiments and habits highly injurious to the welfare of the individuals and of the state.

Many of these laws, by their never-failing effects, speak in a language which no one can misunderstand, and say to the unprotected and untaught. Remain in ignorance, and let your labour be directed by that ignorance, for while you can Procure what is sufficient to support life by such labour, although that life should be an existence in abject poverty, disease, and misery, we will not trouble ourselves with you, or any of your proceedings; when, however, you can no longer procure work, or obtain the means to support nature, then apply for relief to the parish, and you shall be maintained in idleness.'

And in ignorance and idleness, even in this country, where manual labour is or always might be made valuable, hundreds of thousands of men, women, and children are daily supported. No one acquainted with human nature will suppose that men, women, and children, can be long maintained in ignorance and idleness, without becoming habituated to crime. (It would, perhaps, prove an interesting calculation, and useful to government, to estimate how much its finances would be improved, by giving proper employment to a million of its subjects, rather than by supporting that million in ignorance, idleness, and crime.

Will it exceed the bounds of moderation to say, that a million of the population so employed, under the direction of an intelligent government, might earn to the state ten pounds each annually, or ten millions sterling per annum? Ten millions per year would be obtained, by each individual earning less than four shillings per week; and any part of the population of these kingdoms, including within the average the too young and the too old for labour, may be made to earn, under proper arrangements, more than four shillings per week to the state, besides creating an innumerable train of other more beneficial consequences.)

Why then, are there any idle poor in these kingdoms? Solely because so large a part of the population have been permitted to grow up to manhood in gross ignorance; and because, when they are, or easily may be trained to be willing to labour, useful and productive employment has not been provided for them. All men may, by judicious and proper laws and training, readily acquire knowledge and habits which will enable them, if they be permitted, to produce far more than they need for their support and enjoyment: and thus any population, in the fertile parts of the earth, may be taught to live in plenty and in happiness, without the checks of vice and misery.

Mr Malthus is, however, correct, when he says that the population of the world is ever adapting itself to the quantity of food raised for its support; but he has not told us how much more food an intelligent and industrious people will create from the same soil, than will be produced by one ignorant and ill-governed. It is, however, as one to infinity. For man knows not the limit to his power of creating food. How much has this power been latterly increased in these islands! And in them such knowledge is in its infancy. Yet compare even this power of raising food with the efforts of the Bosgemens or other savages, and it will be found, perhaps, as one to a thousand.

Food for man may also be considered as a compound of the original elements, of the qualities, combinations, and control of which, chemistry is daily adding to our knowledge; nor is it yet for man to say to what this knowledge may lead, or where it may end.

The sea, it may be remarked also, affords an inexhaustible source of food. It may then be safely asserted that the population of the world may be allowed naturally to increase for many thousand years; and yet, under a system of government founded on the principles for the truth of which we contend, the whole may continue to live in abundance and happiness, without one check of vice or misery; and under the guidance of these principles, human labour, properly directed, may be made far more than sufficient to enable the population of the world to live in the highest state of human enjoyment.

Shall we then continue to allow misery to predominate, and the labour of man to be most absurdly applied or wasted, when it might be easily directed to remove that misery? The labour of every man, woman, and child, possessing sufficient bodily strength, may be advanta-geously employed for the public; and there is not, perhaps, a stronger evidence of the extreme ignorance and fallacy of the systems which have hitherto governed the world, than that the rich, the active, and the powerful, should, by tacit consent, support the ignorant in idleness and crime, without making the attempt to train them into industrious, intelligent, and valuable members of the community; although the means by which the change could be easily effected have been always at their command!

It is not, however, intended to propose that the British Government should now give direct employment to all its working population. On the contrary, it is confidently expected that a national system for the training and education of the poor and lower orders will be so effectual, that ere long they will all find employment sufficient to support themselves, except in cases of great sudden depression in the demand for, and consequent depreciation in the value of labour.

To prevent the crime and misery which ever follow these unfavourable fluctuations in the demand for and value of labour, it ought to be a primary duty of every government that sincerely interests itself in the well-being of its subjects, to provide perpetual employment of real national utility, in which all who apply may be immediately occupied. In order that those only who could not obtain employment from private individuals should be induced to avail themselves of these national works, the rate of the public labour might be in general fixed at some proportion less than the average rate of private labour in the district in which such public labour should be performed. These rates might be readily ascertained and fixed, by reference to the county or district quarterly returns of the average rate of labour.

This measure, judiciously managed, would have a similar effect on the price of labour, that the sinking fund produces on the Stock Exchange; and, as the price of public labour should never fall below the means of temperate existence, the plan proposed would perpetually tend to prevent an excess of nationally injurious pressure on the most unprotected part of society.

The most obvious, and, in the first place, the best source, perhaps, of employment, would be the making and repairing of roads. Such employment would be perpetual over the whole kingdom; and it will be found true national economy to keep the public roads at all times in a much higher state of repair than, perhaps, any of them are at present. If requisite, canals, harbours, docks, shipbuilding, and materials for the navy, may be afterwards resorted to; it is not, however, supposed that many of the latter resources would be necessary.

A persevering attention, without which, indeed, not anything beneficial in practice can ever be attained, will soon overcome all the difficulties which may at first appear to obstruct this plan for introducing occasional national employment into the polity of the kingdom.

In times of very limited demand for labour, it is truly lamentable to witness the distress which arises among the industrious for want of regular employment and their customary wages. In these periods, innumerable applications are made to the superintendents of extensive manual operations, to obtain any kind of employment, by which a subsistence may be procured. Such applications are often made by persons who, in search of work, have travelled from one extremity of the island to the other! During these attempts to be useful and honest, in the common acceptation of the terms, the families of such wandering individuals accompany them, or remain at home; in either case they generally experience sufferings and privations which the gay and splendid will hesitate to believe it possible that human nature could endure.

Yet, after this extended and anxious endeavour to procure employment, the applicant often returns unsuccessful; he cannot, by his most strenuous exertions, procure an honest and independent existence; therefore, with intentions perhaps as good, and a mind as capable of great and benevolent actions as the remainder of his fellow men, he has no other resources left but to starve, apply to his parish for relief, and thus suffer the greatest degradation, or rely on his own native exertions, and, to supply himself and family with bread, resort to what are termed dishonest means.

Some minds thus circumstanced are so delicately formed, that they will not accept the one or adopt the other of the two latter modes to sustain life, and in consequence they actually starve.

These, however, it is to be hoped, are not very numerous. But the number is undoubtedly great, of those whose health is ruined by bad and insufficient food, clothing, and shelter; who contract lingering diseases, and suffer premature death, the effect of partial starvation.

The most ignorant and least enterprising of them apply to the parish for support; soon lose the desire of exertion; become permanently dependent; conscious of their degradation in society; and henceforward, with their offspring, remain a burden and grievous evil to the state; while those among this class who yet possess strength and energy of body and mind, with some undestroyed powers of reasoning, perceive, in part, the glaring errors and injustice of society towards themselves and their fellow sufferers.

Can it then create surprise that feelings like those described should force human nature to endeavour to retaliate? Multitudes of our fellow men are so goaded by these reflections and circumstances, as to be urged, even while incessantly and closely pursued by legal death almost without a chance of escape, to resist those laws under which they suffer; and thus the private depredator on society is formed, fostered, and matured.

Shall we then longer withhold national instruction from our fellow men, who, it has been shown, might easily be trained to be industrious, intelligent, virtuous, and valuable members of the state?

True, indeed, it is, that all the measures now proposed are only a compromise with the errors of the present systems; but as these errors now almost universally exist, and must be overcome solely by the force of reason; and as reason, to effect the most beneficial purposes, makes her advance by slow degrees, and progressively substantiates one truth of high import after another, it will be evident, to minds of comprehensive and accurate thought, that by these and similar compromises alone can success be rationally expected in practice. For such compromises bring truth and error before the public; and whenever they are fairly exhibited together, truth must ultimately prevail. As many of the inconsistencies of the present systems are evident to the most intelligent and well-disposed minds, the way for the public admission of the important truths which have now been in part unfolded seems to be rendered easy', and it is confidently expected that the period is at hand, when man, through ignorance, shall not' much longer inflict unnecessary misery on man; because the mass of mankind will become enlightened, and will clearly discern that by so acting they will inevitably create misery to themselves. (As soon as the public mind shall be sufficiently prepared to receive it, the practical detail of this system shall be fully developed.)

For the extensive knowledge of the facts which present themselves on the globe, makes it evident to those whose reasoning faculties have not been entirely paralysed, that all mankind firmly believe, that everybody except themselves has been grievously deceived in his fundamental principles; and feel the utmost astonishment that the nations of the world could embrace such gross inconsistencies for divine or political truths. Most persons are now also prepared to understand, that these weaknesses are firmly and conscientiously fixed in the minds of millions, who, when born, possessed equal faculties with themselves. And although they plainly discern in others what they deem inconceivable aberrations of the mental powers, yet, in despite of such facts, they are taught to believe that they themselves could not have been so deceived; and this impression is made upon the infant mind with the greatest ease, whether it be to create followers of the most ignorant, or of the most enlightened systems.

The inhabitants of the world are, therefore, abundantly conscious of the inconsistencies contained in those systems in which all have been trained out of the pale of their own peculiar, and, as they are taught to believe, highly favoured sect: and yet the number of the largest sect in the world is small, when compared with the remaining sects which have been instructed to think the notions of that larger division an error of the grossest kind, proceeding alone from the ignorance or deception of their predecessors.

All that is now requisite, previous to withdrawing the last mental bandage by which hitherto the human race has been kept in darkness and misery, is, by calm and patient reasoning to tranquillize the public mind, and thus prevent the evil effects which otherwise might arise from the too sudden prospect of freely enjoying rational liberty of mind.

To withdraw that bandage without danger, reason must be judiciously applied to lead men of every sect (for all have been in part abused to reflect that if untold myriads of beings, formed like themselves, have been so grossly deceived as they believe them to have been, what power in nature was there to prevent them from being equally deceived?

Such reflections, steadily pursued by those who are anxious to follow the plain and simple path of reason, will soon make it obvious that the inconsistencies which they behold in all other sects out of their own pale, are precisely similar to those which all other sects can readily discover within that pale.

It is not, however, to be imagined, that this free and open exposure of the gross errors in which the existing generation has been instructed, should be forthwith palatable to the world; it would be contrary to reason to form any such expectations. Yet, as evil exists, and as man cannot be rational, nor of course happy, until the cause of it shall be removed; the writer, like a physician who feels the deepest interest in the welfare of his patient, has hitherto administered of this unpalatable restorative the smallest quantity which he deemed sufficient for the purpose. He now waits to see the effects which that may produce.

Should the application not prove of sufficient strength to remove the mental disorder, he promises that it shall be increased, until sound health to the public mind be firmly and permanently established.

2
Principles of Communism

Friedrich Engels

What is Communism?

Communism is the doctrine of the conditions of the liberation of the proletariat.

What is the Proletariat?

The proletariat is that class in society which lives entirely from the sale of its labour and does not draw profit from any kind of capital; whose weal and woe, whose life and death, whose sole existence depends on the demand for labour—hence, on the changing state of business, on the vagaries of unbridled competition. The proletariat, or the class of proletarians, is, in a word, the working class of the 19th century.

Proletarians, then, have not always existed?

No. There have always been poor and working classes; and the working class have mostly been poor. But there have not always been workers and poor people living under conditions as they are today; in other words, there have not always been proletarians, any more than there has always been free unbridled competitions.

How did the proletariat originate?

The proletariat originated in the Industrial Revolution, which took place in England in the last half of the last (18th) century, and which has since then been repeated in all the civilized countries of the world.

This Industrial Revolution was precipitated by the discovery of the steam engine, various spinning machines, the mechanical loom, and a whole series of other mechanical devices. These machines, which were very expensive and hence could be bought only by big capitalists, altered the whole mode of production and displaced the former workers, because the machines turned out cheaper and better commodities than the workers could produce with their inefficient spinning wheels and handlooms. The machines delivered industry wholly into the hands of the big capitalists and rendered entirely worthless the meagre property of the workers (tools, looms, etc.). The result was that the capitalists soon had everything in their hands and nothing remained to the workers. This marked the introduction of the factory system into the textile industry.

Once the impulse to the introduction of machinery and the factory system had been given, this system spread quickly to all other branches of industry, especially cloth and book-printing, pottery, and the metal industries.

Labour was more and more divided among the individual workers so that the worker who previously had done a complete piece of work now did only a part of that piece. This division of labour made it possible to produce things faster and cheaper. It reduced the activity of the individual worker to simple, endlessly repeated mechanical motions which could be performed not only as well but much better by a machine. In this way, all these industries fell, one after another, under the dominance of steam, machinery, and the factory system, just as spinning and weaving had already done.

But at the same time, they also fell into the hands of big capitalists, and their workers were deprived of whatever independence remained to them. Gradually, not only genuine manufacture but also handicrafts came within the province of the factory system as big capitalists increasingly displaced the small master craftsmen by setting up huge workshops, which saved many expenses and permitted an elaborate division of labour.

This is how it has come about that in civilized countries at the present time nearly all kinds of labour are performed in factories—and, in nearly all branches of work, handicrafts and manufacture have been superseded. This process has, to an ever greater degree, ruined the old middle class, especially the small handicraftsmen; it has entirely transformed the condition of the workers; and two new classes have been created which are gradually swallowing up all the others. These are:

(i) The class of big capitalists, who, in all civilized countries, are already in almost exclusive possession of all the means of subsistence and of the instruments (machines, factories) and materials necessary for the production of the means of subsistence. This is the bourgeois class, or the bourgeoisie.

(ii) The class of the wholly propertyless, who are obliged to sell their labour to the bourgeoisie in order to get, in exchange, the means of subsistence for their support. This is called the class of proletarians, or the proletariat.

Under what conditions does this sale of the labour of the proletarians to the bourgeoisie take place?

Labour is a commodity, like any other, and its price is therefore determined by exactly the same laws that apply to other commodities. In a regime of big industry or of free competition—as we shall see, the two come to the same thing—the price of a commodity is, on the average, always equal to its cost of production. Hence, the price of labour is also equal to the cost of production of labour.

But, the costs of production of labour consist of precisely the quantity of means of subsistence necessary to enable the worker to continue working, and to prevent the working class from dying out. The worker will therefore get no more for his labour than is necessary for this purpose; the price of labour, or the wage, will, in other words, be the lowest, the minimum, required for the maintenance of life.

However, since business is sometimes better and sometimes worse, it follows that the worker sometimes gets more and sometimes gets less for his commodities. But, again, just as the industrialist, on the average of good times and bad, gets no more and no less for his commodities than what they cost, similarly on the average the worker gets no more and no less than his minimum.

This economic law of wages operates the more strictly the greater the degree to which big industry has taken possession of all branches of production.

What working classes were there before the Industrial Revolution?

The working classes have always, according to the different stages of development of society, lived in different circumstances and had different relations to the owning and ruling classes.

In antiquity, the workers were the slaves of the owners, just as they still are in many backward countries and even in the southern part of the United States.

In the Middle Ages, they were the serfs of the land-owning nobility, as they still are in Hungary, Poland, and Russia. In the Middle Ages, and indeed right up to the Industrial Revolution, there were also journeymen in the cities who worked in the service of petty bourgeois masters. Gradually, as manufacture developed, these journeymen became manufacturing workers who were even then employed by larger capitalists.

In what way do proletarians differ from slaves?

The slave is sold once and for all; the proletarian must sell himself daily and hourly.

The individual slave, property of one master, is assured an existence, however miserable it may be, because of the master's interest. The individual proletarian, property as it were of the entire bourgeois class which buys his labour only when someone has need of it, has no secure existence. This existence is assured only to the class as a whole.

The slave is outside competition; the proletarian is in it and experiences all its vagaries.

The slave counts as a thing, not as a member of society. Thus, the slave can have a better existence than the proletarian, while the proletarian belongs to a higher stage of social development and, himself, stands on a higher social level than the slave.

The slave frees himself when, of all the relations of private property, he abolishes only the relation of slavery and thereby becomes a proletarian; the proletarian can free himself only by abolishing private property in general.

In what way do proletarians differ from serfs?

The serf possesses and uses an instrument of production, a piece of land, in exchange for which he gives up a part of his product or part of the services of his labour.

The proletarian works with the instruments of production of another, for the account of this other, in exchange for a part of the product.

The serf gives up, the proletarian receives. The serf has an assured existence, the proletarian has not. The serf is outside competition, the proletarian is in it.

The serf liberates himself in one of three ways: either he runs away to the city and there becomes a handicraftsman; or, instead of products and and services, he gives money to his lord and thereby becomes a free tenant; or he overthrows his feudal lord and himself becomes a property owner. In short, by one route or another, he gets into the owning class and enters into competition. The proletarian liberates himself by abolishing competition, private property, and all class differences.

In what way do proletarians differ from manufacturing workers?

The manufacturing worker of the 16th to the 18th centuries still had, with but few exception, an instrument of production in his own possession—his loom, the family spinning wheel, a little plot of land which he cultivated in his spare time. The proletarian has none of these things.

The manufacturing worker almost always lives in the countryside and in a more or less patriarchal relation to his landlord or employer; the proletarian lives, for the most part, in the city and his relation to his employer is purely a cash relation.

The manufacturing worker is torn out of his patriarchal relation by big industry, loses whatever property he still has, and in this way becomes a proletarian.

What were the immediate consequences of the Industrial Revolution and of the division of society into bourgeoisie and proletariat?

First, the lower and lower prices of industrial products brought about by machine labour totally destroyed, in all countries of the world, the old system of manufacture or industry based upon hand labour.

In this way, all semi-barbarian countries, which had hitherto been more or less strangers to historical development, and whose industry had been based on manufacture, were violently forced out of their isolation. They bought the cheaper commodities of the English and allowed their own manufacturing workers to be ruined. Countries which had known no progress for thousands of years—for example, India—were thoroughly revolutionized, and even China is now on the way to a revolution.

We have come to the point where a new machine invented in England deprives millions of Chinese workers of their livelihood within a year's time.

In this way, big industry has brought all the people of the earth into contact with each other, has merged all local markets into one world market, has spread civilization and progress everywhere and has thus ensured that whatever happens in civilized countries will have repercussions in all other countries.

It follows that if the workers in England or France now liberate themselves, this must set off revolution in all other countries— revolutions which, sooner or later, must accomplish the liberation of their respective working class.

Second, wherever big industries displaced manufacture, the bourgeoisie developed in wealth and power to the utmost and made itself the first class of the country. The result was that wherever this happened, the bourgeoisie took political power into its own hands and displaced the hitherto ruling classes, the aristocracy, the guild-masters, and their representative, the absolute monarchy.

The bourgeoisie annihilated the power of the aristocracy, the nobility, by abolishing the entailment of estates—in other words, by making landed property subject to purchase and sale, and by doing away with the special privileges of the nobility. It destroyed the power of the guild-masters by abolishing guilds and handicraft privileges. In their place, it put competition—that is, a state of society in which everyone has the right to enter into any branch of industry, the only obstacle being a lack of the necessary capital.

The introduction of free competition is thus public declaration that from now on the members of society are unequal only to the extent that their capitals are unequal, that capital is the decisive power, and that therefore the capitalists, the bourgeoisie, have become the first class in society.

Free competition is necessary for the establishment of big industry, because it is the only condition of society in which big industry can make its way.

Having destroyed the social power of the nobility and the guild-masters, the bourgeois also destroyed their political power. Having raised itself to the actual position of first class in society, it proclaims itself to be also the dominant political class. This it does through the introduction of the representative system which rests on bourgeois equality before the law and the recognition of free competition, and in European countries takes the form of constitutional monarchy. In these constitutional monarchies, only those who possess a certain capital are voters—that is to say, only members of the bourgeoisie. These bourgeois voters choose the deputies, and these bourgeois deputies, by using their right to refuse to vote taxes, choose a bourgeois government.

Third, everywhere the proletariat develops in step with the bourgeoisie. In proportion, as the bourgeoisie grows in wealth, the proletariat grows in numbers. For, since the proletarians can be employed only by capital, and since capital extends only through employing labour, it follows that the growth of the proletariat proceeds at precisely the same pace as the growth of capital.

Simultaneously, this process draws members of the bourgeoisie and proletarians together into the great cities where industry can be carried on most profitably, and by thus throwing great masses in one spot it gives to the proletarians a consciousness of their own strength.

Moreover, the further this process advances, the more new labour-saving machines are invented, the greater is the pressure exercised by big industry on wages, which, as we have seen, sink to their minimum and therewith render the condition of the proletariat increasingly unbearable. The growing dissatisfaction of the proletariat thus joins with its rising power to prepare a proletarian social revolution.

What were the further consequences of the Industrial Revolution?

Big industry created in the steam engine, and other machines, the means of endlessly expanding industrial production, speeding it up, and cutting its costs. With production thus facilitated, the free competition, which is necessarily bound up with big industry, assumed the most extreme forms; a multitude of capitalists invaded industry, and, in a short while, more was produced than was needed.

As a consequence, finished commodities could not be sold, and a so-called commercial crisis broke out. Factories had to be closed, their owners went bankrupt, and the workers were without bread. Deepest misery reigned everywhere.

After a time, the superfluous products were sold, the factories began to operate again, wages rose, and gradually business got better than ever.

But it was not long before too many commodities were again produced and a new crisis broke out, only to follow the same course as its predecessor.

Ever since the beginning of this (19th) century, the condition of industry has constantly fluctuated between periods of prosperity and periods of crisis; nearly every five to seven years, a fresh crisis has intervened, always with the greatest hardship for workers, and always accompanied by general revolutionary stirrings and the direct peril to the whole existing order of things.

What follows from these periodic commercial crises?

First:

- That, though big industry in its earliest stage created free competition, it has now outgrown free competition;
- that, for big industry, competition and generally the individualistic organization of production have become a fetter which it must and will shatter;
- that, so long as big industry remains on its present footing, it can be maintained only at the cost of general chaos every seven years, each time threatening the whole of civilization and not only plunging the proletarians into misery but also ruining large sections of the bourgeoisie;

- hence, either that big industry must itself be given up, which is an absolute impossibility, or that it makes unavoidably necessary an entirely new organization of society in which production is no longer directed by mutually competing individual industrialists but rather by the whole society operating according to a definite plan and taking account of the needs of all.

Second: That big industry, and the limitless expansion of production which it makes possible, bring within the range of feasibility a social order in which so much is produced that every member of society will be in a position to exercise and develop all his powers and faculties in complete freedom.

It thus appears that the very qualities of big industry which, in our present-day society, produce misery and crises are those which, in a different form of society, will abolish this misery and these catastrophic depressions.

We see with the greatest clarity:

(i) That all these evils are from now on to be ascribed solely to a social order which no longer corresponds to the requirements of the real situation; and

(ii) That it is possible, through a new social order, to do away with these evils altogether.

What will this new social order have to be like?

Above all, it will have to take the control of industry and of all branches of production out of the hands of mutually competing individuals, and instead institute a system in which all these branches of production are operated by society as a whole—that is, for the common account, according to a common plan, and with the participation of all members of society.

It will, in other words, abolish competition and replace it with association.

Moreover, since the management of industry by individuals necessarily implies private property, and since competition is in reality merely the manner and form in which the control of industry by private property owners expresses itself, it follows that private property cannot be separated from competition and the individual management of industry. Private property must, therefore, be abolished and in its place must come the common utilization of all instruments of production and the distribution of all products according to common agreement—in a word, what is called the communal ownership of goods.

In fact, the abolition of private property is, doubtless, the shortest and most significant way to characterize the revolution in the whole social order which has been made necessary by the development of industry—and for this reason it is rightly advanced by communists as their main demand.

Was not the abolition of private property possible at an earlier time?

No. Every change in the social order, every revolution in property relations, is the necessary consequence of the creation of new forces of production which no longer fit into the old property relations.

Private property has not always existed.

When, towards the end of the Middle Ages, there arose a new mode of production which could not be carried on under the then existing feudal and guild forms of property, this manufacture, which had outgrown the old property relations, created a new property form, private property. And for manufacture and the earliest stage of development of big industry, private property was the only possible property form; the social order based on it was the only possible social order.

So long as it is not possible to produce so much that there is enough for all, with more left over for expanding the social capital and extending the forces of production—so long as this is not possible, there must always be a ruling class directing the use of society's productive forces, and a poor, oppressed class. How these classes are constituted depends on the stage of development.

The agrarian Middle Ages give us the baron and the serf; the cities of the later Middle Ages show us the guild-master and the journeyman and the day laborer; the 17th century has its manufacturing workers; the 19th has big factory owners and proletarians.

It is clear that, up to now, the forces of production have never been developed to the point where enough could be developed for all, and that private property has become a fetter and a barrier in relation to the further development of the forces of production.

Now, however, the development of big industry has ushered in a new period. Capital and the forces of production have been expanded to an unprecedented extent, and the means are at hand to multiply them without limit in the near future. Moreover, the forces of production have been concentrated in the hands of a few bourgeois, while the great mass of the people are more and more falling into the proletariat, their situation becoming more wretched and intolerable in proportion to the increase of wealth of the bourgeoisie. And finally, these mighty and easily extended forces of production have so far outgrown private property and the bourgeoisie, that they threaten at any moment to unleash the most violent disturbances of the social order.

Now, under these conditions, the abolition of private property has become not only possible but absolutely necessary.

Will the peaceful abolition of private property be possible?

It would be desirable if this could happen, and the communists would certainly be the last to oppose it. Communists know only too well that all conspiracies are not only useless, but even harmful. They know all too well that revolutions are not made intentionally and arbitrarily, but that, everywhere and always, they have been the necessary consequence of conditions which were wholly independent of the will and direction of individual parties and entire classes.

But they also see that the development of the proletariat in nearly all civilized countries has been violently suppressed, and that in this way the opponents of communism have been working towards a revolution with all their strength. If the oppressed proletariat is finally driven to revolution, then we communists will defend the interests of the proletarians with deeds as we now defend them with words.

Will it be possible for private property to be abolished at one stroke?

No, no more than existing forces of production can at one stroke be multiplied to the extent necessary for the creation of a communal society.

In all probability, the proletarian revolution will transform existing society gradually and will be able to abolish private property only when the means of production are available in sufficient quantity.

What will be the course of this revolution?

Above all, it will establish a democratic constitution, and through this, the direct or indirect dominance of the proletariat. Direct in England, where the proletarians are already a majority of the people. Indirect in France and Germany, where the majority of the people consists not only of proletarians, but also of small peasants and petty bourgeois who are in the process of falling into the proletariat, who are more and more dependent in all their political interests on the proletariat, and who must, therefore, soon adapt to the demands of the proletariat. Perhaps this will cost a second struggle, but the outcome can only be the victory of the proletariat.

Democracy would be wholly valueless to the proletariat if it were not immediately used as a means for putting through measures directed against private property and ensuring the livelihood of the proletariat. The main measures, emerging as the necessary result of existing relations, are the following:

(i) Limitation of private property through progressive taxation, heavy inheritance taxes, abolition of inheritance through collateral lines (brothers, nephews, etc.) forced loans, etc.

(ii) Gradual expropriation of landowners, industrialists, railroad magnates and shipowners, partly through competition by state industry, partly directly through compenzation in the form of bonds.

(iii) Confiscation of the possessions of all emigrants and rebels against the majority of the people.

(iv) Organization of labour or employment of proletarians on publicly owned land, in factories and workshops, with competition among the workers being abolished and with the factory owners, in so far as they still exist, being obliged to pay the same high wages as those paid by the state.

(v) An equal obligation on all members of society to work until such time as private property has been completely abolished. Formation of industrial armies, especially for agriculture.

(vi) Centralization of money and credit in the hands of the state through a national bank with state capital, and the suppression of all private banks and bankers.

(vii) Education of the number of national factories, workshops, railroads, ships; bringing new lands into cultivation and improvement of land already under cultivation—all in proportion to the growth of the capital and labour force at the disposal of the nation.

(viii) Education of all children, from the moment they can leave their mother's care, in national establishments at national cost. Education and production together.

(ix) Construction, on public lands, of great palaces as communal dwellings for associated groups of citizens engaged in both industry and agriculture and combining in their way of life the advantages of urban and rural conditions while avoiding the one-sidedness and drawbacks of each.

(x) Destruction of all unhealthy and jerry-built dwellings in urban districts.

(xi) Equal inheritance rights for children born in and out of wedlock.

(xii) Concentration of all means of transportation in the hands of the nation.

It is impossible, of course, to carry out all these measures at once. But one will always bring others in its wake. Once the first radical attack on private property has been launched, the proletariat will find itself forced to go ever further, to concentrate increasingly in the hands of the state all capital, all agriculture, all transport, all trade. All the foregoing measures are directed to this end; and they will become practicable and feasible, capable of producing their centralizing effects to precisely the degree that the proletariat, through its labour, multiplies the country's productive forces.

Finally, when all capital, all production, all exchange have been brought together in the hands of the nation, private property will disappear of its own accord, money will become superfluous, and production will so expand and man so change that society will be able to slough off whatever of its old economic habits may remain.

Will it be possible for this revolution to take place in one country alone?

No. By creating the world market, big industry has already brought all the peoples of the earth, and especially the civilized peoples, into such close relation with one another that none is independent of what happens to the others.

Further, it has coordinated the social development of the civilized countries to such an extent that, in all of them, bourgeoisie and proletariat have become the decisive classes, and the struggle between them the great struggle of the day. It follows that the communist revolution will not merely be a national phenomenon but must take place simultaneously in all civilized countries—that is to say, at least in England, America, France, and Germany.

It will develop in each of the these countries more or less rapidly, according as one country or the other has a more developed industry, greater wealth, a more significant mass of productive forces. Hence, it will go slowest and will meet most obstacles in Germany, most rapidly and with the fewest difficulties in England. It will have a powerful impact on the other countries of the world, and will radically alter the course of development which they have followed up to now, while greatly stepping up its pace.

It is a universal revolution and will, accordingly, have a universal range.

What will be the consequences of the ultimate disappearance of private property?

Society will take all forces of production and means of commerce, as well as the exchange and distribution of products, out of the hands of private capitalists and will manage them in accordance with a plan based on the availability of resources and the needs of the whole society. In this way, most important of all, the evil consequences which are now associated with the conduct of big industry will be abolished.

There will be no more crises; the expanded production, which for the present order of society is overproduction and hence a prevailing cause of misery, will then be insufficient and in need of being expanded much further. Instead of generating misery, overproduction will reach beyond the elementary requirements of society to assure the satisfaction of the needs of all; it will create new needs and, at the same time, the means of satisfying them. It will become the condition of, and the stimulus to, new progress, which will no longer throw the whole social order into confusion, as progress has always done in the past. Big industry, freed from the pressure of private property, will undergo such an expansion that what we now see will seem as petty in comparison as manufacture seems when put beside the big industry of our own day. This development of industry will make available to society a sufficient mass of products to satisfy the needs of everyone.

The same will be true of agriculture, which also suffers from the pressure of private property and is held back by the division of privately owned land into small parcels. Here, existing improvements and scientific procedures will be put into practice, with a resulting leap forward which will assure to society all the products it needs.

In this way, such an abundance of goods will be able to satisfy the needs of all its members.

The division of society into different, mutually hostile classes will then become unnecessary. Indeed, it will be not only unnecessary but intolerable in the new social order. The existence of classes originated in the division of labour, and the division of labour, as it has been known up to the present, will completely disappear. For mechanical and chemical processes are not enough to bring industrial and agricultural production up to the level we have described; the capacities of the men who make use of these processes must undergo a corresponding development.

Just as the peasants and manufacturing workers of the last century changed their whole way of life and became quite different people when they were impressed into big industry, in the same way, communal control over production by society as a whole, and the resulting new development, will both require an entirely different kind of human material.

People will no longer be, as they are today, subordinated to a single branch of production, bound to it, exploited by it; they will no longer develop one of their faculties at the expense of all others; they will no longer know only one branch, or one branch of a single branch, of production as a whole. Even industry as it is today is finding such people less and less useful.

Industry controlled by society as a whole, and operated according to a plan, presupposes well-rounded human beings, their faculties developed in balanced fashion, able to see the system of production in its entirety.

The form of the division of labour which makes one a peasant, another a cobbler, a third a factory worker, a fourth a stock-market operator, has already been underminded by machinery and will completely disappear. Education will enable young people quickly to familiarize themselves with the whole system of production and to pass from one branch of production to another in response to the needs of society or their own inclinations. It will, therefore, free them from the one-sided character which the present-day division of labour impresses upon every individual. Communist society will, in this way, make it possible for its members to put their comprehensively developed faculties to full use. But, when this happens, classes will necessarily disappear. It follows that society organized on a communist basis is incompatible with the existence of classes on the one hand, and that the very building of such a society provides the means of abolishing class differences on the other.

A corollary of this is that the difference between city and country is destined to disappear. The management of agriculture and industry by the same people rather than by two different classes of people is, if only for purely material reasons, a necessary condition of communist association. The dispersal of the agricultural population on the land, alongside the crowding of the industrial population into the great cities, is a condition which corresponds to an undeveloped state of both agriculture and industry and can already be felt as an obstacle to further development.

The general cooperation of all members of society for the purpose of planned exploitation of the forces of production, the expansion of production to the point where it will satisfy the needs of all, the abolition of a situation in which the needs of some are satisfied; at the expense of the needs of others, the complete liquidation of classes and their conflicts, the rounded development of the capacities of all members of society through the elimination of the present division of labour, through industrial education, through engaging in varying activities, through the participation by all in the enjoyments produced by all, through the combination of city and country—these are the main consequences of the abolition of private property.

What will be the influence of communist society on the family?

It will transform the relations between the sexes into a purely private matter which concerns only the persons involved and into which society has no occassion to intervene. It can do this since it does away with private property and educates children on a communal basis, and in this way removes the two bases of traditional marriage —the dependence rooted in private property, of the women on the man, and of the children on the parents.

And here is the answer to the outcry of the highly moral philistines against the "community of women". Community of women is a condition which belongs entirely to bourgeois society and which today finds its complete expression in prostitution. But prostitution is based on private property and falls with it. Thus, communist society, instead of introducing the community of women, in fact abolishes it.

How do communists differ from socialists?

The so-called socialists are divided into three categories.

Reactionary Socialists

The first category consists of adherents of a feudal and patriarchal society which has already been destroyed, and is still daily being destroyed, by big industry and world trade and their creation, bourgeois society. This category concludes, from the evils of existing society, that feudal and patriarchal society must be restored because it was free of such evils. In one way or another, all their proposals are directed to this end.

This category of reactionary socialists, for all their seeming partisanship and their scalding tears for the misery of the proletariat, is nevertheless energetically opposed by the communists for the following reasons:

(i) It strives for something which is entirely impossible.

(ii) It seeks to establish the rule of the aristocracy, the guildmasters, the small producers, and their retinue of absolute or feudal monarchs, officials, soldiers, and priests—a society which was, to be sure, free of the evils of present-day society but which brought it at least as many evils without even offering to the oppressed workers the prospect of liberation through a communist revolution.

(iii) As soon as the proletariat becomes revolutionary and communist, these reactionary socialists show their true colours by immediately making common cause with the bourgeoisie against the proletarians.

Bourgeois Socialists

The second category consists of adherents of present-day society who have been frightened for its future by the evils to which it necessarily gives rise. What they want, therefore, is to maintain this society while getting rid of the evils which are an inherent part of it.

To this end, some propose mere welfare measures—while others come forward with grandiose systems of reform which, under the pretence of re-organizing society, are in fact intended to preserve the foundations, and hence the life, of existing society.

Communists must unremittingly struggle against these bourgeois socialists because they work for the enemies of communists and protect the society which communists aim to overthrow.

Democratic Socialists

Finally, the third category consists of democratic socialists who favour some of the same measures the communists advocate, as described in Question 18, not as part of the transition to communism, however, but as measures which they believe will be sufficient to abolish the misery and evils of present-day society.

These democratic socialists are either proletarians who are not yet sufficiently clear about the conditions of the liberation of their class, or they are representatives of the petty bourgeoisie, a class which, prior to the achievement of democracy and the socialist measures to which it gives rise, has many interests in common with the proletariat.

It follows that, in moments of action, the communists will have to come to an understanding with these democratic socialists, and in general to follow as far as possible a common policy with them—provided that these socialists do not enter into the service of the ruling bourgeoisie and attack the communists.

It is clear that this form of cooperation in action does not exclude the discussion of differences.

What is the attitude of the communists to the other political parties of our time?

This attitude is different in the different countries.

In England, France, and Belgium, where the bourgeoisie rules, the communists still have a common interest with the various democratic parties, an interest which is all the greater the more closely the socialistic measures they champion approach the aims of the communists —that is, the more clearly and definitely they represent the interests of the proletariat and the more they depend on the proletariat for support. In England, for example, the working-class Chartists are infinitely closer to the communists than the democratic petty bourgeoisie or the so-called Radicals.

In America, where a democratic constitution has already been established, the communists must make the common cause with the party which will turn this constitution against the bourgeoisie and use it in the interests of the proletariat—that is, with the agrarian National Reformers.

In Switzerland, the Radicals, though a very mixed party, are the only group with which the communists can co-operate, and, among these Radicals, the Vaudois and Genevese are the most advanced.

In Germany, finally, the decisive struggle now on the order of the day is that between the bourgeoisie and the absolute monarchy. Since the communists cannot enter upon the decisive struggle between themselves and the bourgeoisie until the bourgeoisie is in power, it follows that it is in the interest of the communists to help the bourgeoisie to power as soon as possible in order the sooner to be able to overthrow it. Against the governments, therefore, the communists must continually support the radical liberal party, taking care to avoid the self-deceptions of the bourgeoisie and not fall for the enticing promises of benefits which a victory for the bourgeoisie would allegedly bring to the proletariat. The sole advantages which the proletariat would derive from a bourgeois victory would consist.

(i) in various concessions which would facilitate the unification of the proletariat into a closely knit, battle-worthy, and organized class; and

(ii) in the certainty that, on the very day the absolute monarchies fall, the struggle between bourgeoisie and proletariat will start. From that day on, the policy of the communists will be the same as it now is in the countries where the bourgeoisie is already in power.

3

The Communist Manifesto

Karl Marx and Friedrich Engels

A spectre is haunting Europe—the spectre of Communism. All the powers of old Europe have entered into a holy alliance to exorcise this spectre: Pope and Tsar, Metternich and Guizot, French Radicals and German police-spies.

Where is the party in opposition that has not been decried as communistic by its opponents in power? Where is the opposition that has not hurled back the branding reproach of communism, against the more advanced opposition parties, as well as against its reactionary adversaries?

Two things result from this fact:

I. Communism is already acknowledged by all European powers to be itself a power.

II. It is high time that Communists should openly, in the face of the whole world, publish their views, their aims, their tendencies, and meet this nursery tale of the spectre of communism with a manifesto of the party itself.

To this end Communists of various nationalities have assembled in London and sketched the following manifesto, to be published in the English, French, German, Italian, Flemish and Danish languages.

I. Bourgeois and Proletarians

The history of all hitherto existing society[2] is the history of class struggles.

Freeman and slave, patrician and plebian, lord and serf, guild-master[3] and journeyman, in a word, oppressor and oppressed, stood in constant opposition to one another, carried on an uninterrupted, now hidden, now open fight, a fight that each time ended, either in a revolutionary reconstitution of society at large, or in the common ruin of the contending classes.

In the earlier epochs of history, we find almost everywhere a complicated arrangement of society into various orders, a manifold gradation of social rank. In ancient Rome we have patricians, knights, plebeians, slaves; in the Middle Ages, feudal lords, vassals, guild-masters, journeymen, apprentices, serfs; in almost all these classes, again, subordinate gradations.

The modern bourgeois society that has sprouted from the ruins of feudal society has not done away with class antagonisms. It has but established new classes, new conditions of oppression, new forms of struggle in place of the old ones.

Our epoch, the epoch of the bourgeoisie, possesses, however, this distinct feature: it has simplified class antagonisms. Society as a whole is increasingly splitting up into two great hostile camps, into two great classes directly facing each other—bourgeoisie and proletariat.

From the serfs of the Middle Ages sprang the chartered burghers of the earliest towns. From these burgesses the first elements of the bourgeoisie were developed.

The discovery of America, the rounding of the Cape, opened up fresh ground for the rising bourgeoisie. The East Indian and Chinese markets, the colonization of America, trade with the colonies, the increase in the means of exchange and in commodities generally, gave to commerce, to navigation, to industry, an impulse never before known, and thereby, to the revolutionary element in the tottering feudal society, a rapid development.

The feudal system of industry, in which industrial production was monopolized by closed guilds, now no longer suffices for the growing wants of the new markets. The manufacturing system took its place. The guild-masters were pushed aside by the manufacturing middle class; division of labour between the different corporate guilds vanished in the face of division of labour in each single workshop.

In the meantime, the markets kept ever growing, the demand ever rising. Even manufacturers no longer sufficed. Thereupon, steam and machinery revolutionized industrial production. The place of manufacture was taken by the giant, modern industry; the place of the industrial middle class by industrial millionaires, the leaders of the whole industrial armies, the modern bourgeois.

Modern Industry has established the world market, for which the discovery of America paved the way. This market has given an immense development to commerce, to navigation, to communication by land. This development has, in turn, reacted on the extension of industry; and in proportion as industry, commerce, navigation, railways extended, in the same proportion the bourgeoisie developed, increased its capital, and pushed into the background every class handed down from the Middle Ages.

We see, therefore, how the modern bourgeoisie is itself the product of a long course of development, of a series of revolutions in the modes of production and of exchange.

Each step in the development of the bourgeoisie was accompanied by a corresponding political advance in that class. An oppressed class under the sway of the feudal nobility, an armed and self-governing association of medieval commune: here independent urban republic (as in Italy and Germany); there taxable "third estate" of the monarchy (as in France); afterwards, in the period of manufacturing proper, serving either the semi-feudal or the absolute monarchy as a counterpoise against the nobility, and, in fact, cornerstone of the great monarchies in general—the bourgeoisie has at last, since the establishment of Modern Industry and of the world market, conquered for itself, in the modern representative state, exclusive political sway. The executive of the modern state is but a committee for managing the common affairs of the whole bourgeoisie.

The bourgeoisie, historically, has played a most revolutionary part.

The bourgeoisie, wherever it has got the upper hand, has put an end to all feudal, patriarchal, idyllic relations. It has pitilessly torn asunder the motley feudal ties that bound man to his "natural superiors", and has left no other nexus between man and man than naked self-interest, than callous "cash payment". It has drowned out the most heavenly ecstasies of religious fervour, of chivalrous enthusiasm, of philistine sentimentalism, in the icy water of egotistical calculation. It has resolved personal worth into exchange value, and in place of the numberless indefeasible chartered freedoms, has set up that single, unconscionable freedom—Free Trade. In one word, for exploitation, veiled by religious and political illusions, it has substituted naked, shameless, direct, brutal exploitation.

The bourgeoisie has stripped of its halo every occupation hitherto honoured and looked up to with reverent awe. It has converted the physician, the lawyer, the priest, the poet, the man of science, into its paid wage labourers.

The bourgeoisie has torn away from the family its sentimental veil, and has reduced the family relation into a mere money relation.

The bourgeoisie has disclosed how it came to pass that the brutal display of vigour in the Middle Ages, which reactionaries so much admire, found its fitting complement in the most slothful indolence. It has been the first to show what man's activity can bring about. It has accomplished wonders far surpassing Egyptian pyramids, Roman aqueducts, and Gothic cathedrals; it has conducted expeditions that put in the shade all former exoduses of nations and crusades.

The bourgeoisie cannot exist without constantly revolutionizing the instalments of production, and thereby the relations of production, and with them the whole relations of society. Conservation of the old modes of production in unaltered form, was, on the contrary, the first condition of existence for all earlier industrial classes. Constant revolutionizing of production, uninterrupted disturbance of all social conditions, everlasting uncertainty and agitation distinguish the bourgeois epoch from all earlier ones. All fixed, fast frozen relations, with their train of ancient and venerable prejudices and opinions, are swept away, all new-formed ones become antiquated before they can ossify. All that is solid melts into air, all that is holy is profaned, and man is at last compelled to face with sober senses his real condition of life and his relations with his kind.

The need of a constantly expanding market for its products chases the bourgeoisie over the entire surface of the globe. It must nestle everywhere, settle everywhere, establish connections everywhere.

The bourgeoisie has, through its exploitation of the world market, given a cosmopolitan character to production and consumption in every country. To the great chagrin of reactionaries, it has drawn from under the feet of industry the national ground on which it stood. All old-established national industries have been destroyed or are daily being destroyed. They are dislodged by new industries, whose introduction becomes a life and death question for all civilized nations, by industries that no longer work up indigenous raw material, but raw material drawn from the remotest zones; industries whose products are consumed, not only at home, but in every quarter of the globe. In place of the old wants, satisfied by the production of the country, we find new wants, requiring for their satisfaction the products of distant lands and climes. In place of the old local and national seclusion and self-sufficiency, we have intercourse in every direction, universal inter-dependence of nations. And as in material, so also in intellectual production. The intellectual creations of individual nations become common property. National one-sidedness and narrow-mindedness become more and more impossible, and from the numerous national and local literatures, there arises a world literature.

The bourgeoisie, by the rapid improvement of all instruments of production, by the immensely facilitated means of communication, draws all, even the most barbarian, nations into civilization. The cheap prices of commodities are the heavy artillery with which it forces the barbarians' intensely obstinate hatred of foreigners to capitulate. It compels all nations, on pain of extinction, to adopt the bourgeois mode of production; it compels them to introduce what it calls civilization into their midst, i.e. to become bourgeois themselves. In one word, it creates a world after its own image.

The bourgeoisie has subjected the country to the rule of the towns. It has created enormous cities, has greatly increased the urban population as compared with the rural, and has thus rescued a considerable part of the population from the idiocy of rural life. Just as it has made the country dependent on the towns, so it has made barbarian and semi-barbarian countries dependent on the civilized ones, nations of peasants on nations of bourgeois, the East on the West.

The bourgeoisie keeps more and more doing away with the scattered state of the population, of the means of production, and of property. It has agglomerated population, centralized the means of production, and has concentrated property in a few hands. The necessary consequence of this was political centralization. Independent, or but loosely connected provinces, with separate interests, laws, governments, and systems of taxation, became lumped together into one nation, with one government, one code of laws, one national class interest, one frontier, and one customs tariff.

The bourgeoisie, during its rule of scarce one hundred years, has created more massive and more colossal productive forces than have all preceding generations together. Subjection of nature's forces to man, machinery, application of chemistry to industry and agriculture, steam navigation, railways, electric telegraphs, clearing of whole continents for cultivation, canalization or rivers, whole populations conjured out of the ground—what earlier century had even a presentiment that such productive forces slumbered in the lap of social labour?

We see then: the means of production and of exchange, on whose foundation the bourgeoisie built itself up, were generated in feudal society. At a certain stage in the development of these means of production and of exchange, the conditions under which feudal society produced and exchanged, the feudal organization of agriculture and manufacturing industry, in one word, the feudal relations of property became no longer compatible with the already developed productive forces; they became so many fetters. They had to be burst asunder; they were burst asunder.

Into their place stepped free competition, accompanied by a social and political constitution adapted in it, and the economic and political sway of the bourgeois class.

A similar movement is going on before our own eyes. Modern bourgeois society, with its relations of production, of exchange and of property, a society that has conjured up such gigantic means of production and of exchange, is like the sorcerer who is no longer able to control the powers of the nether world whom he has called up by his spells. For many a decade past, the history of industry and commerce is but the history of the revolt of modern productive forces against modern conditions of production, against the property relations that are the conditions for the existence of the bourgeois and of its rule. It is enough to mention the commercial crises that, by their periodical return, put the existence of the entire bourgeois society on its trial, each time more threateningly. In these crises, a great part not only of the existing products, but also of the previously created productive forces, are periodically destroyed. In these crises, there breaks out an epidemic that, in all earlier epochs, would have seemed an absurdity—the epidemic of over-production. Society suddenly finds itself put back into a state of momentary barbarism; it appears as if a famine, a universal war of devastation, had cut off the supply of every means of subsistence; industry and commerce seem to be destroyed. And why? Because there is too much civilization, too much means of subsistence, too much industry, too much commerce. The productive forces at the disposal of society no longer tend to further the development of the conditions of bourgeois property; on the contrary, they have become too powerful for these conditions, by which they are fettered, and so soon as they overcome these fetters, they bring disorder into the whole of bourgeois society, endanger the existence of bourgeois property. The conditions of bourgeois society are too narrow to comprise the wealth created by them. And how does the bourgeoisie get over these crises? One the one hand, by enforced destruction of a mass of productive forces; on the other, by the conquest of new markets, and by the more thorough exploitation of the old ones. That is to say, by paving the way for more extensive and more destructive crises, and by diminishing the means whereby crises are prevented.

The weapons with which the bourgeoisie felled feudalism to the ground are now turned against the bourgeoisie itself.

But not only has the bourgeoisie forged the weapons that bring death to itself; it has also called into existence the men who are to wield those weapons—the modern working class—the proletarians.

In proportion as the bourgeoisie, i.e. capital, is developed, in the same proportion is the proletariat, the modern working class, developed—a class of labourers, who live only so long as they find work, and who find work only so long as their labour increases capital. These labourers, who must sell themselves piecemeal, are a commodity, like every other article of commerce, and are consequently exposed to all the vicissitudes of competition, to all the fluctuations of the market.

Owing to the extensive use of machinery, and to the division of labour, the work of the proletarians has lost all individual character, and, consequently, all charm for the workman. He becomes an appendage of the machine, and it is only the most simple, most monotonous, and most easily acquired knack, that is required of him. Hence, the cost of production of a workman is restricted, almost entirely, to the means of subsistence that he requires for maintenance, and for the propagation of his race. But the price of a commodity, and therefore also of labour, is equal to its cost of production. In proportion, therefore, as the repulsiveness of the work increases, the wage decreases. What is more, in proportion as the use of machinery and division of labour increases, in the same proportion the burden of toil also increases, whether by prolongation of the working hours, by the increase of the work exacted in a given time, or by increased speed of machinery, etc.

Modern Industry has converted the little workshop of the patriarchal master into the great factory of the industrial capitalist. Masses of labourers, crowded into the factory, are organized like soldiers. As privates of the industrial army, they are placed under the command of a perfect hierarchy of officers and sergeants. Not only are they slaves of the bourgeois class, and of the bourgeois state; they are daily and hourly enslaved by the machine, by the overlooker, and, above all, in the individual bourgeois manufacturer himself. The more openly this despotism proclaims gain to be its end and aim, the more petty, the more hateful and the more embittering it is.

The less the skill and exertion of strength implied in manual labour, in other words, the more Modern Industry becomes developed, the more is the labour of men superseded by that of women. Differences of age and sex have no longer any distinctive social validity for the working class. All are instruments of labour, more or less expensive to use, according to their age and sex.

No sooner is the exploitation of the labourer by the manufacturer, so far at an end, that he receives his wages in cash, than he is set upon by the other portion of the bourgeoisie, the landlord, the shopkeeper, the pawnbroker, etc.

The lower strata of the middle class—the small tradespeople, shopkeepers, and retired tradesmen generally, the handicraftsmen and peasants—all these sink gradually into the proletariat, partly because their diminutive capital does not suffice for the scale on which Modern Industry is carried on, and is swamped in the competition with the large capitalists, partly because their specialized skill is rendered worthless by new methods of production. Thus, the proletariat is recruited from all classes of the population.

The proletariat goes through various stages of development. With its birth begins its struggle with the bourgeoisie. At first, the contest is carried on by individual labourers, then by the work of people of a factory, then by the operative of one trade, in one locality, against the individual bourgeois who directly exploits them. They direct their attacks not against the bourgeois condition of production, but against the instruments of production themselves; they destroy imported wares that compete with their labour, they smash to pieces machinery, they set factories ablaze, they seek to restore by force the vanished status of the workman of the Middle Ages.

At this stage, the labourers still form an incoherent mass scattered over the whole country, and broken up by their mutual competition. If anywhere they unite to form more compact bodies, this is not yet the consequence of their own active union, but of the union of the bourgeoisie, which class, in order to attain its own political ends, is compelled to set the whole proletariat in motion, and is moreover yet, for a time, able to do so. At this stage, therefore, the proletarians do not fight their enemies, but the enemies of their enemies, the remnants of absolute monarchy, the landowners, the non-industrial bourgeois, the petty bourgeois. Thus, the whole historical movement is concentrated in the hands of the bourgeoisie; every victory so obtained is a victory for the bourgeoisie.

But with the development of industry, the proletariat not only increases in number; it becomes concentrated in greater masses, its strength grows, and it feels that strength more. The various interests and conditions of life within the ranks of the proletariat are more and more equalized, in proportion as machinery obliterates all distinctions of labour, and nearly everywhere reduces wages to the same low level. The growing competition among the bourgeois, and the resulting commercial crises, make the wages of the workers ever more fluctuating. The increasing improvement of machinery, ever more rapidly developing, makes their livelihood more and more precarious; the collisions between individual workmen and individual bourgeois take more and more the character of collisions between two classes. Thereupon, the workers begin to form combinations (trade unions) against the bourgeois; they club together in order to keep up the rate of wages; they found permanent associations in order to make provision beforehand for these occasional revolts. Here and there, the contest breaks out into riots.

Now and then the workers are victorious, but only for a time. The real fruit of their battles lie not in the immediate result, but in the ever expanding union of the workers. This union is helped on by the improved means of communication that are created by Modern Industry, and that place the workers of different localities in contact with one another. It was just this contact that was needed to centralize the numerous local struggles, all of the same character, into one national struggle between classes. But every class struggle is a political struggle. And that union, to attain which the burghers of the Middle Ages, with their miserable highways, required centuries, the modern proletarian, thanks to railways, achieve in a few years.

This organization of the proletarians into a class, and, consequently, into a political party, is continually being upset again by the competition between the workers themselves. But it ever rises up again, stronger, firmer, mightier. It compels legislative recognition of particular interests of the workers, by taking advantage of the divisions among the bourgeoisie itself. Thus, the Ten-Hours Bill in England was carried.

Altogether, collisions between the classes of the old society further in many ways the course of development of the proletariat. The bourgeoisie finds itself involved in a constant battle. At first with the aristocracy; later on, with those portions of the bourgeoisie itself, whose interests have become antagonistic to the progress of industry; at all time with the bourgeoisie of foreign countries. In all these battles, it sees itself compelled to appeal to the proletariat, to ask for help, and thus to drag it into the political arena. The bourgeoisie itself, therefore, supplies the proletariat with its own elements of political and general education, in other words, it furnishes the proletariat with weapons for fighting the bourgeoisie.

Further, as we have already seen, entire sections of the ruling class are, by the advance of industry, precipitated into the proletariat, or are at least threatened in their conditions of existence. These also supply the proletariat with fresh elements of enlightenment and progress.

Finally, in times when the class struggle nears the decisive hour, the progress of dissolution going on within the ruling class, in fact within the whole range of old society, assumes such a violent, glaring character, that a small section of the ruling class cuts itself adrift, and joins the revolutionary class, the class that holds the future in its hands. Just as, therefore, at an earlier period, a section of the nobility went over to the bourgeoisie, so now a portion of the bourgeoisie goes over to the proletariat, and in particular, a portion of the bourgeois ideologists, who have raised themselves to the level of comprehending theoretically the historical movement as a whole.

Of all the classes that stand face to face with the bourgeoisie today, the proletariat alone is a genuinely revolutionary class. The other classes decay and finally disappear in the face of Modern Industry; the proletariat is its special and essential product.

The lower middle class, the small manufacturer, the shopkeeper, the artisan, the peasant, all these fight against the bourgeoisie, to save from extinction their existence as fractions of the middle class. They are therefore not revolutionary, but conservative. Nay, more, they are reactionary, for they try to roll back the wheel of history. If, by chance, they are revolutionary, they are only so in view of their impending transfer into the proletariat; they thus defend not their present, but their future interests; they desert their own standpoint to place themselves at that of the proletariat.

The "dangerous class", the social scum, that passively rotting mass thrown off by the lowest layers of the old society, may, here and there, be swept into the movement by a proletarian revolution; its conditions of life, however, prepare it far more for the part of a bribed tool of reactionary intrigue.

In the condition of the proletariat, those of old society at large are already virtually swamped. The proletarian is without property; his relation to his wife and children has no longer anything in common with the bourgeois family relations; modern industry labour, modern subjection to capital, the same in England as in France, in America as in Germany, has stripped him of every trace of national character. Law, morality, religion, are to him so many bourgeois prejudices, behind which lurk in ambush just as many bourgeois interests.

All the preceding classes that got the upper hand sought to fortify their already acquired status by subjecting society at large to their conditions of appropriation. The proletarians cannot become masters of the productive forces of society, except by abolishing their own previous mode of appropriation, and thereby also every other previous mode of appropriation. They have nothing of their own to secure and to fortify; their mission is to destroy all previous securities for, and insurances of, individual property.

All previous historical movements were movements of minorities, or in the interest of minorities. The proletarian movement is the self-conscious, independent movement of the immense majority, in the interest of the immense majority. The proletariat, the lowest stratum of our present society, cannot stir, cannot raise itself up, without the whole superincumbent strata of official society being sprung into the air.

Though not in substance, yet in form, the struggle of the proletariat with the bourgeoisie is at first a national struggle. The proletariat of each country must, of course, first of all settle matters with its own bourgeoisie.

In depicting the most general phases of the development of the proletariat, we traced the more or less veiled civil war, raging within existing society, up to the point where that war breaks out into open revolution, and where the violent overthrow of the bourgeoisie lays the foundation for the sway of the proletariat.

Hitherto, every form of society has been based, as we have already seen, on the antagonism of oppressing and oppressed classes. But in order to oppress a class, certain conditions must be assured to it under which it can, at least, continue its slavish existence. The serf, in the period of serfdom, raised himself to membership in the commune, just as the petty bourgeois, under the yoke of the feudal absolutism, managed to develop into a bourgeois. The modern labourer, on the contrary, instead of rising with the process of industry, sinks deeper and deeper below the conditions of existence of his own class. He becomes a pauper, and pauperism develops more rapidly than population and wealth. And here it becomes evident that the bourgeoisie is unfit any longer to be the ruling class in society, and to impose its conditions of existence upon society as an overriding law. It is unfit to rule because it is incompetent to assure an existence to its slave within his slavery, because it cannot help letting him sink into such a state, that it has to feed him, instead of being fed by him. Society can no longer live under this bourgeoisie, in other words, its existence is no longer compatible with society.

The essential conditions for the existence and for the sway of the bourgeois class is the formation and augmentation of capital; the condition for capital is wage labour. Wage labour rests exclusively on competition between the labourers. The advance of industry, whose involuntary promoter is the bourgeoisie, replaces the isolation of the labourers, due to competition, by the revolutionary combination, due to association. The development of Modern Industry, therefore, cuts from under its feet the very foundation on which the bourgeoisie produces and appropriates products. What the bourgeoisie therefore produces, above all, are its own grave-diggers. Its fall and the victory of the proletariat are equally inevitable.

II. Proletarians and Communists

In what relation do the Communists stand to the proletarians as a whole? The Communists do not form a separate party opposed to the other working-class parties.

They have no interests separate and apart from those of the proletariat as a whole.

They do not set up any sectarian principles of their own, by which to shape and mould the proletarian movement.

The Communists are distinguished from the other working-class parties by this only:

1. In the national struggles of the proletarians of the different countries, they point out and bring to the front the common interests of the entire proletariat, independently of all nationality.
2. In the various stages of development which the struggle of the working class against the bourgeoisie has to pass through, they always and everywhere represent the interests of the movement as a whole.

The Communists, therefore, are on the one hand practically, the most advanced and resolute section of the working-class parties of every country, that section which pushes forward all others; on the other hand, theoretically, they have over the great mass of the proletariat the advantage of clearly understanding the lines of march, the conditions, and the ultimate general results of the proletarian movement.

The immediate aim of the Communists is the same as that of all other proletarian parties: Formation of the proletariat into a class, overthrow of the bourgeois supremacy, conquest of political power by the proletariat.

The theoretical conclusions of the Communists are in no way based on ideas or principles that have been invented, or discovered, by this or that would-be universal reformer.

They merely express, in general terms, actual relations springing from an existing class struggle, from a historical movement going on under our very eyes. The abolition of existing property relations is not at all a distinctive feature of communism.

All property relations in the past have continually been subject to historical change consequent upon the change in historical conditions.

The French Revolution, for example, abolished feudal property in favour of bourgeois property.

The distinguishing feature of communism is not the abolition of property generally, but the abolition of bourgeois property. But modern bourgeois private property is the final and most complete expression of the system of producing and appropriating products that is based on class antagonisms, on the exploitation of the many by the few.

In this sense, the theory of the Communists may be summed up in the single sentence: Abolition of private property.

We Communists have been reproached with the desire of abolishing the right of personally acquiring property as the fruit of a man's own labour, which property is alleged to be the groundwork of all personal freedom, activity and independence.

Hard-won, self-acquired, self-earned property! Do you mean the property of petty artisan and of the small peasant, a form of property that preceded the bourgeois form? There is no need to abolish that; the development of industry has to a great extent already destroyed it, and is still destroying it daily.

Or do you mean the modern bourgeois private property?

But does wage labour create any property for the labourer? Not a bit. It creates capital, i.e. that kind of property which exploits wage labour, and which cannot increase except upon conditions of begetting a new supply of wage labour for fresh exploitation. Property, in its present form, is based on the antagonism of capital and wage labour. Let us examine both sides of this antagonism.

To be a capitalist, is to have not only a purely personal, but a social status in production. Capital is a collective product, and only by the united action of many members, nay, in the last resort, only by the united action of all members of society, can it be set in motion.

Capital is therefore not only personal; it is a social power.

When, therefore, capital is converted into common property, into the property of all members of society, personal property is not thereby transformed into social property. It is only the social character of the property that is changed. It loses its class character.

Let us now take wage labour.

The average price of wage labour is the minimum wage, i.e. that quantum of the means of subsistence which is absolutely requisite to keep the labourer in bare existence as a labourer. What, therefore, the wage labourer appropriates by means of his labour merely suffices to prolong and reproduce a bare existence. We by no means intend to abolish this personal appropriation of the products of labour, an appropriation that is made for the maintenance and reproduction of human life, and that leaves no surplus wherewith to command the labour of others. All that we want to do away with is the miserable character of this appropriation, under which the labourer lives merely to increase capital, and is allowed to live only in so far as the interest of the ruling class requires it.

In bourgeois society, living labour is but a means to increase accumulated labour. In communist society, accumulated labour is but a means to widen, to enrich, to promote the existence of the labourer.

In bourgeois society, therefore, the past dominates the present; in communist society, the present dominates the past. In bourgeois society, capital is independent and has individuality, while the living person is dependent and has no individuality.

And the abolition of this state of things is called by the bourgeois, abolition of individuality and freedom! And rightly so. The abolition of bourgeois individuality, bourgeois independence, and bourgeois freedom is undoubtedly aimed at.

By freedom is meant, under the present bourgeois conditions of production, free trade, free selling and buying.

But if selling and buying disappears, free selling and buying disappears also. This talk about free selling and buying, and all the other "brave words" of our bourgeois about freedom in general, have a meaning, if any, only in contrast with restricted selling and buying, with the fettered traders of the Middle Ages, but have no meaning when opposed to the communist abolition of buying and selling, or the bourgeois conditions of production, and of the bourgeoisie itself.

You are horrified at our intending to do away with private property. But in your existing society, private property is already done away with for nine-tenths of the population; its existence for the few is solely due to its non-existence in the hands of those nine-tenths. You reproach us, therefore, with intending to do away with a form of property, the necessary condition for whose existence is the non-existence of any property for the immense majority of society.

In one word, you reproach us with intending to do away with your property. Precisely so; that is just what we intend.

From the moment when labour can no longer be converted into capital, money, or rent, into a social power capable of being monopolized, i.e. from the moment when individual property can no longer be transformed into bourgeois property, into capital, from that moment, you say, individuality vanishes.

You must, therefore, confess that by "individual" you mean no other person than the bourgeois, than the middle class owner of property. This person must, indeed, be swept out of the way, and made impossible.

Communism deprives no man of the power to appropriate the products of society; all that it does is to deprive him of the power to subjugate the labour of others by means of such appropriations.

It has been objected that upon the abolition of private property, all work will cease, and universal laziness will overtake us.

According to this, bourgeois society ought long ago to have gone to the dogs through sheer idleness; for those who acquire anything, do not work. The whole of this objection is but another expression of the tautology: There can no longer be any wage labour when there is no longer any capital.

All objections urged against the communistic mode of producing and appropriating material products, have, in the same way, been urged against the communistic mode of producing and appropriating intellectual products. Just as to the bourgeois, the disappearance of class property is the disappearance of production itself, so the disappearance of class culture is to him identical with the disappearance of all culture.

That culture, the loss of which he laments, is, for the enormous majority, a mere training to act as a machine.

But don't wrangle with us so long as you apply, to our intended abolition of bourgeois property, the standard of your bourgeois notions of freedom, culture, law, etc. Your very ideas are but the outgrowth of the conditions of your bourgeois production and bourgeois property, just as your jurisprudence is but the will of your class made into a law for all, a will whose essential character and direction are determined by the economical conditions of existence of your class.

The selfish misconception that induces you to transform into eternal laws of nature and of reason the social forms stringing from your present mode of production and form, of property—historical relations that rise and disappear in the progress of production—this misconception you share with every ruling class that has preceded you. What you see clearly in the case of ancient property, what you admit in the case of feudal property, you are of course forbidden to admit in the case of your own bourgeois form of property.

Abolition of the family! Even the most radical flare up at this infamous proposal of the Communists.

On what foundation is the present family, the bourgeois family, based? On capital, on private gain. In its completely developed form, this family exists only among the bourgeoisie. But this state of things finds its complement in the practical absence of the family among proletarians, and in public prostitution.

The bourgeois family will vanish as a matter of course when its complement vanishes, and both will vanish with the vanishing of capital.

Do you charge us with wanting to stop the exploitation of children by their parents? To this crime we plead guilty.

But, you say, we destroy the most hallowed of relations, when we replace home education by social.

And your education! Is not that also social, and determined by the social conditions under which you educate, by the intervention direct or indirect, of society, by means of schools, etc.? The Communists have not intended the intervention of society in education; they do but seek to alter the character of that intervention, and to rescue education from the influence of the ruling class.

The bourgeois claptrap about the family and education, about the hallowed correlation of parents and child, becomes all the more disgusting, the more, by the action of Modern Industry, all the family ties among the proletarians are torn asunder, and their children transformed into simple articles of commerce and instruments of labour.

But you Communists would introduce community of women, screams the bourgeoisie in chorus.

The bourgeois sees his wife as a mere instrument of production. He hears that the instruments of production are to be exploited in common, and, naturally, can come to no other conclusion that the lot of being common to all will likewise fall to the women.

He has not even a suspicion that the real point aimed at is to do away with the status of women as mere instruments of production.

For the rest, nothing is more ridiculous than the virtuous indignation of our bourgeois at the community of women which, they pretend, is to be openly and officially established by the Communists. The Communists have no need to introduce free love; it has existed almost from time immemorial.

Our bourgeois, not content with having wives and daughters of their proletarians at their disposal, not to speak of common prostitutes, take the greatest pleasure in seducing each other's wives. (Ah, those were the days!)

Bourgeois marriage is, in reality, a system of wives in common and thus, at the most, what the Communists might possibly be reproached with is that they desire to introduce, in substitution for a hypocritically concealed, an openly legalized system of free love. For the rest, it is self-evident that the abolition of the present system of production must bring with it the abolition of free love springing from that system, i.e. of prostitution both public and private.

The Communists are further reproached with desiring to abolish countries and nationality.

The working men have no country. We cannot take from them what they have not got. Since the proletariat must first of all acquire political supremacy, must rise to be the leading class of the nation, must constitute itself the nation, it is, so far, itself national, though not in the bourgeois sense of the word.

National differences and antagonism between peoples are daily more and more vanishing, owing to the development of the bourgeoisie, to freedom of commerce, to the world market, to uniformity in the mode of production and in the conditions of life corresponding thereto.

The supremacy of the proletariat will cause them to vanish still faster. United action of the leading civilized countries at least is one of the first conditions for the emancipation of the proletariat.

In proportion as the exploitation of one individual by another will also be put an end to, the exploitation of one nation by another will also be put an end to. In proportion as the antagonism between classes within the nation vanishes, the hostility of one nation to another will come to an end.

The charges against communism made from a religious, a philosophical and, generally, from an ideological standpoint, are not deserving of serious examination.

Does it require deep intuition to comprehend that man's ideas, views, and conception, in one word, man's consciousness, changes with every change in the conditions of his material existence, in his social relations and in his social life?

What else does the history of ideas prove, than that intellectual production changes its character in proportion as material production is changed? The ruling ideas of each age have ever been the ideas of its ruling class.

When people speak of the ideas that revolutionize society, they do but express that fact that within the old society the elements of a new one have been created, and that the dissolution of the old ideas keeps even pace with the dissolution of the old conditions of existence.

When the ancient world was in its last throes, the ancient religions were overcome by Christianity. When Christian ideas succumbed in the 18th century to rationalist ideas, feudal society fought its death battle with the then revolutionary bourgeoisie. The ideas of religious liberty and freedom of conscience merely gave expression to the sway of free competition within the domain of knowledge.

"Undoubtedly," it will be said, "religious, moral, philosophical, and juridicial ideas have been modified in the course of historical development. But religion, morality, philosophy, political science, and law, constantly survived this change."

"There are, besides, eternal truths, such as Freedom, Justice, etc., that are common to all states of society. But communism abolishes eternal truths, it abolishes all religion, and all morality, instead of constituting them on a new basis; it therefore acts in contradiction to all past historical experience."

What does this accuzation reduce itself to? The history of all past society has consisted in the development of class antagonisms, antagonisms that assumed different forms at different epochs.

But whatever form they may have taken, one fact is common to all past ages, viz., the exploitation of one part of society by the other. No wonder, then, that the social consciousness of past ages, despite all the multiplicity and variety it displays, moves within certain common forms, or general ideas, which cannot completely vanish except with the total disappearance of class antagonisms.

The communist revolution is the most radical rupture with traditional relations; no wonder that its development involved the most radical rupture with traditional ideas.

But let us have done with the bourgeois objections to communism.

We have seen above that the first step in the revolution by the working class is to raise the proletariat to the position of ruling class to win the battle of democracy.

The proletariat will use its political supremacy to wrest, by degree, all capital from the bourgeoisie, to centralize all instruments of production in the hands of the state, i.e., of the proletariat organized as the ruling class; and to increase the total productive forces as rapidly as possible.

Of course, in the beginning, this cannot be effected except by means of despotic inroads on the rights of property, and on the conditions of bourgeois production; by means of measures, therefore, which appear economically insufficient and untenable, but which, in the course of the movement, outstrip themselves, necessitate further inroads upon the old social order, and are unavoidable as a means of entirely revolutionizing the mode of production.

These measures will, of course, be different in different countries.

Nevertheless, in most advanced countries, the following will be pretty generally applicable.

1. Abolition of property in land and application of all rents of land to public purposes.
2. A heavy progressive or graduated income tax.
3. Abolition of all rights of inheritance.
4. Confiscation of the property of all emigrants and rebels.
5. Centralization of credit in the banks of the state, by means of a national bank with state capital and an exclusive monopoly.
6. Centralization of the means of communication and transport in he hands of the state.
7. Extension of factories and instruments of production owned by the state; the bringing into cultivation of waste lands, and the improvement of the soil generally in accordance with a common plan.
8. Equal obligation of all to work. Establishment of industrial armies, especially for agriculture.
9. Combination of agriculture with manufacturing industries; gradual abolition of all the distinction between town and country by a more equable distribution of the populace over the country.
10. Free education for all children in public schools. Abolition of children's factory labour in its present form. Combination of education with industrial production, etc.

When, in the course of development, class distinctions have disappeared, and all production has been concentrated in the hands of a vast association of the whole nation, the public power will lose its political character. Political power, properly so called, is merely the organized power of one class for oppressing another. If the proletariat during its contest with the bourgeoisie is compelled, by the force of circumstances, to organize itself as a class; if, by means of a revolution, it makes itself the ruling class, and, as such, sweeps away by force the old conditions of production, then it will, along with these conditions, have swept away the conditions for the existence of class antagonisms and of classes generally, and will thereby have abolished its own supremacy as a class.

In place of the old bourgeois society, with its classes and class antagonisms, we shall have an association in which the free development of each is the condition for the free development of all.

III. Socialist and Communist Literature

1. Reactionary Socialism

(a) Feudal Socialism

Owing to their historical position, it became the vocation of the aristocracies of France and England to write pamphlets against modern bourgeois society. In the French Revolution of July 1830, and in the English reform agitation, these aristocracies again succumbed to the hateful upstart. Thenceforth, a serious political struggle was altogether out of the question. A literary battle alone remained possible. But even in the domain of literature, the old cries of the restoration period had become impossible.[5]

In order to arouse sympathy, the aristocracy was obliged to lose sight, apparently, of its own interests, and to formulate its indictment against the bourgeoisie in the interest of the exploited working class alone. Thus, the aristocracy took their revenge by singing lampoons on their new masters and whispering in his ears sinister prophecies of coming catastrophes.

In this way arose feudal socialism: half lamentation, half lampoon; half an echo of the past, half menace of the future; at times, by its bitter, witty and incisive criticism, striking the bourgeoisie to the very heart's core, but always ludicrous in its effect, through total incapacity to comprehend the march of modern history.

The aristocracy, in order to rally the people to them, waved the proletarian alms-bag in front for a banner. But the people, so often as it joined them, saw on their hindquarters the old feudal coats of arms, and deserted with loud and irreverent laughter.

One section of the French Legitimists and "Young England" exhibited this spectacle:

In pointing out that their mode of exploitation was different to that of the bourgeoisie, the feudalists forget that they exploited under circumstances and conditions that were quite different and that are now antiquated. In showing that, under their rule, the modern proletariat never existed, they forget that the modern bourgeoisie is the necessary offspring of their own form of society.

For the rest, so little do they conceal the reactionary character of their criticism that their chief accuzation against the bourgeois amounts to this: that under the bourgeois regime a class is being developed which is destined to cut up, root and branch, the old order of society.

What they upbraid the bourgeoisie with is not so much that it creates a proletariat as that it creates a *revolutionary* proletariat.

In political practice, therefore, they join in all corrective measures against the working class; and in ordinary life, despite their high faluting phrases, they stoop to pick up the golden apples dropped from the tree of industry, and to barter truth, love, and honor, for traffic in wool, beetroot-sugar, and potato spirits.[6]

As the parson has ever gone hand in hand with the landlord, so has clerical socialism with feudal socialism.

Nothing is easier than to give Christian asceticism a socialist tinge. Has not Christianity declaimed against private property, against marriage, against the state? Has it not preached in the place of these, charity and poverty, celibacy and mortification of the flesh, monastic life and Mother Church? Christian socialism is but the holy water with which the priest consecrates the heart-burnings of the aristocrat.

(b) Petty-Bourgeois Socialism

The feudal aristocracy was not the only class that was ruined by the bourgeoisie, not the only class whose conditions of existence pined and perished in the atmosphere of modern bourgeois society. The medieval burgesses and the small peasant proprietors were the precursors of the modern bourgeoisie. In those countries which are but little developed, industrially and commercially, these two classes still vegetate side by side with the rising bourgeoisie.

In countries where modern civilization has become fully developed, a new class of petty bourgeois has been formed, fluctuating between proletariat and bourgeoisie, and ever renewing itself a supplementary part of bourgeois society. The individual members of this class, however, as being constantly hurled down into the proletariat by the action of competition, and, as Modern Industry develops, they even see the moment approaching when they will completely disappear as an independent section of modern society, to be replaced in manufactures, agriculture and commerce, by overlookers, bailiffs and shopmen.

In countries like France, where the peasants constitute far more than half of the population, it was natural that writers who sided with the proletariat against the bourgeoisie should use, in their criticism of the bourgeois regime, the standard of the peasant and petty bourgeois, and from the standpoint of these intermediate classes, should take up the cudgels for the working class. Thus arose petty-bourgeois socialism. Sismondi was the head of this school, not only in France but also in England.

This school of socialism dissected with great acuteness the contradictions in the conditions of modern production. It laid bare the hypocritical apologies of economists. It proved, incontrovertibly, the disastrous effects of machinery and division of labour, the concentration of capital and land in a few hands; overproduction and crises; it pointed out the inevitable ruin of the petty bourgeois and peasant, the misery of the proletariat, the anarchy in production, the crying inequalities in the distribution of wealth, the industrial war of extermination between nations, the dissolution of old moral bonds, of the old family relations, of the old nationalities.

In it positive aims, however, this form of socialism aspires either to restoring the old means of production and of exchange, and with them the old property relations, and the old society, or to cramping the modern means of production and of exchange within the framework of the old property relations that have been, and were bound to be, exploded by those means. In either case, it is both reactionary and Utopian.

Its last words are: corporate guilds for manufacture; patriarchal relations in agriculture.

Ultimately, when stubborn historical facts had dispersed all intoxicating effects of self-deception, this form of socialism ended in a miserable hangover.

(c) German or "True" Socialism

The socialist and communist literature of France, a literature that originated under the pressure of a bourgeoisie in power, and that was the expressions of the struggle against this power, was introduced into Germany at a time when the bourgeoisie in that country had just begun its contest with feudal absolutism.

German philosophers, would-be philosophers, and beaux esprits (men of letters), eagerly seized on this literature, only forgetting that when these writings immigrated from France into Germany, French social conditions had not immigrated along with them. In contact with German social conditions, this French literature lost all its immediate practical significance and assumed a purely literary aspect. Thus, to the German philosophers of the 18th century, the demands of the first French Revolution were nothing more than the demands of "Practical Reason" in general, and the utterance of the will of the revolutionary French bourgeoisie signified, in their eyes, the laws of pure will, of will as it was bound to be, of true human will generally.

The work of the German literati consisted solely in bringing the new French ideas into harmony with their ancient philosophical conscience, or rather, in annexing the French ideas without deserting their own philosophic point of view.

This annexation took place in the same way in which a foreign language is appropriated, namely, by translation.

It is well known how the monks wrote silly lives of Catholic saints *over* the manuscripts on which the classical works of ancient heathendom had been written. The German literati reversed this process with the profane French literature. They wrote their philosophical nonsense beneath the French original. For instance, beneath the French criticism of the economic functions of money, they wrote "alienation of humanity", and beneath the French criticism of the bourgeois state they wrote "dethronement of the category of the general", and so forth.

The introduction of these philosophical phrases at the back of the French historical criticisms, they dubbed "Philosophy of Action", "True Socialism", "German Science of Socialism", "Philosophical Foundation of Socialism", and so on.

The French socialist and communist literature was thus completely emasculated. And, since it ceased, in the hands of the German, to express the struggle of one class with the other, he felt conscious of having overcome "French one-sidedness" and of representing, not true requirements, but the requirements of truth; not the interests of the proletariat, but the interests of human nature, of man in general, who belongs to no class, has no reality, who exists only in the misty realm of philosophical fantasy.

This German socialism, which took its schoolboy task so seriously and solemnly, and extolled its poor stock-in-trade in such a mountebank fashion, meanwhile gradually lost its pedantic innocence.

The fight of the Germans, and especially of the Prussian bourgeoisie, against feudal aristocracy and absolute monarchy, in other words, the liberal movement, became more earnest.

By this, the long-wished for opportunity was offered to "True" Socialism of confronting the political movement with the socialistic demands, of hurling the traditional anathemas against liberalism, against representative government, against bourgeois competition, bourgeois freedom of the press, bourgeois legislation, bourgeois liberty and equality, and of preaching to the masses that they had nothing to gain, and everything to lose, by this bourgeois movement. German socialism forgot, in the nick of time, that the French criticism, whose silly echo it was, presupposed the existence of modern bourgeois society, with its corresponding economic conditions of existence, and the political constitution adapted thereto, the very things those attainment was the object of the pending struggle in Germany.

To the absolute governments, with their following of parsons, professors, country squires, and officials, it served as a welcome scarecrow against the threatening bourgeoisie.

It was a sweet finish, after the bitter pills of flogging and bullets, with which these same governments, just at that time, dosed the German working-class risings.

While this "True" Socialism thus served the government as a weapon for fighting the German bourgeoisie, it, at the same time, directly represented a reactionary interest, the interest of German philistines. In Germany, the petty-bourgeois class, a relic of the 16th century, and since then constantly cropping up again under the various forms, is the real social basis of the existing state of things.

To preserve this class is to preserve the existing state of things in Germany. The industrial and political supremacy of the bourgeoisie threatens it with certain destruction—on the one hand, from the concentration of capital; on the other, from the rise of a revolutionary proletariat. "True" Socialism appeared to kill these two birds with one stone. It spread like an epidemic.

The robe of speculative cobwebs, embroidered with flowers of rhetoric, steeped in the dew of sickly sentiment, this transcendental robe in which the German Socialists wrapped their sorry "eternal truths", all skin and bone, served to wonderfully increase the sale of their goods amongst such a public. And on its part German socialism recognized, more and more, its own calling as the bombastic representative of the petty-bourgeois philistine.

It proclaimed the German nation to be the model nation, and the German petty philistine to be the typical man. To every villainous meanness of this model man, it gave a hidden, higher, socialistic interpretation, the exact contrary of its real character. It went to the extreme length of directly opposing the "brutally destructive" tendency of communism, and of proclaiming its supreme and impartial contempt of all class struggles. With very few exceptions, all the so-called socialist and communist publications that now (1847) circulate in Germany belong to the domain of this foul and enervating literature.[7]

2. Conservative or Bourgeois Socialism

A part of the bourgeoisie is desirous of redressing social grievances in order to secure the continued existence of bourgeois society.

To this section belong economists, philanthropists, humanitarians, improvers of the condition of the working class, organizers of charity, members of societies for the prevention of cruelty to animals, temperance fanatics, hole-and-corner reformers of every imaginable kind. This form of socialism has, moreover, been worked out into complete systems.

We may cite Proudhon's *Philosophy of Poverty* as an example of this form.

The socialistic bourgeois want all the advantages of modern social conditions without the struggles and dangers necessarily resulting therefrom. They desire the existing state of society, minus its revolutionary and disintegrating elements. They wish for a bourgeoisie without a proletariat. The bourgeoisie naturally conceives the world in which it is supreme to be the best; and bourgeois socialism develops this comfortable conception into various more or less complete systems. In requiring the proletariat to carry out such a system, and thereby to march straightaway into the social New Jerusalem, it but requires in reality that the proletariat should remain within the bounds of existing society, but should cast away all its hateful ideas concerning the bourgeoisie.

A second, and more practical, but less systematic, form of this socialism sought to depreciate every revolutionary movement in the eyes of the working class by showing that no mere political reform, but only a change in the material conditions of existence, in economical relations, could be of any advantage to them. By changes in the material conditions of existence, this form of socialism, however, by no means understands abolition of the bourgeois relations of production, an abolition that can be affected only by a revolution, but administrative reforms, based on the continued existence of these relations; reforms, therefore, that in no respect affect the relations between capital and labour, but, at the best, lessen the cost, and simplify the administrative work of bourgeois government.

Bourgeois socialism attains adequate expression when, and only when, it becomes a mere figure of speech.

Free trade: for the benefit of the working class. Protective duties: for the benefit of the working class. Prison reform: for the benefit of the working class. This is the last word and the only seriously meant word of bourgeois socialism.

It is summed up in the phrase: the bourgeois is a bourgeois—for the benefit of the working class.

3. Critical-Utopian Socialism and Communism

We do not here refer to that literature which, in every great modern revolution, has always given voice to the demands of the proletariat, such as the writings of Babeuf[8] and others.

The first direct attempts of the proletariat to attain its own ends, made in times of universal excitement, when feudal society was being overthrown, necessarily failed, owing to the then undeveloped state of the proletariat, as well as to the absence of the economic conditions for its emancipation, conditions that had yet to be produced, and could be produced by the impending bourgeois epoch alone. The revolutionary literature that accompanied these first movements of the proletariat had necessarily a reactionary character. It inculcated universal asceticism and social leveling in its crudest form.

The socialist and communist systems, properly so called, those of Saint-Simon[9], Fourier[10], Owen[11], and others, spring into existence in the early undeveloped period, described above, of the struggle between proletariat and bourgeoisie (see Section 1. Bourgeois and Proletarians).

The founders of these systems see, indeed, the class antagonisms, as well as the action of the decomposing elements in the prevailing form of society. But the proletariat, as yet in its infancy, offers to them the spectacle of a class without any historical initiative or any independent political movement.

Since the development of class antagonism keeps even pace with the development of industry, the economic situation, as they find it, does not as yet offer to them the material conditions for the emancipation of the proletariat. They therefore search after a new social science, after new social laws, that are to create these conditions.

Historical action is to yield to their personal inventive action; historically created conditions of emancipation to fantastic ones; and the gradual, spontaneous class organization of the proletariat to an organization of society especially contrived by these inventors. Future history resolves itself, in their eyes, into the propaganda and the practical carrying out of their social plans.

In the formation of their plans, they are conscious of caring chiefly for the interests of the working class, as being the most suffering class. Only from the point of view of being the most suffering class does the proletariat exist for them.

The undeveloped state of the class struggle, as well as their own surroundings, causes Socialists of this kind to consider themselves far superior to all class antagonisms. They want to improve the condition of every member of society, even that of the most favoured. Hence, they habitually appeal to society at large, without the distinction of class; nay, by preference, to the ruling class. For how can people when once they understand their system, fail to see in it the best possible plan of the best possible state of society?

Hence, they reject all political, and especially all revolutionary action; they wish to attain their ends by peaceful means, necessarily doomed to failure, and by the force of example, to pave the way for the new social gospel.

Such fantastic pictures of future society, painted at a time when the proletariat is still in a very undeveloped state and has but a fantastic conception of its own position, correspond with the first instinctive yearnings of that class for a general reconstruction of society.

But these socialist and communist publications contain also a critical element. They attack every principle of existing society. Hence, they are full of the most valuable materials for the enlightenment of the working class. The practical measures proposed in them—such as the abolition of the distinction between town and country, of the family, of the carrying on of industries for the account of private individuals, and of the wage system, the proclamation of social harmony, the conversion of the function of the state into a more superintendence of production—all these proposals point solely to the disappearance of class antagonisms which were, at that time, only just cropping up, and which, in these publications, are recognized in their earliest indistinct and undefined forms only. These proposals, therefore, are of a purely Utopian character.

The significance of critical-Utopian socialism and communism bears an inverse relation to historical development. In proportion as the modern class struggle develops and takes definite shape, this fantastic standing apart from the contest, these fantastic attacks on it, lose all practical value and all theoretical justifications. Therefore, although the originators of these systems were, in many respects, revolutionary, their disciples have, in every case, formed mere reactionary sects. They hold fast by the original views of their masters, in opposition to the progressive historical development of the proletariat. They, therefore, endeavour, and that consistently, to deaden the class struggle and to reconcile the class antagonisms. They still dream of experimental realization of their social utopias, of founding isolated phalansteres, of establishing "Home Colonies", or setting up a "Little Icaria"[12]—pocket editions of the New Jerusalem—and to realize all these castles in the air, they are compelled to appeal to the feelings and purses of the bourgeois. By degrees, they sink into the category of the reactionary conservative socialists depicted above, differing from these only by more systematic pedantry, and by their fanatical and superstitious belief in the miraculous effects of their social science.

They, therefore, violently oppose all political action on the part of the working class; such action, according to them, can only result from blind unbelief in the new gospel.

The Owenites in England, and the Fourierists in France, respectively, oppose the Chartists and the Reformistes.

IV. Position of the Communists in Relation to the Various Existing Opposition Parties

Section II has made clear the relations of the Communists to the existing working-class parties, such as the Chartists in England and the Agrarian Reformers in America.

The Communists fight for the attainment of the immediate aims, for the enforcement of the momentary interests of the working class; but in the movement of the present, they also represent and take care of the future of that movement. In France, the Communists ally with the Social Democrats against the conservative and radical bourgeoisie, reserving, however, the right to take up a critical position in regard to phases and illusions traditionally handed down from the Great Revolution.

In Switzerland, they support the Radicals, without losing sight of the fact that this party consists of antagonistic elements, partly of Democratic Socialists, in the French sense, partly of radical bourgeois.

In Poland, they support the party that insists on an agrarian revolution as the prime condition for national emancipation, that party which fomented the insurrection of Krakow in 1846.

In Germany, they fight with the bourgeoisie whenever it acts in a revolutionary way, against the absolute monarchy, the feudal squirearchy, and the petty-bourgeoisie.

But they never cease, for a single instant, to instill into the working class the clearest possible recognition of the hostile antagonism between bourgeoisie and proletariat, in order that the German workers may straightway use, as so many weapons against the bourgeoisie, the social and political conditions that the bourgeoisie must necessarily introduce along with its supremacy, and in order that, after the fall of the reactionary classes in Germany, the fight against the bourgeoisie itself may immediately begin.

The Communists turn their attention chiefly to Germany, because that country is on the eve of a bourgeois revolution that is bound to be carried out under more advanced conditions of European civilization and with a much more developed proletariat than that of England was in the 17th, and France in the 18th century, and because the bourgeois revolution in Germany will be but the prelude to an immediately following proletarian revolution.

In short, the Communists everywhere support every revolutionary movement against the existing social and political order of things.

In all these movements, they bring to the front, as the leading question in each, the property question, no matter what its degree of development at the time.

Finally, they labour everywhere for the union and agreement of the democratic parties of all countries.

The Communists disdain to conceal their views and aims. They openly declare that their ends can be attained only by the forcible overthrow of all existing social conditions. Let the ruling classes tremble at a communist revolution. The proletarians have nothing to lose but their chains. They have a world to win.

Working men of all countries, unite!

Notes

1. By bourgeoisie is meant the class of modern capitalists, owners of the means of social production and employers of wage labour. By proletariat, the class of modern wage labourers who, having no means of production of their own, are reduced to selling their labour power in order to live. *[Note by Engels—1888 English edition]*
2. That is, all *written* history. In 1847, the pre-history of society, the social organization existing previous to recorded history, all but unknown. Since then, August von Haxthausen (1792–1866) discovered common ownership of land in Russia, Georg Ludwig von Maurer proved it to be the social foundation from which all Teutonic races started in history, and, by and by, village communities were found to be, or to have been, the primitive form of society everywhere from India to Ireland. The inner organization of this primitive communistic society was laid bare, in its typical form, by Lewis Henry Morgan's (1818–1861) crowning discovery of the true nature of the gens and its relation to the tribe. With the dissolution of the primeval communities, society begins to be differentiated into separate and finally antagonistic classes. I have attempted to retrace this dissolution in *Der Ursprung der Familie, des Privateigenthumus und des Staats,* second edition, Stuttgart, 1886. [Engels, 1888 English edition]
3. Guild-master, that is, a full member of a guild, a master within, not a head of a guild. *[Engels: 1888 English edition]*
4. This was the name given their urban communities by the townsmen of Italy and France, after they had purchased or conquered their initial rights of self-government from their feudal lords. *[Engels: 1890 German edition]*

   "Commune" was the name taken in France by the nascent towns even before they had conquered from their feudal lords and masters local self-government and political rights as the "Third Estate". Generally speaking, for the economical development of the bourgeoisie, England is here taken as the typical country, for its political development, France. *[Engels: 1888 English edition]*
5. Note by Engels to 1888 English edition: Not the English Restoration (1660–1689), but the French Restoration (1814–1830).

6. Note by Engels to 1888 English edition: This applies chiefly to Germany, where the landed aristocracy and squirearchy have large portions of their estates cultivated for their own account by stewards, and are, moreover, extensive beetroot-sugar manufacturers and distillers of potato spirits. The wealthier British aristocracy are, as yet, rather above that; but they, too, know how to make up for declining rents by lending their names to floaters or more or less shady joint-stock companies.
7. Note by Engels to 1888 German edition: The revolutionary storm of 1848 swept away this whole shabby tendency and cured its protagonists of the desire to dabble in socialism. The chief representative and classical type of this tendency is Mr Karl Gruen.
8. Francois Noel Babeuf (1760–1797): French political agitator; plotted unsuccessfully to destroy the Directory in revolutionary France and established a communistic system.
9. Comte de Saint-Simon, Claude Henri de Rouvroy (1760–1825): French social philosopher; generally regarded as founder of French socialism. He thought society should be reorganized along industrial lines and that scientists should be the new spiritual leaders. His most important work is *Nouveau Christianisme* (1825).
10. Charles Fourier (1772–1837): French social reformer; propounded a system of self-sufficient cooperatives known as Fourierism, especially in his work *Le Nouveau Monde industriel* (1829–30)
11. Robert Owen (1771–1858): Welsh industrialist and social reformer. He formed a model industrial community at New Lanark, Scotland, and pioneered cooperative societies. His books include *New View of Society* (1813).
12. Note by Engels to 1888 English edition: "Home Colonies" were what Owen called his communist model societies. *Phalansteres were socialist colonies on the plan of Charles Fourier; Icaria was the name given by Caber to his Utopia and, later on, to his American communist colony.*

4

Scientific Socialism, 1844–75

Karl Marx

An Epitome

From Economic and Philosophical Manuscripts, 1844

The labourer becomes poorer the more wealth he produces, indeed, the more powerful and wide-ranging his production becomes. Labour does not only produce commodities, it produces itself and the labourer as a commodity, and in relation to the level at which it produces commodities. The product of labour is labour, which fixes itself in the object, it becomes a thing, it is the *objectification* of labour. The *objectification of labour* manifests itself so much as a loss of objects, that the labourer is robbed of the most necessary objects, not only to maintain his own life, but even objects with which to labour. Indeed, labour itself becomes an object, which only with the greatest effort and with random interruptions can be acquired. Appropriation of objects manifests itself so much as estrangement, that, the more objects the labourer produces, the fewer he can own and so he plunges deeper under the mastery of his product: Capital.

In this definition—that the labourer is related to the product of his labour as a strange, foreign object, lies all the consequences. For from this hypothesis the following becomes clear: the more the labourer labours, as well as the more powerful the alien, object world which he builds over himself becomes, the poorer he himself becomes, that is, his inner world, as he owns less. The same thing occurs in religion. The more people place faith in God, the less they retain in themselves. The labourer places his life in the object; but now it [his life] belongs less to him than to the object. Therefore, the more this happens, the more deprived of objects the labourer becomes. What the product of his labour is, he is not. Therefore, the greater this product, the less he becomes. The alienation of the labourer in his product has this significance: since his labour is an object, not only does this labour become a separate existence, but it is also separate from him, independent, *alien* to his existence and a self-sufficient power which exists above him, that the life, which he has bestowed on the object, confronts him as something hostile and strange.

What then makes up the alienation of labour? *First,* that labour is *alien* to the labourer, that is, that it does not make up his existence, that he does not affirm himself in his labour, but rather denies himself; he does not feel happy, but rather unhappy; he does not grow physically or mentally, but rather tortures his body and ruins his mind. The labourer feels himself first to be other than his labour and his labour to be other than himself. He is at home when he is not labouring, and when he is labouring he is not at home. His labour is not voluntary, but *constrained, forced* labour. Therefore, it does not meet a need, but rather it is a means to meet some need alien to it. Its estranged character becomes obvious when one sees that as soon as there is no physical or other coercion, labour is avoided like the plague. This alienated labour, in which human beings alienate themselves from themselves, is a labour of self-denial and self-torture. Finally, the alienation of labour manifests itself to the labourer in that this labour does not belong to him, but to someone else; it does not belong to him; while he is doing it he does not belong to himself, but to another. The activity of the labourer is not his own activity. It belongs to someone else, it is *the loss of his self.* The result, therefore, is that the human being (the labourer) does not feel himself to be free except in his animal functions: eating, drinking, and reproducing, at his best in his dwelling or in his clothing, etc., and in his human functions he is no more than an animal. The animal becomes human and the human becomes animal.

A direct consequence of the estrangement of the humans from the product of their labour, from their life-activity, from their species-being, is *the estrangement of humans from humans.* When a human confronts himself as a stranger, so he confronts another human as a stranger. The relationship of humans to their labour, to the product of their labour, and to themselves, is also the relationship of humans to each other, and to the labour of others and to the objects of others. Moreover, this fact, that the individual is estranged from his species-being means that the individual is estranged from other individuals, since each of them is estranged from their own species-being...

This relationship of the labourer to his labour gives birth to the relationship of that labour to the capitalist, or whatever one wishes to name the "labour-master." Private property is also the product, the result, the *natural consequence* of alienated labour, of the alienated relationship of the labourer to nature and to himself. Therefore, private property arises from the analysis of the idea of alienated labour, that is, of alienated humanity, of estranged labour, of estranged life, of estranged humanity. Wages are an unmediated, direct result of estranged labour, and estranged labour is the unmediated, direct source of private property. If the one falls, the other must fall. From the relationship of estranged labour to private property follows the conclusion that the liberation of society from private property, etc., from servitude, expresses its political form in the emancipation of the labourer, and not only the emancipation of the labourer, for in the emancipation of the labourer is contained the emancipation of all humanity, and it contains this because the entirety of human servitude is involved in the relationship of the labourer to production and all relationships of servitude are only modifications and consequences of this primary relationship...

Communism is the positive supersession of private property as human self-estrangement, and hence the true appropriation of the human essence through and for man; it is the complete restoration of man to himself as a social—i.e. human—being, a restoration which has become conscious and which takes place within the entire wealth of previous periods of development. This communism equals humanism; it is the genuine resolution of the conflict between man and nature, and between man and man, the true resolution of the conflict between existence and being, between objectification and self-affirmation, between freedom and necessity, between individual and species. It is the solution of the riddle of history and knows itself to be the solution.

The entire movement of history is therefore both the actual act of creation of communism—the birth of its empirical existence— and, for its thinking consciousness, the comprehended and known movement of its becoming. Its movement—production and consumption —is the sensuous revelation of the movement of all previous production —i.e. the realization or reality of man. Religion, the family, the state, law, morality, science, art, etc., are only *particular modes of production* and therefore come under its general law. The positive supersession of private property, as the appropriation of human life, is therefore the positive supersession of all estrangement, and the return of man from religion, the family, the state, etc., to his human—i.e. social— existence. Religious alienation as such takes place only in the sphere of consciousness, of man's inner life, but economic alienation is that of real life—its supersession therefore embraces both aspects...

Private property has made us so stupid and one-sided that an object is only ours when we have it, when it exists for us as capital or when we directly possess, eat, drink, wear, inhabit it, etc., in short, when we *use* it. The supersession of private property is therefore the complete emancipation of all human senses and attributes; but it is this emancipation precisely because these senses and attributes have become human, subjectively as well as objectively.

From Theses on Feuerbach, 1845

Feuerbach starts out from the fact of religious self-alienation, of the duplication of the world into a religious world and a secular one. He resolves the religious essence into the human essence. But the human essence is no abstraction inherent in each single individual. In its reality it is the ensemble of the social relations. Feuerbach, consequently, does not see that the *religious sentiment* is itself a social product, and that the abstract individual whom he analyses belongs to a particular form of society.

From the German Ideology, 1846

The various stages of development in the division of labour are just so many different forms of ownership, i.e. the existing stage in the division of labour determines also the relations of individuals to one another with reference to the material, instrument, and product of labour...As soon as the distribution of labour comes into being, each man has a particular, exclusive sphere of activity, which is forced upon him and from which he cannot escape. He is a hunter, a fisherman, a herdsman, or a critical critic, and must remain so if he does not want to lose his means of livelihood; while in communist society, where nobody has one exclusive sphere of activity but each can become accomplished in any branch he wishes, society regulates the general production and thus makes it possible for me to do one thing today and another tomorrow, to hunt in the morning, fish in the afternoon, rear cattle in the evening, criticize after dinner, just as I have a mind, without ever becoming hunter, fisherman, herdsman or critic.

From the Communist Manifesto, 1848

The history of all hitherto existing society is the history of class struggles. Freeman and slave, patrician and plebeian, lord and serf, guild-master and journeyman, in a word, oppressor and oppressed, stood in constant opposition to one another, carried on an uninterrupted, now hidden, now open fight, a fight that each time ended, either in a revolutionary re-constitution of society at large, or in the common ruin of the contending classes. In the earlier epochs of history, we find almost everywhere a complicated arrangement of society into various *orders,* a manifold gradation of social rank. In ancient Rome we have patricians, equites, plebeians, slaves; in the Middle Ages, lords, vassals, guild-masters, journeymen, apprentices, serfs; in almost all these classes, again, subordinate gradations.

What else does the history of ideas prove, than that intellectual production changes its character in proportion as material production is changed? The ruling ideas of each age have ever been the ideas of its ruling class. When people speak of ideas that revolutionize society, they do but express the fact that within the old society the elements of a new one have been created, and that the dissolution of the old ideas keeps even pace with the dissolution of the old conditions of existence. The modern *bourgeois* society that has sprouted from the ruins of feudal society has not done away with clash antagonisms. It has but established *new classes, new conditions of oppression, new forms of struggle* in place of the old ones. Our epoch, the epoch of the bourgeoisie, possesses, however, this distinctive feature: *it has simplified the class antagonisms.* Society as a whole is more and more splitting up into two great hostile camps, into two great classes directly facing each other: *Bourgeoisie* and *Proletariat.*

From the serfs of the Middle Ages sprang the chartered burghers of the earliest towns. From these burgesses the first elements of the bourgeoisie were developed. The discovery of America, the rounding of the Cape, opened up fresh ground for the rising bourgeoisie. The East Indian and Chinese markets, the colonization of America, trade with the colonies, the increase in the means of exchange and in commodities generally, gave to commerce, to navigation, to industry, an impulse never before known, and thereby, to the revolutionary element in the tottering feudal society, a rapid development. The feudal system of industry, under which industrial production was monopolized by closed guilds, now no longer sufficed for the growing wants of the new markets. The manufacturing system took its place. The guild-masters were closed on one side by the manufacturing middle class; division of labour between the different corporate guilds vanished in the face of division of labour in each single workshop.

Meantime the markets kept ever growing, the demand ever rising. Even manufacture no longer sufficed. Thereupon, steam and machinery revolutionized industrial production. The place of manufacture was taken by the giant, Modern Industry, the place of the industrial middle class, by industrial millionaires, the leaders of whole industrial armies, the modern bourgeois. Modern industry has established the world-market, for which the discovery of America paved the way. This market has given an immense development to commerce, to navigation, to communication by land. This development has, in its turn, reacted on the extension of industry; and in proportion as industry, commerce, navigation, railways extended, in the same proportion the bourgeoisie developed, increased its capital, and pushed into the background every class handed down from the Middle Ages. We see, therefore, how the modern bourgeoisie is itself the product of a long course of development, of *a series of revolutions* in the modes of production and of exchange. Each step in the development of the bourgeoisie was accompanied by a corresponding political advance of that class. An oppressed class under the sway of the feudal nobility, an armed and self-governing association in the medieval commune; here an independent *urban republic* (as in Italy and Germany), there a taxable *third estate* of the monarchy (as in France); afterwards, in the period of manufacture proper, serving either the semi-feudal or the absolute monarchy as a counterpoise against the nobility, and, in fact, the cornerstone of the great monarchies in general, the bourgeoisie has at last, since the establishment of Modern Industry and of the world-market, conquered for itself, in the modern representative State, exclusive political sway. *The executive of the modern State is but a committee for managing the common affairs of the whole bourgeoisie...*

We see then: the means of production and of exchange, on whose foundation the bourgeoisie built itself up, were generated in *feudal society*. At a certain stage in the development of these means of production and of exchange, the conditions under which feudal society produced and exchanged, the feudal organization of agriculture and manufacturing industry, in one word, the feudal relations of property became no longer compatible with the already developed productive forces; they became so many fetters. They had to be burst asunder; they were burst asunder. Into their place stepped free competition, accompanied by a social and political constitution adapted to it, and by the economical and political sway of the bourgeois class.

In proportion as the bourgeoisie, i.e. Capital, is developed, in the same proportion is the proletariat, the modern working class, developed—a class of labourers, who live only so long as they find work, and who find work only so long as their labour increases capital. These labourers, who must sell themselves piecemeal, are a commodity, like every other article of commerce, and are consequently exposed to all the vicissitudes of competition, to all the fluctuations of the market. Owing to the extensive use of machinery and to division of labour, the work of the proletarians has lost all individual character, and consequently, all charm for the workman. He becomes an appendage of the machine, and it is only the most simple, most monotonous and most easily acquired knack, that is required of him. Hence, the cost of production of a workman is restricted, almost entirely, to the means of subsistence that he requires for his maintenance, and for the propagation of his race. But the price of a commodity, and therefore also of labour, is equal to its cost of production. In proportion, therefore, as the repulsiveness of the work increases, the wage decreases. Nay more, in proportion as the use of machinery and division of labour increases, in the same proportion the burden of toil also increases, whether by prolongation of the working hours, by increase of the work exacted in a given time or by increased speed of the machinery, etc.

Masses of labourers, crowded into the factory, are organized like soldiers. As privates of the industrial army they are placed under the command of a perfect hierarchy of officers and sergeants. Not only are they slaves of the bourgeois class, and of the bourgeois state; they are daily and hourly enslaved by the machine, by the foreman, and, above all, by the individual bourgeois manufacturer himself. The more openly this despotism proclaims gain to be its end and aim, the more petty, the more hateful and the more embittering it is. Differences of age and sex have no longer any distinctive social validity for the working class. All are instruments of labour, more or less expensive to use, according to their age and sex ... The growing competition among the bourgeoisie, and the resulting commercial crises, make the wages of the workers ever more fluctuating. The unceasing improvement of machinery, ever more rapidly developing, makes their livelihood more and more precarious ... The modern labourer, instead of rising with the progress of industry, sinks deeper and deeper below the conditions of existence of his own class. He becomes a pauper, and paupe-rism develops more rapidly than population and wealth ...

The proletarians have nothing to lose but their chains. They have a world to win.

Workers of the World: Unite!!

From Contributions to the Critique of Political Economy, 1859

In the social production of their life, men enter into definite relations that are indispensable and independent of their will, relations of production which correspond to a definite stage of development of their material productive forces. The sum total of these relations of production constitutes the economic structure of society, the real foundation, on which rises a legal and political superstructure and to which correspond definite forms of social consciousness. The mode of production of material life conditions the social, political and intellectual life process in general. It is not the consciousness of men that determines their being, but, on the contrary, their social being that determines their consciousness. At a certain stage of their development, the material productive forces of society come in conflict with the existing relations of production, or—what is but a legal expression for the same thing—with the property relations within which they have been at work hitherto. From forms of development of the productive forces these relations turn into their fetters. Then begins an epoch of social revolution.

With the change of the economic foundation the entire immense superstructure is more or less rapidly transformed. In considering such transformations a distinction should always be made between the material transformation of the economic conditions of production, which can he determined with the precision of natural science, and the legal, political, religious, aesthetic or philosophic—in short, ideological forms in which men become conscious of this conflict and fight it out ... No social order ever perishes before all the productive forces for which there is room in it have developed; and new, higher relations of production never appear before the material conditions of their existence have matured in the womb of the old society itself. Therefore mankind always sets itself only such tasks as it can solve; since, looking at the matter more closely, it will always be found that the task itself arises only when the material conditions for its solution already exist or are at least in the process of formation.

From Critique of the Gotha Programme, 1875

Since labour is the source of all wealth, no one in society can appropriate wealth except as the product of labour. Therefore, if he himself does not work, he lives by the labour of others and also acquires his culture at the expense of the labour of others. Labour becomes the source of wealth and culture only as social labour, or, what is the same thing, in and through society. In proportion as labour develops socially, and becomes thereby a source of wealth and culture, poverty and destitution develop among the workers, and wealth and culture among the non-workers. This is the law of all history hitherto.

Within the cooperative society based on common ownership of the means of production, the producers do not exchange their products; just as little does the labour employed on the products appear here as the value of these products, as a material quality possessed by them, since now, in contrast to capitalist society, individual labour no longer exists in an indirect fashion but directly as a component part of total labour. What we have to deal with here is a communist society, not as it has developed on its own foundations, but, on the contrary, just as it emerges from capitalist society; which is thus in every respect, economically, morally, and intellectually, still stamped with the birthmarks of the old society from whose womb it emerges. Accordingly, the individual producer receives back from society— after the deductions have been made—exactly what he gives to it. What he has given to it is his individual quantum of labour. For example, he receives a certificate from society that he has furnished such-and-such an amount of labour (after deducting his labour for the common funds); and with this certificate, he draws from the social stock of means of consumption as much as the same amount of labour cost. The same amount of labour which he has given to society in one form, he receives back in another.

This equal right is an unequal right for unequal labour. It recognizes no class differences, because everyone is only a worker like everyone else; but it tacitly recognizes unequal individual endowment, and thus productive capacity, as a natural privilege. It is, therefore, a right of inequality, in its content, like every right. Further, one worker is married, another is not; one has more children than another, and so on and so forth. Thus, with an equal performance of labour, and hence an equal in the social consumption fund, one will in fact receive more than another, one will be richer than another, and so on. To avoid all these defects, right, instead of being equal, would have to be unequal. But these defects are inevitable in the first phase of communist society as it is when it has just emerged after prolonged birth pangs from capitalist society.

In a higher phase of communist society, after the enslaving subordination of the individual to the division of labour, and therewith also the antithesis between mental and physical labour, has vanished; after labour has become not only a means of life but life's prime want; after the productive forces have also increased with the all-around development of the individual, and all the springs of cooperative wealth flow more abundantly—only then can the narrow horizon of bourgeois right be crossed in its entirety and society inscribe on its banners: *From each according to his ability, to each according to his needs!*

A "free state" is by no means the aim of the workers, who have got rid of the narrow mentality of humble subjects, to set the state free. *Freedom* consists in converting the state from an organ superimposed upon society into one completely subordinate to it; and today, too, the forms of state are more free or less free to the extent that they restrict the "freedom of the state." The question then arises: What transformation will the state undergo in communist society? In other words, what social functions will remain in existence there that are analogous to present state functions? This question can only be answered scientifically. Between capitalist and communist society there lies the period of the revolutionary transformation of the one into the other. Corresponding to this is also a political transition period in which the state can be nothing but *the revolutionary dictatorship of the proletariat.*

Bourgeois "freedom of conscience" is nothing but the toleration of all possible kinds of religious freedom of conscience from the witchery of religion. But one chooses not to transgress the "bourgeois" level. The standardization of the working day must include the restriction of female labour, insofar as it relates to the duration, intermissions, etc., of the working day; otherwise, it could only mean the exclusion of female labour from branches of industry that are especially unhealthy for the female body, or are objectionable morally for the female sex.

A general prohibition of child labour is incompatible with the existence of large-scale industry and hence an empty, pious wish. Its realization—if it were possible—would be reactionary, since, with a strict regulation of the working time according to the different age groups and other safety measures for the protection of children, an early combination of productive labour with education is one of the most potent means for the transformation of present-day society.

5

Evolutionary Socialism

Eduard Bernstein

Eduard Bernstein (1850-1932) faced the problem—for Social Democrats—that things did not work out as badly as predicted in the Communist Manifesto. He was a colleague of Engels, and claimed Engel's support in dismissing with revolutionism, and calling for an evolutionary socialism, or as it is more commonly called "revisionism"...

Introduction

It has been maintained in a certain quarter that the practical deductions from my treatises would be the abandonment of the conquest of political power by the proletariat organised politically and economically. That is quite an arbitrary deduction, the accuracy of which I altogether deny.

I set myself against the notion that we have to expect shortly a collapse of the bourgeois economy, and that social democracy should be induced by the prospect of such an imminent, great, social catastrophe to adapt its tactics to that assumption. That I maintain most emphatically.

The adherents of this theory of a catastrophe, base it especially on the conclusions of the *Communist Manifesto*. This is a mistake in every respect.

The theory which the *Communist Manifesto* sets forth of the evolution of modern society was correct as far as it characterized the general tendencies of that evolution. But it was mistaken in several special deductions, above all in the estimate of the time the evolution would take. The last has been unreservedly acknowledged by Friedrich Engels, the joint author with Marx of the *Manifesto,* in his preface to the *Class War in France.* But it is evident that if social evolution takes a much greater period of time than was assumed, it must also take upon itself forms and lead to forms that were not foreseen and could not be foreseen then.

Social conditions have not developed to such an acute opposition of things and classes as is depicted in the *Manifesto.* It is not only useless, it is the greatest folly to attempt to conceal this from ourselves. The number of members of the possessing classes is today not smaller but larger. The enormous increase of social wealth is not accompanied by a decreasing number of large capitalists but by an increasing number of capitalists of all degrees. The middle classes change their character but they do not disappear from the social scale.

The concentration in productive industry is not being accomplished even today in all its departments with equal thoroughness and at an equal rate. In a great many branches of production it certainly justifies the forecasts of the socialist critic of society; but in other branches it lags even today behind them. The process of concentration in agriculture proceeds still more slowly. Trade statistics show an extraordinarily; elaborated graduation of enterprises in regard to size. No rung of the ladder is disappearing from it. The significant changes in the inner structure of these enterprises and their interrelationship cannot do away with this fact.

In all advanced countries we see the privileges of the capitalist bourgeoisie yielding step by step to democratic organizations. Under the influence of this, and driven by the movement of the working classes which is daily becoming stronger, a social reaction has set in against the exploiting tendencies of capital, a counteraction which, although it still proceeds timidly and feebly, yet does exist and is always drawing more departments of economic life under its influence. Factory legislation, the democratizing of local government, and the extension of its area of work, the freeing of trade unions and systems of cooperative trading from legal restrictions, the consideration of standard conditions of labour in the work undertaken by public authorities—all these characterize this phase of the evolution.

But the more the political organizations of modem nations are democratized the more the needs and opportunities of great political catastrophes are diminished. He who holds firmly to the catastrophic theory of evolution must, with all his power, withstand and hinder the evolution described above, which, indeed, the logical defenders of that theory formerly did. But is the conquest of political power by the proletariat simply to be by a political catastrophe? Is it to be the appropriation and utilization of the power of the State by the proletariat exclusively against the whole non-proletarian world?

He who replies in the affirmative must be reminded of two things. In 1872 Marx and Engels announced in the preface to the new edition of the *Communist Manifesto* that the Paris Commune had exhibited a proof that "the working classes cannot simply take possession of the readymade State machine and set it in motion for their own aims." And in 1895 Friedrich Engels stated in detail in the preface to *War of the Classes* that the time of political surprises, of the "revolutions of small conscious minorities at the head of unconscious masses" was today at an end, that a collision on a large scale with the military would be the means of checking the steady growth of social democracy and of even throwing it back for a time–in short, that social democracy would flourish far better by lawful than by unlawful means and by violent revolution. And he points out in conformity with this opinion that the next task of the party should be "to work for an uninterrupted increase of its votes" or to carry on a slow *propaganda of parliamentary activity.*

Thus Engels, who, nevertheless, as his numerical examples show, still somewhat overestimated the rate of process of the evolution! Shall we be told that he abandoned the conquest of political power by the working classes, because he wished to avoid the steady growth of social democracy secured by lawful means being interrupted by a political revolution?

If not, and if one subscribes to his conclusions, one cannot reasonably take any offence if it is declared that for a long time yet the task of social democracy is, instead of speculating on a great economic crash, "to organize the working classes politically and develop them as a democracy and to fight for all reforms in the State which are adapted to raise the working classes and transform the State in the direction of democracy."

In short, Engels is so thoroughly convinced that the tactics based on the presumption of a catastrophe have had their day, that he even considers a revision of them necessary in the Latin countries where tradition is much more favourable to them than in Germany. "If the conditions of war between nations have altered," he writes, "no less have those for the war between classes." Has this already been forgotten?

No one has questioned the necessity for the working classes to gain the control of government. The point at issue is between the theory of a social cataclysm and the question whether with the given social development in Germany and the present advanced state of its working classes in the towns and the country, a sudden catastrophe would be desirable in the interest of the social democracy. I have denied it and deny it again, because in my judgment a greater security for lasting success lies in a steady advance than in the possibilities offered by a catastrophic crash.

And as I am firmly convinced that important periods in the development of nations cannot be leapt over I lay the greatest value on the next tasks of social democracy, on the struggle for the political rights of the working man, on the political activity of working men in town and country for the interests of their class, as well as on the work of the industrial organization of the workers.

In this sense I wrote the sentence that the movement means everything for me and that what is *usually* called "the final aim of socialism" is nothing; and in this sense I write down again today. Even if the word "usually" had not shown that the proposition was only to be understood conditionally, it was obvious that it could not express indifference concerning the final carrying out of socialist principles, but only indifference—or, as it would be better expressed, carelessness—as to the form of the final arrangement of things. I have at no time had an excessive interest in the future beyond general principles; I have not been able to read to the end any picture of the future. My thoughts and efforts are concerned with the duties of the present and the nearest future, and I only busy myself with the perspectives beyond so far as they give me a line of conduct for suitable action now.

The conquest of political power by the working classes, the expropriation of capitalists, are no ends themselves but only means for the accomplishment of certain aims and endeavours. As such they are demands in the programme of social democracy and are not attacked by me. Nothing can be said beforehand as to the circumstances of their accomplishment; we can only fight for their realization. But the conquest of political power necessitates the possession of political *rights;* and the most important problem of tactics which German social democracy has at the present time to solve appears to me to be to devise the best ways for the extension of the political and economic rights of the German working classes.

6
Reformist Socialism

Alexandre Millerand

I touch here a subject which does not fail to excite and even to scandalize a certain number of our friends the national interest the solidarity of classes—are these questions about which a socialist has a right to be anxious without betraying the ideal which he claims to serve, the triumph of a humanity freed from class wars and from wars of nations?

History is made up of elements too numerous and complex for anyone to be able, without vanity to claim to fix a hard-and-fast date for the triumph of his ideas. We fulfill our whole duty if we work in our station, within the limits of our strength, following the law of our nature, to prepare its victory. I have said how high the socialist ideal is, and how it is not enclosed in the narrow bounds which time and circumstances have fixed for any given nation. All the same, it spreads from men to their neighbour and no bad way of working for its extension is to take pains first to win over one's fellow citizens.

How, then, can this propaganda be determined irrespectively of the environment wherein it is carried on? Can method and tactics be the same under different or even opposite regimes? If it is true that the republic is the political formula of socialism, it follows, of course, that in a country where socialism has achieved the immense step forward of realizing its political formula, its action and procedure, once it possesses republican forms and universal suffrage, will assume quite a special aspect and character. This means that it is not only the right but the imperative duty of social democracy in France to adapt its method to the conditions of the political regime in which it moves. It would betray the first of its duties if it took refuge in mere phrases of revolution in order to be saved the responsibilities and burdens implied by the reformist method and the pursuit of immediate results. It would, by the same act, sacrifice the primordial interests of the proletariat by declining the effort which should, little by little, realize the aggregate of improvements which I tried to resume in an exact summary.

But how will the French Socialist Party have the right to call the republican regime its own, how will it handle practically that incomparable instrument of reforms, if it affects keeping outside of the Republican Party's life and means to isolate itself in the barren part of the systematic critic? It will only win that authority over the nation without which our views cannot be realized, on condition that it remains neither alien nor indifferent to any of its emotions and aspirations. In domestic affairs it must take sides in the battle in which the Republic is engaged, and formulate its opinion, inspiring itself—as how should it else?—by its own ideal, but also by the needs, the thoughts, and the traditions of the republican democracy, which it continues and from which it inherits. It will not neglect either the good order and prosperity of the public finances, first condition of all social reform, or the maintenance and development of the national production. Public works, improvements destined to promote industry, commerce, and agriculture, judicious management and utilization of our colonial domain—all these are questions which will claim its scrutiny and retain its attention. It will be the attentive and zealous servant of the nation's greatness and prosperity.

Its patriotism—the more sincere because it hates the noisy declamations of chauvinist politicians—has nothing to fear from its ardent love of peace and of mankind. Until that unknown date when the governments agree to lay aside in concert the heavy burden of military expenses, isolated disarmament would be worse than a folly; it would be a crime against the very ideal whose foremost soldier the socialists see France to be. While applying themselves to uphold and strengthen our diplomacy in the ways of peace, to draw from past conventions every effect of union and concord which they admit, and to get new treaties concluded tightening the bonds of friendship and solidarity between nations, they will watch no less carefully to preserve the country's independence unendangered by any aggression, through the power of its arms and the security of its alliances. While preparing for the future, they will not forget either the duties created for them by the past or the obligations imposed by the present...

I have not dissimulated the end toward which it marches, and I am acquainted with the argument that socialism can, and indeed should, call itself "revolutionary," since in fact the disappearance of the wage system will be the most real and radical of revolutions. Words do not frighten me; but I dread equivocations. And what equivocation could be more unfortunate than that of a party masked by a title which contradicts formally its spirit and its method? If we reckon violence reprehensible as well as useless, if legal reform appear to us at once as our immediate objective and as the sole practical procedures to bring us nearer our distant goal, let us, then, have the courage, not a difficult courage, to call ourselves by our own name, "reformists," since reformists we are. Let us take our courage the whole way; and having declared for the reformist method, let us dare to accept its conditions and consequences. Long before yesterday the French Socialist Party gave the first place in its programme to the capture of government; long before today it passed from theories to acts, and sent its campaigners into town halls, into departmental assemblies, into Parliament; it did not do so without resigning itself to the daily compromises which are the price of action, and allying itself with the parties near to it. Having gone so far, being persuaded more than ever of the utility and necessity of a method which has proved its value in experience, by what aberration should it desert that method at the very moment when it is becoming most effective? By what inconsistency should it consent to canvass every mandate, and yet rigorously forbid itself to join in the government, and take, along with the highest responsi-bilities, the most certain power?

Such an illogical course, if possible to continue, would soon ruin the credit and influence of the Party weak enough and sufficiently uncertain of itself to commit it. To put the people off to the mysterious date when a sudden miracle will change the face of the world, or day by day, reform by reform, by a patient and stubborn effort to win step by step all progress—those are the two methods which we must choose between.

Faithful to its principles and to the method which is its own, equally careful not to arouse chimerical hopes, and not to break its promises, French reformist socialism will be able to assume every responsibility; it will not decline any of the burdens imposed on it by its deep feeling of duty towards its ideal and towards its country.

7

The Historic Basis of Socialism

Sidney Webb

The mainstream which has borne European society towards socialism during the past one hundred years is the irresistible progress of democracy. De Tocqueville drove and hammered this truth into the reluctant ears of the Old World two generations ago; and we have all pretended to carry it about as part of our mental furniture ever since. But like most epigrammatic commonplaces, it is not generally realized; and de Tocqueville's book has, in due course, become a classic which everyone quotes and nobody reads. The progress of democracy is, in fact, often imagined, as by Sir Henry Maine, to be merely the substitution of one kind of political machinery for another; and there are many political democrats today who cannot understand why social or economic matters should be mixed up with politics at all. It was not for this that they broke the power of the aristocracy: they were touched not so much with love of the many as with hatred of the few; and, as has been acutely said—though usually by foolish persons—they are radicals merely because they are not themselves lords. But it will not long be possible for any man to persist in believing that the political organization of society can be completely altered without corresponding changes in economic and social relations. De Tocqueville expressly pointed out that the progress of democracy meant nothing less than a complete dissolution of the nexus by which society was held together under the old regime. This dissolution is followed by a period of anarchic spiritual isolation of the individual from his fellows, and to that extent by a general denial of the very idea of society. But man is a social animal; and after more or less interval there necessarily comes into existence a new nexus, differing so entirely from the old-fashioned organization that the historic fossil goes about denying that it is a nexus at all, or that any new nexus is possible or desirable. To him, mostly through lack of economics, the progress of democracy is nothing more than the destruction of old political privileges; and, naturally enough, few can see any beauty in mere dissolution and destruction. Those few are the purely political radicals abhorred of Comte and Carlyle: they are in social matters the empiricist survivals from a pre-scientific age.

The mere Utopians, on the other hand, who wove the baseless fabric of their visions of reconstructed society on their own private looms, equally failed, as a rule, to comprehend the problem of the age. They were, in imagination, resuscitated Joseph the Seconds benevolent despots who would have poured the old world, had it only been fluid, into their new moulds. Against their crude plans the statesman, the radical, and the political economist were united; for they took no account of the blind social forces which they could not control, and which went on inexorably working out social salvation in ways unsuspected by the Utopian.

In the present socialist movement these two streams are united: advocates of social reconstruction have learnt the lesson of democracy, and know that it is through the slow and gradual turning of the popular mind to new principles that social reorganization bit by bit comes. All students of society who are abreast of their time, socialists as well as individualists, realize that important organic changes can only be (1) democratic, and thus acceptable to a majority of the people, and prepared for in the minds of all; (2) gradual, and thus causing no dislocation, however rapid may be the rate of progress; (3) not regarded as immoral by the mass of the people, and thus not subjectively demoralizing to them; and (4) in this country at any rate, constitutional and peaceful.

Socialists may therefore be quite at one with radicals in their political methods. Radicals, on the other hand, are perforce realizing that mere political levelling is quite insufficient to save a state from anarchy and despair. Both sections have been driven to recognize that the root of the difficulty is economic; and there is every day a wider consensus that the inevitable outcome of democracy is the control by the people themselves, not only of their own political organization but, through that, also of the main instruments of wealth production; the gradual substitution of organized cooperation for the anarchy of the competitive struggle; and the consequent recovery, in the only possible way, of what John Stuart Mill calls "the enormous share which the possessors of the instruments of industry are able to take from the produce." The economic side of the democratic ideal is, in fact, socialism itself.

This new scientific conception of the social organism has put completely out of countenance the cherished principles of the political economist and the philosophic radical. We left them sailing gaily into anarchy on the stream of *laissez faire.* Since then the tide has turned. The publication of John Stuart Mill's *Political Economy* in 1848 marks conveniently the boundary of the old individualist economics. Every edition of Mill's book became more and more socialistic. After his death the world learnt the personal history, penned by his own hand, of his development from a mere political democrat to a convinced socialist.

The change in tone since then has been such that one competent economist, professedly anti-socialist, publishes regretfully to the world that all the younger men are now socialists, as well as many of the older professors. It is, indeed, mainly from these that the world has learnt how faulty were the earlier economic generalizations, and, above all, how incomplete as guides for social or political action. These generalizations are accordingly now to be met with only in leading articles, sermons, or the speeches of ministers or bishops. The economist himself knows them no more.

The result of this development of sociology is to compel a revision of the relative importance of liberty and equality as principles to be kept in view in social administration. In Bentham's celebrated "ends" to be aimed at in a civil code, liberty stands predominant over equality, on the ground that full equality can be maintained only by the loss of security for the fruits of labour. That exposition remains as true as ever; but the question for decision remains, how much liberty? Economic analysis has destroyed the value of the old criterion of respect for the equal liberty of others. Bentham, whose economics were weak, paid no attention to the perpetual tribute on the fruits of others' labour which full private property in land inevitably creates. In his view liberty and security to property meant that every worker should be free to obtain the full result of his own labour; and there appeared no inconsistency between them. The political economist now knows that with free competition and private property in land and capital, no individual can possibly obtain the full result of his own labour. The student of industrial development, moreover, finds it steadily more and more impossible to trace what is precisely the result of each separate man's toil. Complete rights of liberty and property necessarily involved, for example, the spoliation of the Irish cottier tenant for the benefit of Lord Clanricarde. What then becomes of the Benthamic principle of the greatest happiness of the greatest number? When the Benthamite comes to understand the law of rent, which of the two will he abandon? For he cannot escape the lesson of the century, taught alike by the economists, the statesmen, and the "practical men," that complete individual liberty, with unrestrained private ownership of the instruments of wealth production, is irreconcilable with the common weal. The free struggle for existence among ourselves menaces our survival as a healthy and permanent social organism. Evolution, Professor Huxley declares, is the substitution of consciously regulated coordination among the units of each organism, for blind anarchic competition. Thirty years ago Herbert Spencer demonstrated the incompatibility of full private property in land with the modem democratic state;

and almost every economist now preaches the same doctrine. The radical is rapidly arriving, from practical experience, at similar conclusions; and the steady increase of the government regulation of private enterprise, the growth of municipal administration, and the rapid shifting of the burden of taxation directly to rent and interest, mark in treble lines the statesman's unconscious abandonment of the old individualism, and our irresistible glide into collectivist socialism.

It was inevitable that the democracy should learn this lesson. With the masses painfully conscious of the failure of individualism to create a decent social life for four-fifths of the people, it might have been foreseen that individualism could not survive their advent to political power. If private property in land and capital necessarily keeps the many workers permanently poor (through no fault of their own) in order to make the few idlers rich (from no merit of their own), private property in land and capital will inevitably go the way of the feudalism which it superseded. The economic analysis confirms the rough generalization of the suffering people. The history of industrial evolution points to the same result; and for two generations the world's chief ethical teachers have been urging the same lesson. No wonder the heavens of individualism are rolling up before our eyes like a scroll; and even the bishops believe and tremble.

It is, of course, possible, as Sir Henry Maine and others have suggested, that the whole experience of the century is a mistake, and that political power will once more swing back into the hands of a monarch or an aristocratic oligarchy. It is, indeed, want of faith in democracy which holds back most educated sympathizers with socialism from frankly accepting its principles. What the economic side of such political atavism would be it is not easy to forecast. The machine industry and steam power could hardly be dismissed with the caucus and the ballot box. So long, however, as democracy in political administration continues to be the dominant principle, socialism may be quite safely predicted as its economic obverse, in spite of those freaks or aberrations of democracy which have already here and there thrown up a short-lived monarchy or a romantic dictatorship. Every increase in the political power of the proletariat will most surely be used by them for their economic and social protection. In England, at any rate, the history of the century serves at once as their guide and their justification.

8

Anarchism and Socialism

G.V. Plekhanov

The Point of View of the Utopian Socialists

The French Materialists of the 18th century while waging relentless war against all the "infames" whose yoke weighed upon the French of this period, by no means scorned the search after what they called "perfect legislation," i.e. the best of all possible legislations, such legislation as should secure to "human beings" the greatest sum of happiness, and could be alike applicable to all existing societies, for the simple reason that it was "perfect" and therefore the most "natural." Excursions into this domain of "perfect legislation" occupy no small place in the works of a d'Holbach and a Helvetius. On the other hand, the Socialists of the first half of our century threw themselves with immense zeal, with unequalled perseverance, into the search after the best of possible social organizations, after a perfect social organization. This is a striking and notable characteristic which they have in common with the French Materialists of the last century, and it is this characteristic which especially demands our attention in the present work.

In order to solve the problem of a perfect social organization, or what comes to the same thing, of the best of all possible legislation, we must eventually have some criterion by the help of which we may compare the various "legislations" one with the other. And the criterion must have a special attribute. In fact, there is no question of a "legislation" *relatively* the best, i.e. *the best legislation under given conditions.* No, indeed! We have to find a *perfect* legislation, a legislation whose perfection should have nothing relative about it, should be entirely independent of time and place, should be, in a word, absolute. We are therefore driven to make abstraction from history, since everything in history is relative, everything depends upon circumstance, time, and place. But abstraction made of the history of humanity, what is there left to guide us in our "legislative" investigations' Humanity is left us, man in general, human nature—of which history is but the manifestion. Here then we have our criterion definitely settled, a perfect legislation. The best of all possible legislation is that which best harmonizes with human nature. It may be, of course, that even when we have such a criterion we may, for want of "light" or of logic, fail to solve this problem of the best legislation. "Errare humanum est," but it seems incontrovertible that this problem can be solved, that we can, by taking our stand upon an exact knowledge of human nature, find a perfect legislation, a perfect organization.

Such was, in the domain of social science, the point of view of the French Materialists. Man is a sentient and reasonable being, they said; he avoids painful senzations and seeks pleasurable ones. He has sufficient intelligence to recognize what is useful to him as well as what is harmful to him. Once you admit these axioms, and you can in your investigations into the best legislation, arrive, with the help of reflection and good intentions, at conclusions as well founded, as exact, as incontrovertible as those derived from a mathematical demonstration. Thus Condorcet undertook to construct deductively all precepts of healthy morality by starting from the truth that man is a sentient and reasonable being.

It is hardly necessary to say that in this Condorcet was mistaken. If the "philosophers" in this branch of their investigations arrived at conclusions of incontestable though very relative value, they unconsciously owed this to the fact that they constantly abandoned their abstract standpoint of human nature in general, and took up that of a more or less idealized nature of a man of the Third Estate. This man "felt" and "reasoned," after a fashion very clearly defined by his social environment. It was his "nature" to believe firmly in bourgeois property, representative government, freedom of trade ("laissez faire, laissez passer!" the "nature" of this man was always crying out), and so on. In reality, the French philosophers always kept in view the economic and political requirements of the Third Estate; this was their real criterion. But they applied it unconsciously, and only after much wandering in the field of abstraction, did they arrive at it. Their conscious method always reduced itself to abstract considerations of "human nature," and of the social and political institutions that best harmonize with this nature.

Their method was also that of the Socialists. A man of the 18th century, Morelly, "to anticipate a mass of empty objections that would be endless," lays down as an incontrovertible principle "that in morals nature is one, constant, invariable... that its laws never change;" and that "everything that may be advanced as to the variety in the morals of savage and civilized peoples, by no means proves that nature varies;" that at the outside it only shows "that from certain accidental causes which are foreign to it, some nations have fallen away from the laws of nature; others have remained submissive to them, in some respects from mere habit; finally, others are subjected to them by certain reasoned-out laws that are not always in contradiction with nature;" in a word, "man may abandon the True, but the True can never be annihilated! Fourier relies upon the analysis of the human passions; Robert Owen starts from certain considerations on the formation of human character; Saint Simon, despite his deep comprehension of the historical evolution of humanity, constantly returns to "human nature" in order to explain the laws of this evolution; the Saint-Simonians declared their philosophy was "based upon a new conception of human nature." The Socialists of the various schools may quarrel as to the cause of their different conceptions of human nature; all, without a single exception, are convinced that social science has not and cannot have, any other basis than an adequate concept of this nature. In this they in no wise differ from the Materialists of the 18th century. Human nature is the one criterion they invariably apply in their criticism of existing society, and in their search after a social organization as it should be, after a "perfect" legislation.

Morelly, Fourier, Saint Simon, Owen—we look upon all of them today as Utopian Socialists. Since we know the general point of view that is common to them all, we can determine exactly what the Utopian point of view is. This will be the more useful, seeing that the opponents of Socialism use the word "Utopian" without attaching to it any, even approximately, definite meaning.

The Utopian is one who, starting from an abstract principle, seeks for a perfect social organization. The abstract principle which served as starting point of the Utopians was that of human nature. Of course there have been Utopians who applied the principle indirectly through the intermediary of concepts derived from it. Thus, e.g. in seeking for "perfect legislation," for an ideal organization of society, one may start from the concept of the Rights of Man. But it is evident that in its ultimate analysis this concept derives from that of human nature.

It is equally evident that one may be a Utopian without being a Socialist. The bourgeois tendencies of the French Materialists of the last century are most noticeable in their investigations of a perfect legislation. But this in no way destroys the Utopian character of these enquiries. We have seen that the method of the Utopian Socialist does not in the least differ from that of d'Holbach or Helvetius, those champions of the revolutionary French bourgeoisie.

Nay, more. One may have the profoundest contempt for all "music Of the future," one may be convinced that the social world in which one has the good fortune to live is the best possible of all social worlds, and yet in spite of this one may look at the structure and life of the body social from the same point of view as that from which the Utopians regarded it.

This seems a paradox, and yet nothing could be more true. Take but one example.

In 1753 there appeared Morelly's work, *Les Isles Flottantes on la Basiliade du celebre Pelpai, traduit de I, Indien.* Now, note the arguments with which a review, *La Bibliotheque Impartiale,* combatted the communistic ideas of the author:—"One knows well enough that a distance separates the finest speculations of this kind and the possibility of their realization. For in theory one takes imaginary men who lend themselves obediently to every arrangement, and who second with equal zeal the views of the legislator; but as soon as one attempts to put these things into practice one has to deal with men as they are, that is to say, unsubmissive, lazy, or else in the thraldom of some violent passion. The scheme of equality especially is one that seems most repugnant to the nature of man; they are born to command or to serve, a middle term is a burden to them."

Men are born to command or to serve. We cannot wonder, therefore, if in society we see masters and servants, since human nature wills it so. It was all very well for *La Bibliotheque Impartiale* to repudiate these communist speculations. The point of view from which it itself looked upon social phenomena, the point of view of human nature, it had in common with the Utopian Morelly.

And it cannot be urged that this review was probably not sincere in its arguments, and that it appealed to human nature with the single object of saying something in favor of the exploiters, in favour of those who "command." But sincere or hypocritical in its criticism of Morelly, the *Bibliotheque Impartiale* adopted the standpoint common to all the writers of this period. They all of them appeal to human nature conceived of in one form or another, with the sole exception of the retrograde, who, living shadows of passed times, continued to appeal to the will of God.

As we know, this concept of human nature has been inherited by the 19th century from its predecessor. The Utopian Socialists had no other. But here again it is easy to prove that it is not peculiar to the Utopians.

Even at the period of the Restoration, the eminent French historian, Guizot, in his historical studies, arrived at the remarkable conclusion that the political constitution of any given country depended upon the "condition of property" in that country. This was an immense advance upon the ideas of the last century which had almost exclusively considered the action of the "legislator." But what in its turn did these "conditions of property" depend on? Guizot is unable to answer this question, and after long, vain efforts to find a solution of the enigma in historical circumstances, he returns, falls back "nolens volens," upon the theory of human nature. Augustin Thierry, another eminent historian of the Restoration, found himself in almost the same case, or rather he would have done so if only he had tried to investigate this question of the "condition of property" and its historical vicissitudes. In his concept of social life, Thierry was never able to go beyond his master Saint Simon, who, as we have seen above, held firmly to the point of view of human nature.

The example of the brilliant Saint Simon, a man of encyclopaedic learning, demonstrates more clearly perhaps than any other, how narrow and insufficient was this point of view, in what confusion worse confounded of contradictions it landed those who applied it. Says Saint Simon, with the profoundest conviction: "The future is made up of the last terms of a series, the first of which consist of the past. When one has thoroughly mastered the first terms of any series it is easy to put down their successors; thus from the past carefully observed one can easily deduce the future." This is so true that one asks oneself at the first blush why a man who had so clear a conception of the connection between the various phases of historical evolution, should be classed among the Utopians. And yet, look more closely at the historical ideas of Saint Simon, and you will find that we are not wrong in calling him a Utopian. The future is deducible from the past, the historical evolution of humanity is a process governed by law. But what is the impetus, the motive power that sets in motion the human species, that makes it pass from one phase of evolution to another? Of what does this impetus consist? Where are we to seek it? It is here that Saint Simon comes back to the point of view of all the Utopians, to the point of view of human nature. Thus, according to him, the essential fundamental cause of the French Revolution was a change in the temporal and spiritual forces, and, in order to direct it wisely and conclude it rightly, it "was necessary to put into direct political activity the forces which had become preponderant." In other words, the manufacturers and the savants ought to have been called upon to formulate a political system corresponding to the new social conditions. This was not done, and the Revolution which had began so well was almost immediately directed into a false path. The lawyers and metaphysicians became the masters of the situation. How to explain this historical fact? "It is in the nature of man," replies Saint Simon, "to be unable to pass without some intermediate phase from any one doctrine to another. This law applies most stringently to the various political systems, through which the natural advance of civilization compels the human species to pass. Thus the same necessity which in industry has created the element of a new temporal power, destined to replace military power, and which in the positive sciences, has created the element of a new spiritual power called upon to take the place of theological power, must have developed and set in activity (before the change in the conditions of society had begun to be very perceptible) a temporal or spiritual power of an intermediary, bastard, and transitory nature, whose only mission was to bring about the transition from one social system to another."

So we see that the "historical series" of Saint Simon really explained nothing at all; they themselves need explanation, and for this we have again to fall back upon this inevitable human nature. The French Revolution was directed along a certain line, because human nature was so and so.

One of two things. Either human nature is, as Morelly thought, invariable, and then it explains nothing in history, which shows us constant variations in the relations of man to society; or it does vary according to the circumstances in which men live, and then, far from being the *cause,* it is itself the *effect* of historical evolution. The French Materialists knew well enough that man is the product of his social surroundings. "Man is all education," said Helvetius. This would lead one to suppose that Helvetius must have abandoned the human nature point of view in order to study the laws of the evolution of the environment that fashion human nature, giving to socialized man such or such an "education." And indeed Helvetius did make some efforts in this direction. But not he, nor his contemporaries, nor the Socialists of the first half of our century, nor any representatives of science of the same period, succeeded in discovering a new point of view that should permit the study of the evolution of the social environment; the cause of the historical "education" of man, the cause of the changes which occur in his "nature." They were thus forced back upon the human nature point of view as the only one that seemed to supply them with a fairly solid basis for their scientific investigations. But since human nature in its turn varied, it became indispensable to make abstraction from its variations, and to seek in nature only stable properties, fundamental properties preserved in spite of all changes of its secondary properties. And in the end all that these speculations resulted in was a meagre abstraction, like that of the philosophers, e.g. "man is a sentient and reasonable being," which seemed all the more precious a discovery in that it left plenty of room for every gratuitous hypothesis, and every fantastical conclusion.

A Guizot had no need to seek for the best of social organizations for a perfect legislation. He was perfectly satisfied with the existing ones. And assuredly the most powerful argument he could have advanced to defend them from the attacks of the malcontents would still have been human nature, which he would have said renders every serious change in the social and political constitution of France impossible. The malcontents condemned this same constitution, making use of the same abstraction. And since this abstraction, being completely empty, left, as we have said, full room for every gratuitous hypothesis and the logical consequences resulting therefrom, the "scientific" mission of these reformers assumed the appearance of a geometrical problem; given a certain nature, find what structure of society best corresponds with it. So

Morelly complains bitterly because "our old teachers" failed to attempt the solution of "this excellent problem"—"to find the condition in which it should be almost impossible for men to be depraved, or wicked, or at any rate, 'minima de malls.' "We have already seen that for Morelly human nature was "one, constant, invariable."

We now know what was the "scientific" method of the Utopians. Before we leave them let us remind the reader that in human nature, an extremely thin and therefore not very satisfying abstraction, the Utopians really appealed, not to human nature in general, but to the idealized nature of the men of their own day, belonging to the class whose social tendencies they represented. The social reality, therefore, inevitably appears in the words of the Utopians, but the Utopians were unconscious of this. They saw this reality only across an abstraction which, thin as it was, was by no means translucent.

The Point of View of Scientific Socialism

The great idealist philosophers of Germany, Schelling and Hegel, understood the insufficiency of the human nature point of view. Hegel, in his "Philosophy of History," makes fun of the Utopian bourgeoisie in search of the best of constitutions. German Idealism conceived history as a process subject to law, and sought the motive-power of the historical movement *outside the nature of man*. This was a great step towards the truth. But the Idealists saw this motive-power in the absolute idea, in the "Weitgeist;" and as their absolute idea was only an abstraction of "our process of thinking," in their philosophical speculation upon history, they reintroduced the old love of the Materialist philosophers—human nature—but dressed in robes worthy of the respectable and austere society of German thinkers. Drive nature out of the door, she flies in at the window! Despite the great services rendered to social science by the German Idealists, the great problem of that science, its essential problem, was no more solved in the time of the German Idealists than in the time of the French Materialists. What is this hidden force that causes the historic movement of humanity? No one knew anything about it. In this field there was nothing to go upon save a few isolated observations, more or less accurate, more or less ingenious— sometimes indeed, very accurate and ingenious—but always disjointed and always incomplete.

That social science at last emerged from this No Thoroughfare, it owes to Karl Marx.

According to Marx, "legal relations, like forms of State, can neither be understood in themselves nor from the so-called general development of the human mind, but are rather rooted in those material conditions of life, whose totality Hegel, following the English and the French of the 18th century, summed up under the name of 'bourgeois society.'" This is almost the same as Guizot meant when he said that political constitutions had their roots in "the condition of property." But while for Guizot "the condition of property" remained a mystery which he vainly sought to elucidate with the help of reflections upon human nature, for Marx this "condition" had nothing mysterious; it is determined by the condition of the productive forces at the disposal of a given society. "The anatomy of bourgeois society is to be sought in political economy." But Marx himself shall formulate his own conception of history.

"In the social production of their lives, men enter upon certain definite, necessary relations, relations independent of their will, relations of production that correspond with definite degrees of development of their material productive forces. The totality of these relations of production constitute the economic structure of society, the true basis from which arises a juridical and political superstructure to which definite social forms of consciousness correspond. The mode of production of material life determines the social, political, and intellectual processes of life. It is not the consciousness of mankind that determines their being, but, on the contrary, their social being that determines their consciousness. In a certain stage of their development, the material forces of production of society come into contradiction with the existing relations of production, or, which is only a juridicial expression for the same thing, with the relations of property within which they had hitherto moved. From forms for the development of these forces of production, they are transformed into their fetters. We then enter upon an epoch of social revolution.

This completely materialist conception of history is one of the greatest discoveries of our century, so rich in scientific discoveries. Thanks to it alone sociology has at last, and for ever, escaped from the vicious circle in which it had, until then, turned; thanks to it alone this science now possesses a foundation as solid as natural science. The revolution made by Marx in social science may be compared with that made by Copernicus in astronomy. In fact, before Copernicus, it was believed that the earth remained stationary, while the sun turned round it. The Polish genius demonstrated that what occurred was the exact contrary. And so, up to the time of Marx, the point of view taken by social science, was that of "human nature;" and it was from this point of view that men attempted to explain the historical movement of humanity. To this the point of view of the German genius is diametrically opposed. While man, in order to maintain his existence, acts upon nature outside himself, he alters his own nature. The action of man upon the nature outside himself, presupposes certain instruments, certain means of production; according to the character of their means of production men enter into certain relations within the process of production (since this process is a social one), and according to their relations in this social process of production, their habits, their sentiments, their desires, their methods of thought and of action, in a word, their nature, vary. Thus it is not human nature which explains the historical movement; it is the historical movement which fashions diversely human nature.

But if this is so, what is the value of all the more or less laborious, more or less ingenious enquiries into "perfect legislation" and the best of possible social organizations! None; literally none! They can but bear witness to the lack of scientific education in those who pursue them. Their day is gone for ever. With this old point of view of human nature must disappear the Utopias of every shade and colour The great revolutionary party of our day, the International Social-Democracy, is based not upon some "new conception" of human nature, nor upon any abstract principle, but upon a scientifically demonstrable economic necessity. And herein lies the real strength of this party, making it as invincible as the economic necessity itself.

"The means of production and exchange on whose foundation the bourgeoisie built itself up, were generated in feudal society. At a certain stage in the development of these means of production and exchange, the conditions under which feudal society produced and exchanged, the feudal organization of agriculture and manufacturing industry, in one word, the feudal relations of property become no longer compatible with the already developed productive forces, they become so many fetters. They had to be burst asunder; they were burst asunder. Into their place stepped free competition, accompanied by a social and political constitution adapted to it, and by the economical and political sway of the bourgeois class. A similar movement is going on before our own eyes. Modern bourgeois society, with its relations of production, of exchange, and of property, a society that has conjured up such gigantic means of production and of exchange, is like the sorcerer, who is no longer able to control the powers of the nether world whom he has called up by his spells. For many a decade past the history of industry and commerce is but the history of the revolt of modern productive forces against the property relations that are the conditions for the existence of the bourgeoisie and its rule. It is enough to mention the commercial crises that by their periodical return put on its trial, each time more threateningly, the existence of the entire bourgeois society... The weapons with which the bourgeoisie felled feudalism to the ground are now turned against the bourgeoisie itself." *[Communist Manifesto]*

The bourgeoisie destroyed the feudal conditions of property; the proletariat will put an end to the bourgeois conditions of property. Between the proletariat and the bourgeoisie a struggle, an implacable war, a war to the knife, is as inevitable as was, in its way, the struggle between the bourgeoisie and the privileged estates. *But every class war is a political war.* In order to do away with feudal society the bourgeoisie had to seize upon political power. In order to do away with capitalist society the proletariat must do the same. Its political task is therefore traced out for it beforehand by the force of events themselves, and not by any abstract consideration.

It is a remarkable fact that it is only since Karl Marx that Socialism has taken its stand upon the class war. The Utopian Socialists had no notion—even an inexact one—of it. And in this they lagged behind their contemporary theorists of the bourgeoisie, who understood very well the historical significance at any rate of the struggle of the third estate against the nobles.

If every "new conception" of human nature seemed to supply very definite indications as to the organization of "the society of the future," Scientific Socialism is very chary of such speculations. The structure of society depends upon the conditions of its productive forces. What these conditions will be when the proletariat is in power we do not know. We now know but one thing—that the productive forces already at the disposal of civilized humanity imperatively demand the socialization and systematized organization of the means of production. This is enough to prevent our being led astray in our struggle against "the reactionary mass." "The Communists, therefore, are practically the most advanced and resolute section of the working class parties of every country... theoretically they have over the great mass of the proletariat the advantage of clearly understanding the line of march, the conditions, and the ultimate general results of the proletarian movement." [CM.] These words, written in 1848, are today incorrect only in one sense: they speak of "working class parties" independent of the Communist Party; there is today no working class party which does not more or less closely follow the flag of Scientific Socialism, or, as it was called in the Manifesto, "Communism."

Once again, then, the point of view of the Utopian Socialists, as indeed of all social science of their time, was human nature, or some abstract principle deriving from this idea. The point of view of the social science, of the Socialism of our time is that of economic reality, and of the immanent laws of its evolution. It is easy, therefore, to form an idea of the impression made upon modern Socialists by the arguments of the bourgeois theorists who sing ceaselessly the same old song of the incompatibility of human nature and Communism. It is as though one would wage war upon the Darwinians with arms drawn from the scientific arsenal of Cuvier's time. And a most noteworthy fact is that the "evolutionists" like Herbert Spencer, themselves are not above piping to the same tune.

And now let us see what relation there may be between modem Socialism and what is called Anarchism.

9

Socialism and the Political Struggle

G.V. Plekhanov

The present pamphlet may be an occasion for much misunderstanding and even dissatisfaction. People who sympathise with the trend of *Zemlya i Volya* and *Chorny Peredel* (publications in the editing of which I used to take part) may reproach me with having diverged from the theory of what is called Narodism. The supporters of other factions of our revolutionary party may be displeased with my criticism of outlooks which are dear to them. That is why I consider a short preliminary explanation necessary.

The desire to work *among the people* and for the people, the certitude that "the emancipation of the working classes must be conquered by the working classes themselves"—this *practical* tendency of our Narodism is just as dear to me as it used to be. But its *theoretical* propositions seem to me, indeed, erroneous in many respects. Years of life abroad and attentive study of the social question have convinced me that the triumph of a spontaneous popular movement similar to Stepan Razin's revolt or the Peasant Wars in Germany cannot satisfy the social and political needs of modern Russia, that the old forms of our national life carried within them many germs of their disintegration and that they cannot "develop into a higher communist form" except under the immediate influence of a strong and well-organised *workers'* socialist party. For that reason I think that besides fighting absolutism the

Russian revolutionaries must strive at least to work out the elements for the establishment of such a party in the future. In this creative work they will necessarily have to pass on to the basis of modern socialism, for the ideals of Zemlya i Volya do not correspond to the condition of the industrial workers. And that will be very opportune now that the theory of Russian exceptionalism is becoming synonymous with stagnation and reaction and that the progressive elements of Russian society are grouping under the banner of judicious "Occidentalism".

I go on to another point of my explanation. Here I will first of all say in my defence that I have been concerned not with persons but with opinions, and that my personal differences with this or that socialist group do not in the least diminish my respect for all who sincerely fight for the emancipation of the people.

Moreover, the so-called terrorist movement has opened a new epoch in the development of our revolutionary party—the epoch of *conscious political struggle* against the government. This change in the direction of our revolutionaries' work makes it necessary for them to reconsider all views that they inherited from the preceding period. Life demands that we attentively reconsider all our intellectual stock-in-trade when we step on to new ground, and I consider my pamphlet as a contribution which I can make to this matter of criticism which started long ago in our revolutionary literature. The reader has probably not yet forgotten the biography of Andrei Ivanovich Zhelyabov which contained a severe and frequently very correct critical appraisal of the programme and activity of the Zemlya i Volya group. It is quite possible that my attempts at criticism will be less successful, but it would hardly be fair to consider them less timely.

> Every class struggle is a political struggle.
>
> —*Karl Marx*

Since the Russian revolutionary movement finally took the path of open struggle against absolutism, the question of the socialists' political tasks has become the most vital and most burning question for our party. Because of it people have drifted apart who had been attached to each other by many years of joint practical work, because of it whole groups and organizations have fallen to pieces. It can even be said that all Russian socialists have temporarily been split into two camps supporting diametrically opposite views on "politics" Extremes were unavoidable in this matter, as always in such cases. Some considered the political struggle as almost tantamount to betrayal of the people's cause, as a manifestation of bourgeois instincts among our revolutionary intelligentsia and a defilement of socialist programme purity. Others not only recognized that struggle as necessary, they were even ready, for the sake of its imaginary interests, to compromise with the liberally-minded oppositional elements of our society. Some even went to the extent of considering any manifestation of class antagonism in Russia as harmful for the present. Such views were held, for instance, by Zhelyahov, who, as his biographer says, "imagined the Russian Revolution not exclusively as the emancipation of the peasant or even (?) the workers' estate, but as the political regeneration of the whole Russian people generally".[1] In other words, the revolutionary movement against the absolute monarchy merged in his imagination with the working class's social-revolutionary movement for its economic emancipation; the particular, specially Russian task of the present hid from view the general task of the working class in all civilized countries. The difference could not go any farther, a break became inevitable.

Time, however, smoothed out extremes and resolved a considerable number of the disputed questions to the satisfaction of both sides. Little by little all or nearly all recognised that the political struggle which had been taken up must he pursued until a broad emancipation movement in the people and society destroyed the edifice of absolutism as an earthquake destroys a poultry-house, if Marx's forceful expression can be used here. But to very many of our socialists this struggle still appears as some kind of forced compromise, some temporary triumph of "practice" over "theory", a mockery by life of the impotence of thought. Even the politicians, in justifying themselves against the reproaches showered on them, avoided all appeal to the basic propositions of socialism, and referred only to the incontestible demands of reality. At the bottom of their hearts they themselves apparently also believed that political tendencies were by no means suited to them, but they consoled themselves with the consideration that only in a free state could they let the dead bury the dead and, renouncing all political considerations, devote themselves wholly to the cause of socialism. This vague conviction sometimes led to misunderstandings that were not without their curious side. Analysing the speech of "the Russian guest" at the Chur Congress and attempting to justify itself against the allegation that it dabbled in politics, *Narodnaya Volya* noted, among other things, that its supporters were neither socialists nor political radicals, but simply, Narodovoltsi. The terrorist organ presumed that "in the West" the attention of the radicals was absorbed exclusively by political questions while the socialists would not have anything to do with politics. Anybody who knows the programmers of the West European socialists understands, of course, how erroneous such an idea is as far as the enormous majority of them are concerned. It is well known that Social-Democracy in Europe and America never maintained the principle of political "abstention". Its supporters do not ignore "politics". Only they do not consider the task of the socialist revolution to be "the regeneration of the whole people generally". They try to organize the workers into a separate party in order thus to segregate the exploited from the exploiters and give political expression to the economic antagonism. Where in our country did they get the certitude that socialism calls for political indifference—a certitude which is in glaring contradiction with reality? Schiller's Wallenstein tells Max Piccolomini that human reason is broad, whereas the world is narrow, so that thoughts can live at ease together in the former while there are harsh clashes between things in the latter. Must we say that in our brain, on the contrary, concepts of things which in practice not only get on very well together, but are utterly unthinkable without their mutual connection, cannot live side by side? To answer that question we must first of all make clear the conceptions of socialism which our revolutionaries had during the epoch when political tendencies arose among them. Once convinced that these conceptions were erroneous or backward we shall consider what place is given to the political struggle by the doctrine which even its bourgeois opponents do not refuse to call scientific socialism. All that we shall have to do then will be to make in our general conclusions the corrections which are inevitable when we consider the various peculiarities of the contemporary state of affairs in Russia—and our subject will be exhausted; the political struggle of the working class against its enemies belonging to one historical formation or another will finally reveal to us its connection with the general tasks of socialism.

I

Socialist propaganda has enormously influenced the whole course of intellectual development in the civilized countries. There is hardly a single branch of sociology that has not felt its impact in one sense or another. It has in part destroyed old scientific prejudices and in part transformed them from a naive delusion into a sophism. It is understandable that the influence of socialist propaganda must have affected the supporters of the new teaching still more powerfully. All the traditions of previous "political" revolutionaries have been ruthlessly criticized, all methods of social activity have been analysed from the standpoint of the "new Gospel". But as the scientific substantiation of socialism was complete only with the appearance of *Capital*, it is easy to understand that the results of this criticism have by no means always been satisfactory. And as, on the other hand, there were several schools in Utopian socialism which had almost equal influence, little by little a kind of medium socialism, as it were, has been worked out, and this has been adhered to by people who did not claim to found a new school and were not among the particularly zealous supporters of previously existing schools. This eclectic socialism, as Friedrich Engels says, is "a mish-mash of such critical statements, economic theories, pictures of future society by the founders of different sects, as excite a minimum of opposition; a mish-mash which is the more easily brewed the more the definite sharp edges of the individual constituents are rubbed down in the stream of debate, like rounded pebbles in a brook".[2] This medium socialism, the same author notes, still reigns in the heads of most of the worker socialists in England and in France.[3] We Russians could add that exactly the same mish-mash reigned in the first half of the seventies in the minds of our socialists and represented the general background against which two extreme trends stood out: the so-called Vperyod group and the Bakuninists. The former showed a tendency towards German Social-Democracy, the latter were a Russian version of the anarchist faction of the International. Differing very greatly from each other in almost all respects, the two trends were at one—strange as that is—in their negative attitude to "politics". And it must be confessed that the anarchists were more consistent in this respect than the Russian Social-Democrats of the time.

From the anarchist point of view the political question is the touchstone of any working-class programme. The anarchists not only deny any deal with the modern state, they go so far as to exclude from their notions of "future society" anything that recalls the idea of state in one way or another. "Autonomy of the individual in an autonomous community"—such has been the motto of all consistent supporters of this trend. We know that its founder— Proudhon—in his publication *La Voix du peuple* set himself the not quite modest task "to do as regards the government" (which he confused with the state) "what Kant did as regards religion"[4] and carried his anti-state zeal so far as to declare that Aristotle himself was "a sceptic in matters of state".[5] The accomplishment of the task he had set himself was very simple and followed, if you like, quite logically from the economic doctrines of the French Kant. Proudhon was never able to imagine the economic system of the future otherwise than in the form of commodity production, corrected and supplemented by a new, "just" form of exchange on the basis of "constituted value". For all its "justice", this new form of exchange does not, of course, preclude the purchase, sale or promissory notes which go with commodity production and circulation. All these transactions naturally presuppose various contracts and it is these that determine the mutual relations between the transacting sides. But in modern society "contracts" are based on common legal standards compulsory for all citizens and safeguarded by the state. In the "future society" everything would supposedly proceed somewhat differently. Revolution, according to Proudhon, was to abolish "laws", leaving only "contracts". "There is no need for laws voted by a majority or unanimously," he says in his Idèe gènèrale de la Revolution au XIX siecle, "every citizen, every commune and corporation will establish their own particular laws" (p. 259). With such a view of the matter, the political programme of the proletariat was simplified to the extreme. The state, which recognizes only general laws compulsory for all citizens, could not even be a means for attaining socialist ideals. Making use of it for their aims, the socialists only consolidate the evil by the rooting out of which "social liquidation" should begin. The state must "decline", thus affording "every citizen, every commune and corporation" full freedom to decree "their own particular laws" and to conclude the "contracts" which they require. And if the anarchists do not waste time during the period preceding the "liquidation", these "contracts" will be concluded in the spirit of the *System of Economic Contradictions* and the triumph of the *Revolution* will be assured.

The task of the Russian anarchists was simplified still more. "The destruction of the state" (which little by little replaced in the anarchist programme its "decline" recommended by Proudhon) was to clear the way for the development of the "ideals" of the Russian people. And as communal land tenure and organization of crafts into artels occupy a very prominent place in these "ideals", it was presumed that the "autonomous"

Russians of democratic origin would conclude their "contracts" not in the spirit of Proudhon's reciprocity but rather of agrarian communism. As a "born socialist", the Russian people would not be long in understanding that mere communal land tenure and communal ownership of the instruments of production do not guarantee the desired "equality" and would be forced to set about organizing "autonomous communes" on completely communist foundations.

The Russian anarchists, however—at least those of the so-called rebel shade—bothered little about the economic consequences of the popular revolution they preached. They considered it their duty to remove those social conditions which, in their opinion, hindered the normal development of national life; but they did not ask themselves which road that development would take once it was freed from external hindrances. That this peculiar refashioning of the famous motto of the Manchester School, laissez faire, laissez passer, to make it look revolutionary, precluded all possibility of seriously appraising the contemporary condition of our social and economic life and did away with every criterion for determining even the concept of the "normal" course of its development—this did not occur either to "rebels" or to the "Narodniks" who appeared later. At the same time it would be utterly hopeless to attempt such an appraisal as long as Proudhon's teachings remained the point of departure of our revolutionaries' considerations. The weakest point of those teachings, the point in which they offend logic, is the concept of commodity and of exchange value, i.e. those very premises on which alone the correct conclusions about the mutual relations of the producers in the future economic organization can be based. From the standpoint of Proudhon's theories no special importance attaches to the circumstance that contemporary Russian communal land tenure by no means precludes commodity production. The Proudhonist has no inkling of the "inner, inevitable dialectics", which transforms commodity production at a definite stage of its development into... capitalist production.[6] And that is why it did not occur to his Russian cousin to ask himself whether the divided efforts of "autonomous" persons, communes and corporations would suffice for the struggle against this tendency of commodity production which threatens one fine day to supply a certain proportion of the "born" Communists with "honourably acquired" capitals and to turn them into exploiters of the remaining masses of the population. The anarchist denies the creative role of the state in the socialist revolution for the very reason that he does not understand the tasks and the conditions of that revolution.

We cannot enter here into a detailed analysis of anar-chism in general or of Bakuninism in particular.[7] We wish merely to point out to readers that both Proudhon and the Russian anarchists were completely right from their point of view when they raised "political non-interference" to the position of main dogma in their practical programme. The social and political composition of Russian life in particular, it seemed, justified the negation of "politics" which is compulsory for all anarchists. Before entering the field of political agitation the "*inhabitant*" of Russia has to become a *citizen*, i.e. to win for himself at least some political rights, and first of all, of course, the right to think as he pleases and to say what he thinks. Such a task amounts in practice to a "political revolution", and the experience of Western Europe has clearly "shown" all anarchists that such revolutions have not brought, do not and cannot bring any benefit to the people. As for the consideration that the people must be educated politically by taking part in their country's public life, that could not be put into practice, if only for the reason that the anarchists consider, as we have already seen, that such participation is not education, but perversion of the popular masses: it develops in them "belief in the state" and therefore the tendency to statehood, or as the late M.A. Bakunin would have said, "infects them with its official and social venom, and, in any case, distracts them at least for a short time from what is now the only useful and salutary matter—from revolt."[8] And at the same time, according to the philosophy of history of our "rebels", it appeared that the

Russian people had shown its anti-state tendency by a whole series of large and small movements and could therefore be considered mature enough politically. So down with all "dabbling in politics"! Let us help the people in its anti-state struggle. Let us unite its dispersed efforts in one revolutionary stream—and then the awkward edifice of the state will crash, opening by its fall a new era of social freedom and economic equality! These few words expressed the whole programme of our "rebels".

In this sketchy review of the programmes of the different groups of Russian revolutionaries we must not forget that the views according to which "all constitutions" were only more or less unprofitable contracts with the devil, as old F.H. Jacobi put it—such views, we say, were typical not only Friedrich Engels' polemic with P. Titachov,[9] he will probably remember that the editor of *Nabat*, a who disagreed with the Bakuninists on the question of practical struggle, was in perfect agreement with them on their basic views about the social and political condition of our country. He looked at it through the same prism of Russian exceptionalism and the "inborn communist tendencies of the Russian people".[10] Like a genuine Blanquist he did not deny "politics", of course, but he understood it exclusively as a plot whose purpose is to seize state power. This purpose, it seems, occupied the whole field of vision of our Blanquists of that time and led them to many contradictions. To remain consistent they had to admit that their activity could be useful to the cause of progress only in the exceptional case that the blow they dealt would not deviate a hair's breadth from its target. If their planned seizure of power is a failure, if their plot is discovered or the revolutionary government is overthrown by the liberal party, the Russian people, far from winning anything, will risk losing much. The last of the supposed cases is particularly disastrous. The liberals will establish a strong government which will be far more difficult to fight than modern "absolutely absurd" and "absurdly absolute" monarchy, while "the fire of economic progress" will destroy the radical bases of the people's life. Under its influence exchange will develop, capitalism will consolidate itself, the very principle of the village commune will be destroyed—in a word, the river of time will wash away the stone from which the communist heaven is within hand's reach. In cases of failure the Russian Blanquists would be bound to do terrible damage to the cause of popular emancipation and thus fall into the tragic position of William Tell, who had to risk the life of his own son. And as they have hardly distinguished themselves by the skill of the mythic Swiss "seditionary", the Russian people would not shout to them:

Shoot! I fear not!

> if it adopted their view on the "radical bases" of its life and had been invited to give its opinion about their programme.

Such a narrow and hopeless philosophy of Russian history was bound to lead logically to the amazing conclusion that Russia's economic backwardness was a most reliable ally of the revolution and that stagnation was to be blazoned as the first and only paragraph of our "minimum programme". "Every day brings us new enemies, creates new social factors hostile to us," we read in the first, November, issue of *Nabat* for 1875. "Fire is creeping up to our state forms, too. Now these are dead, lifeless. Economic progress will stir life in them, will breathe into them a new spirit, will give them the strength and the fortitude which they have so far lacked", and so forth. But if Joshua succeeded as the Bible relates, in stopping the sun "for ten degrees", the time of miracles has passed and there is not a single party which could shout: "Stop, productive forces! Do not move, capitalism! " History pays as little attention to the fears of revolutionaries as to the jeremiads of reaction. "Economic progress" does its work without waiting for the anarchists or the Blanquists to put their intentions into practice. Every factory founded in Petersburg, every new wage-worker employed by a Yaroslavl handicraftsman strengthens the "flame of progress", which is supposed to be fatal to the revolution, and consequently decreases the probability of popular victory. Can such a view of the mutual relations of the various social forces in Russia be called revolutionary? We do not think so. In order to make themselves revolutionary in substance and not in name alone, the Russian anarchists, Narodniks and Blanquists should first of all have revolutionized their own heads, and to do so they should have learned to understand the course of historical development and been able to lead it instead of asking old mother history to mark time while they laid new, straighter and better beaten roads for her. The Vperyod group understood the immaturity and erroneousness of the outlooks just expounded, and there was a time when it could have obtained dominating intellectual influence among our revolutionaries. That was the time when practical experience had shaken the foundations of the old anarchist Narodism and all its supporters felt that their programme needed to be seriously reconsidered. Then a consistent criticism of all its theoretical and practical principles could have made the impending turn in the movement still more decisive and irrevocable. The Vperyod group could most conveniently have undertaken that criticism; maintaining almost entirely the standpoint of the Social-Democrats, they were completely free from all Narodnik traditions. But in order to be successful, their criticism *should not have condemned, but elucidated and generalized* the vital requirements of Russian life which were more and more driving our revolutionaries on to the road of political struggle. And yet the *Vperyod* group rejected "politics" just as resolutely as the anarchists. I admit that they did not think socialism to be incompatible with interference in the political life of the bourgeois state, and they fully approved of the programme of West European Social-Democracy. But they presumed that in the modern state "founded on law" the possibility of openly organizing the working class into a political party of its own is bought at too high a price—by the final victory of the bourgeoisie and the deterioration of the workers' condition corresponding to the epoch of capitalism. They forgot that in appraising this situation one must take into account not only the distribution of the national income, but also *the whole organization of production and exchange*; not only the average quantity of products consumed by the workers, but also the *form* which those products take[11]; not only the *degree* of exploitation, but also, in particular, *its form*; not only *the fact of the enslavement* of the working masses, but also the *ideas and concepts* which emerge or may emerge in the head of the worker under the influence of this fact.[12] They would hardly have agreed that the factory worker was bound to be more receptive to socialism than the temporarily bound peasant; still less would they have admitted that the transition, for instance, from natural economy to money economy increases the possibility of a conscious movement of the working masses for their own economic emancipation. The philosophical and historical parts of Marx's teaching remained for them an unread chapter in their favourite book; they believed too much in the omnipotent influence of their propaganda to seek support for it in the objective conditions of social life. And like the socialists of the Utopian period, they held that the whole future of their country, including the social revolution, could be achieved by that propaganda. Posing the question in this way, they could have said with the anarchists, parodying Proudhon's well-known saying: la revolution est au-dessus de la politique. But that was just the reason why they could not get our movement out of the state of inertia it had got into at the end of the seventies owing to the rejection of all political struggle, on the one hand, and the impossibility, on the other, of creating a working-class party of any strength under contemporary political conditions.

The honour of giving new scope to our movement belongs beyond dispute to Narodnaya Volya. Everybody still recalls the attacks that the Narodnaya Volya trend drew upon itself. The writer of these lines himself belonged to the resolute opponents of this trend, and although he perfectly admits now that the struggle for political freedom has become a burning issue for modern Russia, he is still far from sharing all the views expressed in Narodnaya Volya publications. That does not prevent him, however, from acknowledging that in the disputes which took place in the Zemlya i Volya organization about the time of its split, the Narodnaya Volya members were perfectly right as long as they did not go beyond our practical experience. That experience was already then leading to amazing and completely unexpected conclusions, although we did not dare to draw them precisely because of their unexpected-ness. Attempts at the practical struggle "against the state" should already then have led fundamentally to the thought that the Russian "rebel" was compelled by the insuperable force of circumstances to direct his agitation not against the state generally, but only against the *absolute* state, to fight not the idea of state, but the idea of bureaucracy, not for the full economic emancipation of the people, but for the removal of the burdens imposed on the people by the tsarist autocracy. Of course, the agrarian question lay at the root of all or nearly all manifestations of popular dissatisfaction. It could not be otherwise among an agricultural population, where the "power of the land" is felt in absolutely the whole make-up and needs of private and social life. This agrarian question kept crying out for a solution, but it did not rouse *political* discontent. The peasants waited calm and confident for this question to be solved from above: they "rebelled" not for a redistribution of the land, but against oppression by the administration, against the excessive burdens of the taxation system, against the Asiatic way in which arrears were collected, and so on and so forth. The formula which applied to a large number of the cases of active protest was the "legal state", not "Land and Freedom" (Zemlya i Volya) as it seemed to everybody at the time. But if that was so, and if revolutionaries considered themselves obliged to take part in the scattered and ill-considered struggle of isolated communes against the absolute monarchy, was it not time they understood the meaning of their own efforts and directed them with greater purposefulness? Was it not time for them to call all the progressive virile forces of Russia to the struggle and, having found a more general expression for it, to attack absolutism in the very centre of its organization? In answering these questions in the affirmative, the members of Narodnaya Volya were only summing up the revolutionary experience of previous years; in raising the banner of political struggle, they only showed that they were not afraid of the conclusions and consciously continued to follow the road which we had taken although we had an erroneous idea of where it led to. "Terrorism" grew quite logically out of our "rebelliousness".

But with the appearance of Narodnaya Volya, the logical development of our revolutionary movement was already entering a phase in which it could no longer be satisfied with the Narodnik theories of the good old time, i.e. a time innocent of political interests. Examples of theory being outgrown by practice are not rare in the history of human thought in general and of revolutionary thought in particular. When revolutionaries introduce some change or other into their tactics or recast their programme one way or another, often they do not even suspect what a serious test they are giving the teachings generally acknowledged among them. Many of them indeed perish in prison or on the gallows, fully confident that they have worked in the spirit of those teachings, whereas in substance they represent new tendencies which took root in the old theories but have already outgrown them and are ready to find new theories to express them. So it has been with us since the Narodnaya Volya trend consolidated. From the standpoint of the old Narodnik theories, this trend could not stand criticism. Narodism had a sharply negative attitude to any idea of the state; Narodnaya Volya counted on putting its social-reform plans into practice with the help of the state machine. Narodism refused to have anything to do with "politics"; Narodnaya Volya saw in "democratic political revolution" the most reliable "means of social reform". Narodism based its programme on the so-called "ideals" and demands of the peasant population; Narodnaya Volya had to address itself mainly to the urban and industrial population, and consequently to give an incomparably larger place in its programme to the interests of that population. Briefly, in reality, the Narodnaya Volya trend was the complete and all-round denial of Narodism, and as long as the disputing parties appealed to the fundamental propositions of the latter, the "innovators" were completely in the wrong: their practical work was in irreconcilable contradiction with their theoretical views. It was necessary completely to reconsider these views, so as to give Narodnaya Volya's programme singleness of purpose and consistency; the practical revolutionary activity of its supporters had to be at least *accompanied* by a theoretical revolution in the minds of our socialists; in blowing up the Winter Palace we had at the same time to blow up our old anarchic and Narodnik traditions. But here, too, the "course of ideas" lagged behind the "course of things" and it is still difficult to foresee when it will catch up at last. Unable to make up their minds to break with Narodism, the new group was obliged to have recourse to fictions which brought with them at least a semblance of a solution of the contradictions inherent in their programme. The idea of Russian exceptionalism received a new elaboration, and whereas previously it had led to the complete rejection of politics, it now turned out that the exceptionalism of Russian social development consisted precisely in economic questions being and having to be solved in our country by means of state interference. The extremely widespread ignorance here in Russia of the economic history of the West provided the reason why nobody was amazed at "theories" of this kind. The period of capitalist accumulation in Russia was contrasted with the period of capitalist production in the West, and the inevitable dissimilarity between these two phases of economic development was cited as a most convincing proof of, first, our exceptionalism and, second, the appropriateness of the "Narodnaya Volya programme" determined by that exceptionalism.

Need it be added that our revolutionary writers, like the majority of Russian writers generally, considered the "West" from the standpoint of the Jewish boy in Weinberg's well-known story. To this poor schoolboy the whole world seemed as though it were divided into two equal parts: "Russia and abroad", notable points of distinction existing for him only between these two "halves" of the globe, but "abroad" seemed to him a completely homogeneous whole. Russian writers, propagandists of "exceptionalism", introduced only one new thing into that clever geographical classification: they divided "abroad" into East and West, and, not stopping long to think, began to compare the latter with our "glorious state", which was ascribed the role of a kind of "Middle Empire". The historical development of Italy was thus identified with that of France and no distinction was seen between England's economic policy and Prussia's; Colbert's activity was lumped together with Richard Cobden's and the peculiarly "patriotic" physiognomy of Friedrich Listz was lost in the crowd of "West European" political economists who followed Turgot's advice and tried "to forget that in the world there are states separated by frontiers and organized in different ways". Just as all cats appear grey and resemble one another perfectly in the dark, so the social relations of the various states in the "West" lost all distinction in the reflected light of our exceptionalism. One thing was evident: the "Franks" had already "gone bourgeois" long ago, whereas the "brave Russians" had preserved the "primitive" innocence and were advancing to their salvation as a chosen people along the road of exceptionalism. To reach the promised land they only had to keep unswervingly to that path of exceptionalism and not be surprised that the Russian socialists' programmes contradicted the scientific principles of West European socialism and sometimes their own premises!

A typical sample of the fictions quickly thought out to conform Narodnaya Volya's practical programme with Narodnik theories was the famous prophecy that if only we managed to achieve universal suffrage, 90 per cent of the deputies in the future Russian Constituent Assembly would be supporters of the social revolution. Here the theory of our exceptionalism reached the limit beyond which it was threatened with ruin by plain common sense. The Narodniks of the "old faith" firmly held to their dogma of exceptiona-lism but all the same admitted that this exceptionalism still needed some finishing touches. Some found that the Russian people still had a too embryonic bump ... sorry! —feeling of bravery and independence; others strove to put the exceptionalist sentiment of the Russian people into practice in the form of a no less original revolutionary organization. But they all equally acknowledged the necessity for preliminary work among the people. Narodnaya Volya went further. In the leading articles of the very first issues of its journal it began to develop the thought that such work is, first, fruitless ("wasting our energy beating about the people like a fish on the ice") and, secondly, superfluous, because 90 per cent of the deputies sympathizing with the social revolution are more than enough to carry out the aspirations of the Russian Narodniks. Narodnaya Volya's programme could not have given itself a Narodnik character otherwise than by carrying to absurd extremes all the typical features of the Narodnik world outlook.

This is what constitutes the negative service of the fictions of Narodnaya Volya. They aroused the critical thought of the Russian revolutionaries by presenting to them in an exaggerated form the "exceptional" features of their Narodnik programme. But one can hardly say anything about the positive service of these fictions. They temporarily strengthened the energy of the fighters, who needed a theoretical foundation for their practical work, but, being strung hastily together, they did not stand the slightest impact of serious criticism, and by their fall they compromised the cause of the struggle waged under their banner. Having dealt the death-blow to all the traditions of orthodox Narodism by its practical activity and having done so much for the development of the revolutionary movement in Russia, Narodnaya Volya cannot find a justification for itself—nor should it seek one—outside modern scientific socialism. But to adopt this new standpoint it must make a thorough review of its programme, for the theoretical errors and gaps in that programme could not but give it a definite one-sidedness in practice.

Before saying in which sense this review must be undertaken, let us endeavour, according to our plan, to elucidate scientific socialism's attitude to the political movements of the working class.

II

But what is scientific socialism? Under that name we understand the communist teaching which began to take shape at the beginning of the forties out of Utopian socialism under the strong influence of Hegelian philosophy on the one side, and of classical economics on the other; the teaching which first really explained the whole course of human cultural development, pitilessly shattered the bourgeois theoreticians' sophisms and, "armed with all the knowledge of its age", came out in defence of the proletariat. This teaching not only showed with complete clarity how unsound scientifically are the opponents of socialism, but pointing out the errors, it at the same time explained them historically and thus, as Haym once said of Hegel's philosophy, "tied to its triumphal chariot every opinion it had defeated". As Darwin enriched biology with his amazingly simple and yet strictly scientific theory of the origin of species, so also the founders of scientific socialism showed us in the development of the productive forces and their struggle against backward "social conditions of production" the great principle of the variation of *species of social organization*. We hardly need to say whom we consider as the founders of this socialism. This merit belongs indisputably to Karl Marx and Friedrich Engels, whose doctrine stands in exactly the same relation to the modern revolutionary movement in civilized humanity as, in the words of one of them, advanced German philosophy stood in its time to the emancipation movement in Germany; it is its *head*, and the proletariat is its *heart*. But it goes without saying that the development of scientific socialism is not complete and can no more stop at the works of Engels and Marx than the theory of the origin of species could be considered as finally elaborated with the publication of the principal works of the English biologist. The establishment of the basic propositions of the new teaching must be followed by the detailed elaboration of questions pertaining to it, an elaboration which will supplement and complete the revolution carried out in science by the authors of the *Manifesto of the Communist Party*.[13] There is not a single branch of sociology which would not acquire a new and extraordinarily vast field of vision by adopting their philosophical and historical views. The beneficial influence of those views is already beginning to be felt in the fields of history, law and so-called primitive culture. But this philosophical and historical aspect of modern socialism is still too little known in Russia, and therefore we do not consider it superfluous to quote a few excerpts here, in order to acquaint our readers with it in Marx's own words.

Incidentally, although scientific socialism traces its genealogy "from Kant and Hegel", it is nevertheless the most deadly and resolute opponent of idealism. It drives it out of its last refuge— sociology—in which it was received with such delight by the positivists. Scientific socialism presupposes the "materialist conception of history", i.e. it explains the spiritual history of humanity by the development of social relations (among other things under the influence of surrounding nature). From this point of view, as also from that of Vico, "the course of ideas corresponds to the course of things", and not inversely. The principal cause of this or that make-up of social relations, this or that direction in their development, is the condition of the productive forces and the economic structure of society corresponding to them. "In the social production of their life," says Marx,[14] "men enter into definite relations that are indispensable and independent of their will, relations of production which correspond to a definite stage of development of their material productive forces. The sum-total of these relations of production constitutes the economic structure of society, the real foundation on which rises a legal and political super-structure and to which correspond definite forms of social consciousness. The mode of production of material life conditions the social, political and intellectual life process in general. It is not the consciousness of men that determines their being, but, on the contrary, their social being that determines their consciousness ... Legal relations as well as forms of state are to be grasped neither from themselves nor from the so-called general development of the human mind, but rather have their roots in the material conditions of life, the sum-total of which Hegel, following the example of the Englishmen and Frenchmen of the 18th century, combines under the name of 'civil society', that, however, the anatomy of civil society is to be sought in political economy ... At a certain stage of their development, the material productive forces of society come in conflict with the existing relations of production, or—what is but a legal expression for the same thing—with the property relations within which they have been at work hitherto. From forms of development of the productive forces these relations turn into their fetters. Then begins an epoch of social revolution. With the change of the economic foundation the entire immense superstructure is more or less rapidly transformed.... No social order ever perishes before all the productive forces for which there is room in it have developed; and new, higher relations of production never appear before the material conditions of their existence have matured in the womb of the old society itself.

> "Therefore mankind always sets itself only such tasks as it can solve; since, looking at the matter more closely, it will always be found that the task itself arises only when the material conditions for its solution already exist or are at least in the process of formation."

It is now understandable why Marx and Engels reacted with such scornful derision to the "true socialists" in Germany at the end of the forties, who adopted a negative attitude to the German bourgeoisie's struggle against absolutism, "preaching to the masses that they had nothing to gain, and everything to lose, by this bourgeois movement". The historical teaching of Marx and Engels is the genuine "algebra of the revolution", as Herzen once called Hegel's philosophy. That is why Marx and Engels sympathized with "every revolutionary movement against the existing social and political order of things"; and for the same reason they warmly sympathized with the Russian movement, which made Russia, as they said, the vanguard of the revolution in Europe. But despite all their clarity and unambiguousness, Marx's views gave occasion for many misunderstandings in the field of revolutionary theory and practice. Thus, it is often said in our country that the theories of scientific socialism, are inapplicable to Russia because they have their root in West European economic relations. To Marx's teaching is attributed the absurd conclusion that Russia must go through exactly the same phases of historical and economic development as the West. Influenced by the conviction that this conclusion is inevitable, more than one Russian philosopher, familiar neither with Marx nor with the history of Western Europe, entered the lists against the author of *Capital* and accused him of narrow and stereotyped views. This, of course, was tilting at windmills. Our Don Quixotes did not understand that the history of West European relations was used by Marx only as the basis of the *history of capitalist production,* which emerged and developed precisely in that part of the world Marx's general philosophical and historical views stand in exactly the same relation to modern Western Europe as to Greece and Rome, India and Egypt. They embrace the entire cultural history of humanity and can be inapplicable to Russia only if they are generally untenable. It goes without saying that neither the author of *Capital* nor his famous friend and colleague lost sight of the economic peculiarities of any particular country; only in those peculiarities do they seek the explanation of all a country's social, political and intellectual movements. That they do not ignore the significance of our village commune is revealed by the fact that as recently as January 1882 they did not consider it possible to make any decisive forecast concerning its destiny. In the preface to our translation of the *Manifesto of the Communist Party* (Geneva, 1882) they even say explicitly that under certain conditions the Russian village commune may "pass directly to the higher form of communist common ownership". These circumstances are, in their opinion, closely connected with the course of the revolutionary movement in the west of Europe and in Russia. "If the Russian Revolution," they say, "becomes the signal for a proletarian revolution in the West, so that both complement each other, the present Russian common ownership of land may serve as the starting-point for a communist development." (*Manifesto of the Communist Party*, VIII.) It will hardly occur to a single Narodnik to deny that the solution of the village commune question depends on such a condition. Hardly anybody will assert that the oppression by the modern state is favourable to the development or even to the mere maintenance of the commune. And in exactly the same way hardly anyone who understands the significance of international relations in the economic life of modern civilised societies can deny that the development of the Russian village commune "into a higher form of communist common ownership" is closely linked with the destiny of the working-class movement in the West. It thus turns out that nothing in Marx's views on Russia contradicts the most obvious reality, and the absurd prejudices concerning his extreme "Occidentalism" have not the slightest trace of reasonable foundation.

But there is another misunderstanding which directly concerns a question interesting us—the significance of political struggle in the reorganization of social relations—and takes root in an erroneous understanding of Marx's view of the role of the economic factor in the human cultural development. This view has often been interpreted by many in the sense that the author of *Capital* attributes only the slightest importance to the political structure of society, considering it as a secondary detail not worth attention and which, far from being the aim, cannot even be a means of fruitful activity. Even now, one not infrequently meets "Marxists" who ignore the political tasks of socialism on these very grounds. Economic relations, they say, are the basis of all social organization. Changes in these relations are the cause of all political reorganization. In order to free itself from capitalist oppression, the working class must bear in mind not the effect, but the cause, not the political, but the economic organization of society. Political organization will not bring the workers nearer to their goal, since political enslavement will continue as long as their economic dependence on the propertied classes is not removed. The *means* of struggle which the workers use must be brought into line with the *aim* of the struggle. An economic revolution can be achieved only by struggle on economic ground.

With a certain amount of consistency, "Marxism" understood in that way should have changed the socialists' views of the aims and the means of the social revolution and brought them back to Proudhon's famous formula: "political revolution is the aim, economic revolution, the means". In exactly the same way it should have brought the socialist-revolutionaries considerably nearer—at least in theory—to the followers of "conservative socialism" which so resolutely opposes independent political action on the part of the working class. Rodbertus, the last honest and intelligent representative of this socialism, was unable to agree with Lassalle precisely because that celebrated agitator endeavoured to advance the German workers along the path of independent political activity. Not Marx, but Rodbertus, not *revolutionary*, but *conservative, monarchist* socialism denies the significance of "political admixtures to the economic aims" of the working class. And the conservatives know full well why they do so; but those who wish to conciliate the revolutionary movement of the working class with the rejection of "politics", those who attribute to Marx the practical tendencies of Proudhon or even of Rodbertus, show clearly that they do not understand the author of *Capital* or that they deliberately distort his teaching. We speak of deliberate distortion because a certain book by the Moscow Professor Ivanyukov is nothing but such a deliberate distortion of the consequences following from the basic propositions of scientific socialism. This book shows that our Russian *police* socialists are not averse to exploiting for their reactionary aims even a theory under whose banner the most revolutionary movement of our age is proceeding. This alone could make a detailed elucidation of modern socialism's *political* programme indispensable. We will now begin that elucidation, without, however, entering into a controversy with Messrs. Ivanyukov, for it is sufficient to bring out the true sense of a given theory in order to refute deliberate distortions of it. And besides, we are far more interested here in those revolutionaries who, for all the sincerity of their aspirations, are still permeated, although perhaps unconsciously, with anarchist teachings and are therefore prepared to see in Marx's works thoughts which are in place only in *The General Idea of the Revolution in the Nineteenth Century*. The criticism of the conclusions they draw from Marx's philosophical and historical views will logically take us on to the question of the so-called *seizure of power* and will show us how far they are right who see in that act a crime against the idea of human liberty, and also those who, on the contrary, see it as the Alpha and the Omega of the whole social-revolutionary movement.

Let us first consider what the concepts of cause and effect signify when applied to social relations.

If we push a billiard ball with the hand or a cue, it is set in motion; if we strike steel against a flint, a spark appears. In each of these cases it is very easy to determine which phenomenon acts as the cause and which is the effect. But the task is easy only because it is extremely simple. If instead of two isolated phenomena we take a process in which several phenomena or even several series of phenomena are observed simultaneously, the matter is more complicated. Thus, the burning of a candle is, relatively speaking, a fairly complicated process as a result of which light and heat are produced. Hence it would seem that we run no risk of error if we call the heat given off by the flame one of the effects of this chemical process. That is, indeed, the case to a certain extent. But if we contrived in some way to deprive the flame of the heat which it gives off, the combustion would immediately cease, for the process we are considering cannot take place at the ordinary temperature. Therefore, it would also be right to a certain extent to say that heat is the cause of combustion. In order not to deviate from the truth in one direction or the other we should say that heat, while it is the *effect* of combustion at a particular moment, is its cause the moment following. This means that when we speak of a combustion process lasting a certain time we must say that heat is *both* its *effect* and its *cause*, or, in other words, *neither effect nor cause*, but simply one of the phenomena arising from that process and constituting, in turn, a necessary condition for it. Let us take another example. Everybody, "even if he has not been trained in a seminary", knows that what are called the vegetative processes of the human organism exert great influence on psychic phenomena. One mental disposition or other proves to be the effect of a particular physical condition of the organism. But once a certain mental disposition exists, the same vegetative processes are often influenced by it, and it thus becomes the cause of the particular changes in the physical condition of the organism. In order not to go wrong here in one direction or the other, we should say that the psychic phenomena and the vegetative life of the organism constitute two series of coexisting processes, each of which is influenced by the other. If a doctor were to ignore psychic influences on the grounds that man's mental disposition is the effect of the physical condition of his organism, we would infer that schoolboy logic had made him unfit for rational medical practice.

Social life is distinguished by still greater intricacy than the life of the individual organism. That is why the relativity of the concepts of cause and effect is more noticeable here. According to the teaching of classical economics, the size of wages is determined, on the average, by the level of the worker's primary requirements. This means that a given size of wages is the *effect* of a given condition of the worker's requirements. But these requirements, in turn, can grow only if there is a rise in wages, because otherwise there would not be sufficient cause to change their level. Consequently, a given size of wages is the *cause* of a given condition of the worker's requirements. One cannot get out of this logical circle by means of the schoolboy categories of cause and effect. We shall fall into it at every step in our sociological considerations if we forget that "cause and effect are conceptions which only hold good in their application to individual cases; but as soon as we consider the individual cases in their general connection with the universe as a whole, they run into each other, and they become confounded when we contemplate that universal action and reaction in which causes and effects are eternally changing places, so that what is effect here and now will be cause there and then, and vice versa". (Friedrich Engels.)[15]

Having made this reservation, let us endeavour to determine in what sense the causal connection between the economic relations and the political structure of a given society must be understood.

What does history teach us in this respect? It shows that whenever and wherever the process of economic development gave rise to a splitting of society into classes, the contradictions between the interests of those classes invariably led them to struggle for political domination. This struggle arose not only between the various strata of the dominating classes, but also between those classes, on the one hand, and the people, on the other, provided the latter was given conditions at all favourable to intellectual development. In the states of the ancient Orient we see the struggle between the soldiers and the priests; all the drama in the history of the ancient world is in the struggle between the aristocracy and the *demos*, the patricians and the plebeians; the Middle Ages bring forth the burghers, who strive to conquer political mastery within the bounds of their communes; finally, the present-day working class wages a political struggle against the bourgeoisie, which has achieved complete domination in the modern state. Always and everywhere, political power has been the lever by which a class, having achieved domination, has carried out the social upheaval necessary for its welfare and development. So as not to go too far afield, let us consider the history of the "third estate", the class that can look with pride at its past, full of brilliant achievements in all branches of life and thought. It will hardly occur to anybody to reproach the bourgeoisie with lack of tact or ability to attain its aims by the most appropriate means. Nor will anybody deny that its strivings have always had a quite definite economic character. But that did not prevent it from following the path of political struggle and political gains. Now by arms, now by peace treaties, sometimes for the republican independence of its towns, sometimes for the strengthening of royal power, the rising bourgeoisie waged a hard, uninterrupted struggle against feudalism for whole centuries, and long before the French Revolution it could proudly draw its enemies' attention to its successes. "The chances were different and the success varying in the great struggle of the burghers against the feudal lords," the historian says,[16] "and not only was the sum of privileges wrested from them by force or obtained by agreement not the same everywhere, but even when the political forms were the same there were different degrees of liberty and independence for the towns." Nevertheless, the sense of the movement was identical everywhere—it meant the beginning of the social emancipation of the third estate and the decline of the aristocracy, secular and ecclesiastical.[17] In general this movement brought the burghers "municipal independence, the right to elect all the local authorities, the exact fixing of duties", guaranteed the rights of the individual inside the town communes,[18] gave the bourgeoisie a more elevated position in the estate-based states of the "ancien regime", and finally, by a series of continuous gains, brought it to complete domination in modern society. Setting itself social and economic aims which were perfectly defined although they changed with time, and drawing means to continue the struggle from the advantages of the economic position which it had already attained, the bourgeoisie did not miss an opportunity of giving legal expression to the stages in economic progress which it had reached; on the contrary, it made just as skilful a use of each political gain for new conquests in the economic field. No further back than in the middle forties of this century the English Anti-Corn Law League, following Richard Cobden's clever plan, aimed at increasing its political influence in the shires in order to secure the abolition of the "monopoly" it hated and which, apparently, was exclusively *economic*.

History is the greatest of dialecticians. If in the course of its progress, reason, as Mephistopheles says, is changed into irrationality and blessings become a plague, not less often in the historical process does an effect become a cause and a cause prove to be an effect. Arising from the economic relations of its time, the political might of the bourgeoisie in its turn served, and still serves, as an indispensable factor for the further development of those relations.

Now that the bourgeoisie is nearing the end of its historical role and that the proletariat is becoming the only representative of progressive strivings in society, we can observe a phenomenon similar to the one referred to above, but taking place in changed conditions. In all the advanced states of the civilized world, in Europe as well as America, the working class is entering the arena of political struggle and the more it is conscious of its economic tasks, the more resolutely it separates into a political party of its own. "As the existing political parties have always acted only in the interests of property-owners for the preservation of their economic privileges," we read in the programme of the North American Socialist Workers' Party, "the working class must organize into a big workers' party to *achieve political power in the state* and gain economic independence; for the emancipation of the working class can be effected only by the workers themselves."[19] The French Workers' Party expresses itself in the same spirit and in complete agreement with the programme of German Social-Democracy, acknowledging that the proletariat must aspire to an economic revolution "by all means in its power, including universal franchise, thus transformed from a weapon of deceit, which it has been up to now, into a *weapon of emancipation*". The Spanish Workers' Party also strives to "conquer political power" in order to remove the obstacles in the way of the emancipation of the working class.[20]

In England, where, with the ending of the chartist movement, the struggle of the proletariat has been concentrated exclusively on the economic field, the political aspirations of the workers have begun to revive of late. Only a few years ago, the German economist Lujo Brentano noted with triumph in his book *Das Arbeitsverhaltniss, etc.* the complete disappearance of the Social-Democratic trends in England, and philosophized profoundly and with true bourgeois self-satisfaction on the subject that "at present England again constitutes a *single* nation", that "the English workers of our time again form part of the great Liberal Party" and do not strive to seize state power in order, by means of it, "to reorganise society in their own interests" (p. 110). The recently published *Manifesto* of the British Democratic Federation shows that the bourgeois economist's joy was somewhat premature. The Democratic Federation aims at causing the exploited to break away politically from the exploiters and calls from the first of these "nations" precisely to seize state power for the purpose of reconstructing society in the interests of the workers. "The time has come," says the *Manifesto,* "when the mass of the people must necessarily take the management of matters which concern it in its own hands; at present, political and social power is the monopoly of people who live by the labour of their fellow-citizens. The landowners and capitalists who have control of the Upper House and have filled the Lower House aspire only to safeguard their own interests. Take your fate in your own hands, remove the rich parasites of these two groups and rely only on yourselves! "The *Manifesto* demands *"full franchise for all adult men and women "* in the United Kingdom, and other political reforms which "would only show that the men and women of this country have become the masters at home." Then comes a list–representing the immediate demands of the British Democratic Federation—of measures necessary for the development of a "healthy, independent and soundly educated generation, ready to organize the labour of each for the good of all and to *take control, ultimately. Of the entire social and political machine of the state,* in which class differences and privileges will then cease to exist".

Thus, the British proletariat, too, is again entering on the path which the workers of other civilized states entered upon long ago.

But, as the bourgeoisie not only fought the aristocracy on the basis of already existing political relations, but aspired to reshape those relations in its own interests, so also the proletariat does not restrict its political programme to the seizure of the modern state machine. The conviction is more and more spreading among its members that "every order of things which determines the relations of citizens to one another and governs their labour and property relations corresponds to a particular form of government which is at the same time the means of implementing and preserving that order".[21] While the representative (monarchic or republican) system was the progeny of the bourgeoisie, the proletariat demands *direct popular legislation* as the only political form under which its social aspirations can be put into effect. This demand of the working class is among the first in the programme of Social-Democracy in all countries and is very closely related to all the other points in its programme.[22] In spite of Proudhon, the proletariat continues to see in the "political revolution" the most powerful means of achieving an economic revolution.

This testimony of history alone should incline us to think that the political tendencies of the various social classes are based on a correct practical instinct, and not on an erroneous theory. If, despite the complete dissimilarity in all other respects, all classes which wage a conscious struggle against their opponents begin at a definite stage in their development to strive to ensure for themselves political influence and later domination, it is clear that the political structure of society is a far from indifferent condition for their development. If, moreover, we see that not a single class which has achieved political domination has had cause to regret its interest in "politics", but on the contrary, that each one of them attained the highest, the culminating point of its development only after it had acquired political domination, then we must admit that the political struggle is an instrument of social reconstruction whose effectiveness is proved by history. Every teaching which runs counter to this historical induction loses a considerable part of its power of conviction, and if modern socialism were in fact to condemn the political striving of the working class as inexpedient, that would be sufficient reason not to call it scientific.

Let us now check our induction by the deductive method, taking Marx's philosophical and historical views as the premises for our conclusions.

Imagine a society in which a particular class is completely dominant. It secured this domination thanks to the advantages of its economic position which, according to our premises, open before it the path to all other successes in social life. In its capacity as the *ruling* class it naturally reshapes social organization to provide the most favourable conditions for its own existence and carefully removes from it all that can in any way weaken its influence. "Those in power, the mighty, in every period," Schäffle correctly notes, "are also the ones who create law and morality. They only apply the urge of self-preservation inherent in all when they exploit the consequences of their victory, install themselves as rulers at the top and endeavour to maintain domination hereditary as long as possible, as the means to a privileged situation and the exploitation and subjection of those who are not free... There is hardly another section of positive law for which the dominating estates in every period have such great respect and for which they vindicate so much the character of 'eternal' institutions or even 'sacred' foundations of society as that which has consolidated and safeguards the right of their estate and the domination of their class."[23] And as long as the dominating class is the vehicle of the most progressive social ideals, the system it has set up will satisfy all the demands of social development. But as soon as the economic history of a particular society brings forward new elements of a progressive movement, as soon as the "productive forces of society come in conflict with the existing relations of production, or—what is but a legal expression for the same thing— with the property relations within which they have been at work hitherto", the progressive role of the ruling class in question will be over. From a representative of progress it will become its sworn enemy and, of course, it will make use of the state machine for self-defence. In its hands political power will become the most powerful weapon of reaction. To free the road for the development of the productive forces of society it is necessary to remove the property relations which hinder that development, i.e. as Marx says, to carry out a social revolution. But that is impossible as long as legislative power is in the hands of the old order, in other words, as long as it safeguards the interests of the ruling class. It is therefore not astonishing that innovators, i.e. representatives of the oppressed class or classes, will strive to wrest this terrible weapon out of the hands of their opponents and turn it against them. The very logic of things will bring them out on to the road of political struggle and seizure of state power, although they set themselves the task of an economic revolution. Lassalle uttered a profound truth when he said in the preface to his *System of Acquired Rights:* "...where juridical right as private right seems to become entirely detached from the political element, *it is far more political than the political element.* For there it is the *social* element".[24]

In practical life, of course, things are far from going as fast as one might suppose, judging *a priori.* Only gradually does the oppressed class become clear about the connection between its economic position and its *political* role in the state. For a long time it does not understand even its economic task to the full. The individuals composing it wage a hard struggle for their daily subsistence without even thinking which aspects of the social organization they owe their wretched condition to. They try to avoid the blows aimed at them without asking where they come from or by whom, in the final analysis, they are aimed. As yet they have no class consciousness and there is no guiding idea in their struggle against individual oppressors. The oppressed class does not yet exist *for itself;* in time it *will* be the advanced class in society, but it is not yet *becoming* such. Facing the consciously organized power of the ruling class are separate individual strivings of isolated individuals or isolated groups of individuals. Even now, for example, we frequently enough meet a worker who hates the particularly intensive exploiter but does not yet suspect that the whole class of exploiters must be fought and the very possibility of exploitation of man by man removed.

Little by little, however, the process of generalization takes effect, and the oppressed begin to be conscious of themselves as a class. But their understanding of the specific features of their class position still remains too one-sided: the springs and motive forces of the social mechanism as a whole are still hidden from their mind's eye. The class of exploiters appears to them as the simple sum of individual employers, not connected by the threads of political organization. At this stage of development it is not yet clear in the minds of the oppressed—any more than in Professor Lorenz von Stein's—what connection exists between "society" and "state". State power is presumed to stand above the antagonisms of the classes; its representatives appear to be the natural judges and conciliators of the hostile sides. The oppressed class has complete trust in them and is extremely surprised when its requests for help remain unanswered by them. Without dwelling on particular examples, we will merely note that such confusion of concepts was displayed even recently by the British workers, who waged quite an energetic struggle in the economic field and yet considered it possible to belong to one of the bourgeois political parties.

Only in the next and last stage of development does the oppressed class come to a thorough realization of its position. It now realizes the connection between society and state, and it does not appeal for the curbing of its exploiters to those who constitute the political organ of that exploitation. It knows that the state is a fortress serving as the bulwark and defence of its oppressors, a fortress which the oppressed can and must capture and reorganize for their own defence and which they cannot bypass, counting on its neutrality. Relying only on themselves, the oppressed begin to understand that "*political* self-help", as Lange says, "is the most important of all forms of *social* self-help". They then fight for political domination in order to help themselves by changing the existing social relations and adapting the social system to the conditions of their own development and welfare. Neither do they, of course, achieve domination immediately; they only gradually become a formidable power precluding all thought of resistance by their opponents. For a long time they fight only for concessions, demand only such reforms as would give them not domination, but merely the possibility to develop and mature for future domination; reforms which would satisfy the most urgent and immediate of their demands and extend, if only slightly, the sphere of their influence over the country's social life. Only by going through the hard school of the struggle for separate little pieces of enemy territory does the oppressed class acquire the persistence, the daring, and the development necessary for the decisive battle. But once it has acquired those qualities it can look at its opponents as at a class finally condemned by history; it need have no doubt about its victory. What is called the revolution is only the last act in the long drama of revolutionary class struggle which becomes conscious only in so far as it becomes a *political* struggle.[25]

The question is now: would it be expedient for the socialists to hold the workers back from "politics" on the grounds that the political structure of society is determined by its economic relations? Of course not! They would be depriving the workers of a fulcrum in their struggle, they would be depriving them of the possibility of concentrating their efforts and aiming their blows at the social organization set up by the exploiters. Instead, the workers would have to wage guerrilla warfare against individual exploiters, or at most separate groups of those exploiters, who would always have on their side, the organized power of the state. This was the kind of mistake the Russian socialists from among the so-called intelligentsia made when they censured the Northern Union of Russian Workers (in No. 4 of *Zemlya i Volya)* for having included certain political demands in its programme. The same mistake was repeated by Zerno when it recommended that the workers should wage the struggle on economic ground, fight for a shorter working day, higher wages, etc., that they should kill spies and particularly hated foremen and employers, but did not say a word about the *political* tasks of the Russian workers. This lack of synthesis in our socialists' revolutionary views and programmes could not fail to have the most damaging effect on the results of their work. By preserving the political indifference of the workers as a most important sign of the radical nature of their economic demands, we gave indirect support to modern absolutism. Moreover, by cutting short our programmes at the very point where we should have summed up politically the social demands of the working class, we were diminishing the practical significance of those programmes in the eyes of the workers, who understood better than we did the utter futility of the divided struggle against individual exploiters. Fortunately, our working-class movement very soon outgrew this first phase of its development. The answer given by the Northern Union of Russian Workers to the editors of *Zemlya i Volya* (see No. 5 of that publication) showed that at least the members of the Union had understood earlier than our "intelligentsia" how inappropriate was this "political non-interference" of the working class.

All that is very well, some readers may say, but your arguments are not to the point. We do not deny, they may argue, that it would be *useful* for the working class to gain political influence and take state power in its own hands; we only maintain that at present that is *impossible* for many reasons. Your reference to the history of the bourgeoisie proves nothing, for the position of the proletariat in bourgeois society is nothing like that of the third estate in the states of the "ancien regime"! Even Marx admits the difference and formulates it as follows in the *Manifesto of the Communist Party:* "The serf, in the period of serfdom, raised himself to membership in the commune, just as the petty bourgeois, under the yoke of feudal absolutism, managed to develop into a bourgeois. The modern labourer, on the contrary, instead of rising with the progress of industry, sinks deeper and deeper below the conditions of existence of his own class. He becomes a pauper, and pauperism develops more rapidly than population and wealth in bourgeois countries." There is nothing surprising in the fact that every progressive step made by the bourgeoisie in the domain of production and exchange was accompanied by the "corresponding political conquests"; everybody knows that improvement in the material welfare of any particular class is accompanied by the growth of its political influence. But the very fact that the political gains of the bourgeoisie presupposed an increase in its wealth makes us abandon any hopes in the political movements of the working class. Falling deeper and deeper into "pauperism", the workers apparently must lose even the little influence which they won in the struggle for the interests of the bourgeoisie, "fighting the enemies of their enemies—the remnants of absolute monarchy, the landowners, the non-industrial bourgeois", and so on. The political struggle of the working class is purposeless because it is doomed to failure by virtue of the economic position of the workers.

For all its inner untenability, this objection seems at first glance so decisive as not to be passed over in silence. It is the last argument of those supporters of the theory of political non-interference who consider themselves followers of Marx.[26] Therefore, if it is disposed of, the theory of non-interference falls away altogether and the political tasks of modern socialism stand out in their true light.

The working class's share in the national product is constantly diminishing—there is not a shade of doubt about that. The working class is becoming poorer not only relatively, but absolutely too; its income, far from increasing in the same progression as those of other classes in society, is falling; the real wages of the modern proletarian (the quantity of consumer goods falling to his share) are less than the worker's pay was five hundred years ago—this has been proved by the studies of Rogers, Du Chatelet and others.[27] But it by no means follows from this that the economic conditions are at present less favourable to the political movement of the working class than they were in the 14th century. We have already said that in thus appraising the economic conditions in a particular country one must take into account not only the distribution of the national income, but mainly the organization of production and the mode of exchange of products. The strength of the rising bourgeoisie lay not so much in its wealth as in the social and economic progress of which it was once the vehicle. It was not the increase in its income that impelled it to take the path of revolutionary struggle and guaranteed the growth of its political influence; it was the contradiction between the productive forces it brought into existence and the conditions under which the production and exchange of products took place in feudal society. Having once become the representative of progressive demands in that society, the bourgeoisie rallied all the dissatisfied elements under its banner and led them to fight against a regime which the overwhelming majority of the people hated. Not money, but the immaturity of the working class gave the bourgeoisie the leading role in that emancipation movement. Its wealth and its already fairly high social position were naturally indispensable for the fulfilment of this role; but what was that indispensability determined by? First of all by the fact that the bourgeoisie could not destroy the old order without assistance from the lower strata of the population. In this its wealth helped it by giving it influence over the masses which were to fight for its domination. Had the bourgeoisie not been rich it would have had no influence, and without influence over the people it would not have defeated the aristocracy; for the bourgeoisie was strong not of itself, but by virtue of the power which it had already mastered and which it commanded thanks to its capital. The question now arises, *is it possible* for the proletariat to have such influence over another class of the population, and *does it need* such influence to be victorious? It is enough to ask the question and we hear a resolute "No!" from everybody who understands the present position of the working class. It is *impossible* for the proletariat to influence lower classes in the way the bourgeoisie once influenced it, for the simple reason that there are no classes below it; the proletariat itself is the very lowest economic group in modern society. *Nor is there any need* for it to aim at such influence, because it is at the same time the *most numerous* section in society, because precisely the proletariat, with other sections of the working population, has always been the agent whose intervention has decided political issues. We say the most numerous class because all "the other classes decay and finally disappear in the face of modern industry; the proletariat is its special and essential product. The lower middle class, the small manufacturer, the shopkeeper, the artisan, the peasant, all these fight against the bourgeoisie, to save from extinction their existence as fractions of the middle class. They are therefore conservative.

Nay more, they are reactionary, for they try to roll back the wheel of history. If by chance they are revolutionary, they are so only in view of their impending transfer into the proletariat, they thus defend not their present, but their future interests, they desert their own standpoint to place themselves at that of the proletariat".

Formerly the working class was victorious under the command of the bourgeoisie, and it only naively wondered at the strange fact that nearly all the difficulties in the struggle fell to its lot while nearly all the advantages and honours of victory went to its ally. Now it is not satisfied with this auxiliary role and it turns against the bourgeoisie the very strength which once secured the latter's victory. But that strength is now much greater. It has grown and is continuing to grow in the same measure as the concentration of capital and the spread of large-scale production. Besides, it has grown in the same measure as the political experience of the working class, which the bourgeoisie itself brought into the social arena. Can there be any doubt that the proletariat, which, when led by the bourgeoisie, was once strong enough to destroy feudal absolutism, will in time be strong enough to smash the political domination of the bourgeoisie on its own initiative? The bourgeoisie was able to defeat feudalism only thanks to its wealth, the proletariat will defeat the bourgeoisie for the very reason that its lot—"pauperism"—is becoming the lot of an ever-increasing portion of modern society.

But in the history of its development the bourgeoisie received from its wealth another and indeed extremely "*productive* service", as its economists would say. It received knowledge and became the most advanced and educated section of society at that time. Can the proletariat acquire that knowledge, can it be at the same time the poorest and the most advanced of all classes in society? Without this condition political domination is out of the question for the proletariat, for without knowledge there is no strength.

We have already said that the bourgeoisie itself began the political education of the proletariat. It took care of the education of the proletariat as much as this was necessary for the struggle against its own enemies. It shattered the proletariat's religious beliefs whenever this was required to weaken the political significance of the clergy; it broadened the proletariat's legal outlook wherever it needed to oppose "natural" law to the written law of the estate-based state. Now the economic question is on the agenda and political economy now plays—as a very clever German[28] said—just as important a role as natural law played in the 18th century. Will the bourgeoisie agree to be the working class's leader in the investigation of the relations between labour and capital, that question of questions of the whole of social economy? It is reluctant to take upon itself even that role, advantageous as it is to itself, because merely to raise that question means to threaten the bourgeoisie's domination. But *can* it fulfil that role, if only in the way it once did in regard to religion and law? No, it cannot be blinded by their class interests, its representatives in science lost long ago all ability to investigate social questions objectively, scientifically. Therein lies the whole secret of the present decay of bourgeois economics. Ricardo was the last economist who, though still a bourgeois in heart and soul, was intelligent enough to understand the diametrical opposition of interests between labour and capital. Sismondi was the last bourgeois economist who had enough feeling to deplore that antagonism sincerely. After them, the *general* theoretical studies of bourgeois economists in the main lost all scientific significance. To convince oneself of this it is sufficient to recall the history of political economy since Ricardo and to look through the works of Bastiat, Carey, Leroy-Beaulieu or the modern Katheder Sozialisten. From peaceful and objective thinkers the bourgeois economists have become militant guardians and watchdogs of capital who devote all their efforts to reconstructing the very edifice of science for the purpose of war. But in spite of these warlike exertions, they continually retreat and leave in their enemies' hands the scientific territory over which they once had uncontrolled sway. Nowadays people who display no "demagogic" strivings whatever try to assure us that the workers are "better able than any Smith or

Faucher to master the most abstract concepts" in the science of economics. Such was the opinion, for instance, of a man who has the highest authority among German economists but who, for his part, had the deepest scorn for them. "We look upon the workers as children," this man added, "whereas they are already head and shoulders above us."[29]

But is there no exaggeration in what he says? Can the working class understand "abstract" questions of social economics and socialism at least as well as, if not better than, people who have spent years and years on their education?

What are the principles of modern scientific socialism founded on? Are they the concoctions of some leisurely benefactor of humanity, or are they the summing up of those very phenomena which we all come up against, one way or another, in our daily life, the explanation of the very laws which determine our participation in the production, the exchange, or simply the distribution of products? Whoever answers this question will agree that the working class has many chances of understanding correctly the "most abstract" laws of social economics and of mastering the most abstract principles of scientific socialism. The difficulty in understanding the laws of some particular science is caused by incomplete knowledge of the data underlying those laws. Wherever it is only a question of everyday phenomena in which the scientific law only generalizes facts that everybody knows, people in the practical field not only understand perfectly the theoretical principles, they can sometimes even teach the theoreticians themselves. Ask the farmer about the influence that the distance to the market has on the price of his products or the effect the fertility of the soil has on the size of the land rent. Ask the manufacturer how the expansion of the market influences the cheapening of production. Or ask the worker where the employer gets his profits from. ...You will see that all these people know Ricardo, although they have never even seen the cover of his works. Yet these questions are reputed to be very intricate and "abstract", whole seas of ink have been used upon them and such a tremendous number of volumes have been written about them that they are enough to terrify you when you begin to study economics. The same in each and every part of social economics. Take the theory of exchange value. You can explain to the worker in a couple of words what it is determined by and how but many of Messrs, the bourgeois economists are still unwilling or unable to understand this perfectly simple theory, and in their disputes about it they fall into gross errors of logic for which no teacher of arithmetic would hesitate to give an elementary school pupil a bad mark. That is why we think that the writer we quoted was correct and that the only understanding audience today on urgent social problems is one of proletarians or of people who have adopted the proletarian stand point. Once the fundamental principles of social economics are mastered, the understanding of scientific socialism no longer presents any difficulty: here too the worker will only follow the directions of his practical experience. This aspect of the question was magnificently explained by Marx. "By heralding the dissolution of the *hitherto existing world order*" we read in *A Contribution to the Critique of Hegel's Philosophy of Law,* "the proletariat merely proclaims the secret of its own existence, for it is the *factual dissolution* of that world order. By demanding the *negation of private property,* the proletariat merely raises to the rank of *a principle of society* what society has raised to the rank of *its* principle, what is already embodied in it as the negative result of society without its own participation."[30] So we see that the proletariat needs no material wealth to attain to an understanding of the conditions of its emancipation. Its pauperism, determined *not by the poverty of the barbarism of society, but by defects in the social organization*—this pauperism, far from making the understanding of these conditions more difficult, makes it easier.

The laws governing the distribution of products in capitalist society are extremely unfavourable to the working class. But the organization of production and the form of exchange characteristic of capitalism provide for the first time both the objective and the subjective possibility for the emancipation of the working people. Capitalism broadens the worker's outlook and removes all the prejudices he inherited from the old society; it impels him to fight and at the same time ensures his victory by increasing his numbers and putting at his disposal the economic possibility of organizing the kingdom of labour. Technical progress increases man's power over nature and raises labour productivity to such a degree that the necessity of labour cannot become a hindrance, but, on the contrary, will be an indispensable condition for the all-round development of the members of socialist society. At the same time, the socialization of *production* characteristic of capitalism paves the way for the conversion of its *instruments and products* into common property. The joint-stock company, the highest form of organization for industrial enterprises at the present time, excludes the capitalists from any active role in the economic life of society and turns them into drones whose disappearance cannot cause the slightest disorganization in the course of that life. "If the energetic race of major-demos once succeeded without difficulty in deposing a royal dynasty which had grown indolent," the conservative Rodbertus says, "why should a living and energetic organization of workers (the staff of companies is composed of qualified workers), why should not such an organization in time remove owners who have become mere *rentiers?...* And yet capital cannot turn off this road! Having outlived its period of prosperity, capital is becoming its own grave-digger!

"Why, we ask, in our turn, should not the same organization of workers which will be in a position "to remove owners who have become mere *rentiers"*—why should not such an organization be in a position to seize state power and thus achieve political domination? For the former presumes the latter: only such an organization can "remove" the owners as can overcome their *political* resistance.

But that is not all: there are other social phenomena which also increase the probability of the proletariat's *political* victory.

> "...Entire sections of the ruling classes are, by the advance of industry, precipitated into the proletariat, or are at least

threatened in their conditions of existence. These also supply the proletariat with fresh elements of enlightenment and progress.

"Finally, in times when the class struggle nears the decisive hour, the process of dissolution going on within the ruling class, in fact within the whole range of old society, assumes such a violent, glaring character, that a small section of the ruling class cuts itself adrift, and joins the revolutionary class, the class that holds the future in its hands. Just as, therefore, at an earlier period, a section of the nobility went over to the bourgeoisie, so now a portion of the bourgeoisie goes over to the proletariat, and in particular, a portion of the bourgeois ideologists, who have raised themselves to the level of comprehending theoretically the historical movement as a whole."

There is a very remarkable legend among the Negroes of North Guinea. "One day," it says, "God summoned the two sons of the first human couple. One of them was white, the other dark-skinned. Placing before them a heap of gold and a book, God ordered the dark-skinned brother, as being the elder, to choose one of the two. He chose the gold, so the younger brother received the book. An unknown force immediately transported the younger one with the book to a cold, distant country. But thanks to his book he became learned, terrifying and strong. As for the elder brother, he remained in his native country and lived long enough to see how superior science is to wealth."

The bourgeoisie once had both knowledge and wealth. Unlike the dark-skinned brother in the Negro legend, it obtained possession of both gold and book, because history, the god of human societies, does not recognize the right of classes which are under age, and commits them to the guardianship of their elder brothers. But the time came when the working class, slighted by history, grew out of childhood and the bourgeoisie had to share with it. The bourgeoisie kept the gold, while the younger brother received the "book", thanks to which, despite the darkness and cold of his cellars, he has now become "strong and terrifying". Little by little, scientific socialism is ousting the bourgeois theories from the pages of this magic book, and soon the proletariat will read in the book how they can gain material sufficiency. Then they will throw off the shameful yoke of capitalism and show the bourgeoisie "how superior science is to wealth".

III

In the first chapter we endeavoured to explain historically the origin of the conviction that socialism is incompatible with any politics". We saw that this conviction was based on Proudhon's and Bakunin's teaching on the state, on the one hand, and on a certain inconsistency in our Social-Democrats of the seventies, on the other. Moreover, it was supported by the general tone of the background against which both the tendencies mentioned above stood out. That background consisted, as we said quoting Engels, in a mish-mash of manifold theories of the founders of different socialist sects. The Utopian socialists, we know, had an entirely negative attitude to the political movements of the working class, seeing in them nothing but "blind unbelief in the new Gospel". This negative view of "politics" came to us with the teachings of the Utopians. Long before revolutionary movement of any strength began in Russia, our socialists, like the "true" socialists in Germany at the end of the forties (see the *Manifesto of the Communist Party),* were ready "to hurl the traditional anathemas against liberalism, against representative government, against bourgeois competition, bourgeois freedom of the press, bourgeois legislation, bourgeois liberty and equality", forgetting entirely that all these attacks "presupposed the existence of modern bourgeois society, with its corresponding economic conditions of existence, and the political constitution adapted thereto", i.e. the very conditions that it should still have been a question of assuring in our country.[31]

As a result of all these influences there arose such a firm conviction of the inexpediency of any political struggle except the revolutionary struggle in the narrow and vulgar sense of the word, that we began to regard with prejudice the socialist parties in Western Europe which saw electoral campaigns, for instance, as a powerful means of educating and organising the working masses. All the political and economic gains those campaigns brought seemed to us unpardonable opportunism, a ruinous deal with the demon of the bourgeois state, tantamount to renouncing bliss in future socialist life. We ourselves did not even notice that our theories were involving us in a vicious circle of insoluble contradictions. We regarded the village commune as the point of departure of Russia's social and economic development and, at the same time, renouncing political struggle, we voluntarily deprived ourselves of all possibility of safeguarding that commune against the present destructive influences by state interference. We were thus forced to remain indifferent spectators of a process which was destroying the very foundation on which we wished to erect the edifice of the future.

We saw, however, that the logic of events had led the Russian movement on to another road and forced the Russian revolutionaries, as represented by the Narodnaya Volya party, to fight for political influence and even dominance as one of the most powerfactors of economic revolution. We also saw that having entered upon that road our movement was growing to such an extent that the social and political theories of different varieties of Proudhonism were too narrow and cramping for it. The course of events peculiar to Russian social life clashed with the course of the ideas dominating among our revolutionaries and thus provoked a new trend of thought.

This trend, we said further, will not rid itself of its characteristic contradictions until it merges with the incomparably deeper and wider current of modern socialism. The Russian revolutionaries must adopt the standpoint of Western Social-Democracy and break with "rebel" *theories* just as a few years ago they renounced "rebel" *practice,* introducing a new, *political* element into their programme. This will not be difficult for them to do if they endeavour to adopt the correct view of the political side of Marx's teaching and are willing to reconsider the methods and immediate aims of their struggle by applying this new criterion to them.

We saw as early as in the second chapter what false conclusions were prompted by the philosophical and historical premises of modern socialism. *Narodnaya Volya* itself apparently did not notice the erroneousness of those conclusions and was inclined "even to defend Dühring's sociological standpoint on the predominant influence of the political and legal element in the social structure over the economic", as P.L. Lavrov put it in describing the most recent tendencies in the Russian revolutionary movement.[32] And it is only by this inclination that we can explain the polemic contained in the home review of Narodnaya Volya No. 6 against some kind of "immediate interpreters of Marx's historical theory", who, according to the author, based their views "mainly on Hegel's famous triad", not having "any other inductive material" for their conclusions and explaining "Hegel's law in the sense evil, merely in its extreme development, will lead to good".[33] It is sufficient to acquaint oneself with the programme of the German Social-Democrats or the French collectivists to see how "Marx's historical theory" is understood by his West European followers and, if you like, by his "immediate interpreters". We, for our part, can assure our Russian comrades that these "interpreters" understand "Hegel's law" by no means "in the sense that evil, merely in its extreme development, will lead to good", and, besides, that they use it as *"inductive* material" only when they study the history of German philosophy, in which this law has a very prominent place and which, *in any case,* it cannot be left out of, just as, according to the popular saying, you cannot leave words out of a song. The passage we quoted is an almost word-for-word repetition of the reproach addressed by Dühring to Marx that in his historical scheme "the Hegelian negation of negation plays, for want of better and clearer means, the role of a midwife with whose help the future emerges from the womb of the present".[34] But this trick has already received the punishment it deserved from Engels, who showed the utter scientific worthlessness of the former Berlin *Dozent's* works. Why, then, repeat other people's errors and adopt, on such shifting grounds, a negative attitude towards the greatest and most revolutionary social theory of the 19th century? For without revolutionary theory there is no revolutionary movement in the true sense of the word. Any class which strives for its emancipation, any political party which aims at dominance, is revolutionary only insofar as it represents the most progressive social trends and consequently is a vehicle of the most progressive ideas of its time. An idea which is inherently revolutionary is a kind of dynamite which no other explosive in the world can replace. And as long as our movement is under the banner of backward or erroneous theories it will have revolutionary significance only by some, but by no means all of its aspects. At the same time, without its members knowing it, it will bear in itself the germs of reaction which will deprive it even of that little significance in the more or less near future, because, as Heine said, "New time needs a new garment for the new job it's got to do."

And indeed that really new time will come at last—for our country too.

Incorrect understanding of some principles of modern socialism is not, however, the main obstacle preventing our revolutionary movement from taking the road paved by the working class in the West. A closer acquaintance with the literature of "Marxism" will show our socialists what a powerful weapon they have deprived themselves of by refusing to understand and master the theory of the great teacher of the "workers of all countries". They will then see that our revolutionary movement, far from losing anything, will gain a lot if the Russian Narodniks and the Russian Narodnaya Volya at last become Russian Marxists and a new, higher standpoint reconciles all the groups existing among us, which are all right each in its own way, because despite their one-sidedness each of them expresses a definite vital need of Russian social life.

Another obstacle prevents our movement from developing in the direction just indicated. It consists in our lacking sense of proportion in politics. Since the very beginning of our movement this has prevented our revolutionaries from bringing their immediate tasks into line with their strength and it is due to nothing else than lack of political experience on the part of Russian public figures. Whether we went among the people to disseminate socialist publications, settled in the villages to organize the protesting elements of our peasantry or joined directly in the fight against the representatives of absolutism, we repeated one and the same mistake everywhere. We always overestimated our strength and never fully took account of the resistance that would be offered by the social environment, we hastened to raise a method of action temporarily favoured by circumstances into a universal principle precluding all other ways and means. As a result, all our programmes were in a state of absolutely unstable equilibrium which could be upset by the most insignificant change in the surrounding atmosphere. We changed those programmes almost every couple of years and could not keep to anything *lasting* because we always kept to something *narrow* and *one-sided.* Just as, according to Belinsky's words, Russian society had experience of all literary trends even before it had any literature, so the Russian socialist movement managed to try out all possible shades of West European socialism despite the fact that it had not yet become a movement of our working class.

The struggle against absolutism that Narodnaya Volya has undertaken will undoubtedly help greatly to eliminate the one-sidedness of the study *groups* by bringing our revolutionaries out on to a broader path and compelling them to strive to set up a real *party.* But in order to put a stop to the continual changing of programmes, to rid themselves of these habits of political nomads and to acquire intellectual stability at last, the Russian revolutionaries must complete the criticism which began with the rise of conscious political trends among them. They must adopt a critical attitude to the very programme which has made necessary the criticism of *all* previous programmes and theories. The "Narodnaya Volya party" is the child of a time of transition. Its programme is the last produced in the conditions which made our one-sidedness inevitable and therefore legitimate. Although it broadens the political horizon of the Russian socialists, this programme in itself is not yet free from one-sidedness. The lack of sense of proportion in politics, of the ability to line up the immediate aims of the party with its actual or potential strength is also still conspicuous in it. The Narodnaya Volya party reminds one of a man who is going along a real road but has no idea of distances and therefore feels sure that he can leave "miles and leagues behind— twenty thousand leagues, ere night, covered in a single flight". Practice will, of course, shatter his illusion, but that shattering may cost him a great deal. It would be better for him to ask himself whether seven-league strides do not belong to the realm of fantasy.

By seven-league strides we mean the element of fantasy whose existence in the programme referred to we have already pointed out and which was manifested in the second issue of *Narodnaya Volya* by assurances concerning the social-revolutionary (we do not say *socialist)* majority in the future Russian Constituent Assembly, 55 and in No. 8-9 by considerations on "the seizure of power by the provisional revolutionary government". We are profoundly convinced that this element of fantasy is highly dangerous for the "Narodnaya Volya party" itself. Dangerous to it as a socialist party because it diverts attention of the working class from the immediate tasks in Russia; dangerous to it as a party which has assumed the initiative of our emancipation movement because it will alienate from the party great resources and forces which, in other circumstances, would accrue to it out of the so-called society. Let us explain this in greater detail.

To whom does Narodnaya Volya appeal, to whom can it and should it appeal in fighting absolutism? "The enlistment in the organization"—Narodnaya Volya—*"of individuals from the peasantry* capable of joining it," we read in Kalendar Narodnoi Voli,[35] "has naturally always been acknowledged as very desirable ... But as for a mass peasant organization at present, that was considered completely fantastic when our programme was drawn up, and, if we are not mistaken, subsequent practice was unable to change the opinion of our socialists on this subject." Perhaps the "Narodnaya Volya party" intends to rely on the more progressive section of our labouring population, i.e. on the town workers? It does actually attach great importance to propaganda and organization among them, it considers that "the urban working population must be the object of the party's serious attention". But the very reason on which it bases this necessity shows that in the party's conception the town workers must be only one of the elements in our revolutionary movement. They "are of particular significance for the revolution, both by their position and by their relatively greater maturity", the same document explains; "the success of the first attack depends entirely on the conduct of the workers and the troops." So the impending revolution will not be a working-class revolution in the full sense of the term, but the workers must take part in it because they "are of particular significance *for it*". Which other elements, then, will be included in this movement? We have already seen that one of these elements will be the "troops", but in the army "in present conditions propaganda among the men is so difficult that great hope can hardly be placed upon It. Action on *the officer corps* is far more convenient: being more educated and having greater liberty they are more susceptible to influence"! That is quite correct, of course, but we will not stop at that for the moment, we will go further. Besides the workers and "the officer corps", the Narodnaya Volya party has in mind the liberals and "Europe", in relation to which "the policy of the party must strive to ensure the sympathy of the peoples for the Russian revolution, to rouse sympathy for the revolution among the European public". To attain this aim "the party must make known to Europe all the disastrous significance of Russian absolutism for European civilization itself, and also the party's true aims and the significance of our revolutionary movement as the expression of the protest of the whole nation". As far as the "liberals" are concerned, "we must point out, without concealing our radicalism, that given the present setting of our party tasks, our interests and theirs compel us to act jointly against the government."

Thus we see that the Narodnaya Volya party relies not only, nor even mainly, on the working and peasant classes. It also has in mind society and the officer corps, which, in substance, is the very flesh and bone" of that society. It wants to convince the liberal part of that society that "given the present setting of our party tasks" the interests of Russian liberalism coincide with those of the Russian social-revolutionary party. What, then, does it do to that conviction upon the Russian liberals? First of all it publishes the programme of the Executive Committee which says that "the *people's will* would be sufficiently well expressed and Implemented by a Constituent Assembly freely elected by universal suffrage and receiving instructions from the electors". In its famous "Letter to Alexander III" the Executive Committee also demanded "the convocation of representatives of the whole Russian people to reconsider the existing forms of statehood and public life and to refashion them according to the desires of the people".[36] That programme does indeed coincide with the interests of the Russian liberals, and in order to carry it out they would probably be reconciled even to universal suffrage, which the Executive Committee cannot fail to demand. In all this, the programme of the said Committee displays far greater maturity than all those which preceded it. But, not to mention such a huge blunder as to demand freedom of assembly, of speech, of the press and of electoral programmes only "as a temporary measure", let us recall other statements of the Narodnaya Volya party. The party organ hastened to warn its readers that the majority of the deputies to the Constituent Assembly would be supporters of radical economic revolution. We have already said above that this assurance was no more than a fiction invented to conciliate incompatible elements in the Narodnaya Volya programme. Let us now consider the printed expression of that assurance from the stand-point of tactics. The question is: does an economic revolution suit the interests of Russian liberalism? Does our liberal society sympathize with the agrarian revolution which Narodnaya Volya says the peasant deputies will aim at? West European history tells us most convincingly that whenever the "red spectre" took at all threatening forms the "liberals" were ready to seek protection in the embraces of the most unceremonious military dictatorship. Did the terrorist organ think that our Russian liberals would be an exception to this general rule? If so, on what did it base its conviction? Did it also think that contemporary "public opinion in Europe" was so imbued with socialist ideas that it would sympathize with the convocation of a social-revolutionary Constituent Assembly? Or did it think that although the European bourgeoisie trembled at the red spectre in their own countries they would cheer its appearance in Russia? It goes without saying that it thought nothing of the sort and forgot nothing of the sort. But why, in that case, make such a risky statement? Or was the Narodnaya Volya party organ so convinced of the inevitable realization of its prophecy that it considered it necessary to rouse the members of the organization to take steps corresponding to the importance of the anticipated event? Bearing in mind the fact that the same organ declared work among the people useless, we think the statement was intended rather to calm than to rouse: a social-revolutionary majority in the Constituent Assembly was expected *despite* the fact that the work referred to now recalls the "Danaides filling bottomless barrels".

In itself the statement could have been regarded as unimportant, especially as *Narodnaya Volya* itself had apparently given up its exaggeratedly optimistic hopes about the future composition of the Russian Constituent. We think so, because the leading article in No. 8-9 speaks of the economic revolution which, in the absence of social-revolutionary initiative among the people themselves, must be accomplished by the "provisional revolutionary government" before the convocation of the Constituent Assembly. The author of the article quite rightly sees such a revolution as the only guarantee that "the Zemsky Sobor which is convoked will be attended by true representatives of the people". Thus, *Narodnaya Volya's* former illusion has been shattered completely. But, unfortunately, it has only disappeared to give place to a new one, still more harmful for the cause of the Narodnaya Volya party. The element of fantasy in the programme has not been removed but has only assumed a new form, being now called that very *"seizure of power by the provisional revolutionary government"* which is supposed to give the party the possibility to carry out the economic revolution referred to. It is obvious that the new "setting of the party tasks" can on no account impress upon either Russian liberalism or bourgeois Europe the idea that they have common interests with the Russian revolutionary movement. However downtrodden and crushed Russian society may be it is by no means deprived of the instinct of self-preservation and in no case will it voluntarily meet the "red spectre" half-way; to point out to it such a formulation of the party tasks means to deprive oneself of its support and to rely only on one's own strength. But is that strength great enough to warrant the risk of alienating such an ally? Can our revolutionaries really seize power and retain it, if only for a short time, or is all talk of this nothing else than cutting the skin of a bear that has not been killed and which, by force of circumstances, is not even going to be killed? That is a question which has recently become an urgent one for revolutionary Russia....

Let us hasten to make a reservation. The previous pages must already have convinced the reader that we do not belong to the opponents in principle of such an act as the seizure of power by a revolutionary party. In our opinion that is the last, and what is more, the absolutely inevitable conclusion to be drawn from the political struggle which every class striving for emancipation must undertake at a definite stage in social development. Having gained political domination, a revolutionary class will retain that domination and be relatively secure against the blows of reaction only when it uses against reaction the mighty weapon of state power. "Den Teufel halte, wer inn halt!" says Faust.

But there is no more difference between heaven and earth than between the dictatorship of a class and that of a group of revolutionary *raznochintsi.* This applies in particular to the dictatorship of the working class, whose present task is not only to overthrow the political domination of the unproductive classes in society, but also to do away with the anarchy now existing in production and consciously to organise all functions of social and economic life. The mere *understanding* of this task calls for an advanced working class with political experience and education, a working class free from bourgeois prejudices and able to discuss its situation by itself. In addition to this, its *solution* presupposes that socialist ideas are spread among the proletariat and that the proletariat is conscious of its own strength and confident in victory. But *such* a proletariat *will not allow* even the sincerest of its well-wishers to seize power. It will not allow it for the simple reason that it has been to the school of political education with the firm intention of finishing it at some time and coming forward as an independent figure in the arena of historical life, instead of passing eternally from one guardianship to another; it will not allow it because such a guardianship would be unnecessary, as the proletariat could then solve the problem of the socialist revolution itself; and finally it will not allow it because such a guardianship would be harmful, for the conscious participation of the producers in organizing production cannot be replaced by any conspiratorial skill, any daring or self-sacrifice on the part of the conspirators. The mere thought that the social problem can be solved in practice by anybody but the workers themselves shows complete misunderstanding of this problem, irrespective of whether the idea is held by an "Iron Chancellor" or a revolutionary organization. Once the proletariat has understood the conditions of its emancipation and is mature to emancipate itself, it will take state power in its own hands in order to finish off its enemies and build up social life, not, of course, on the basis of *an*-archy, which would bring new disasters, but of pan-archy, which will give all adult members of society the possibility to take part in the discussion and settlement of social matters. And until the working class is sufficiently developed to be able to fulfil its great historical task, the duty of its supporters is to accelerate the process of its development, to remove the obstacles preventing its strength and its consciousness from growing, and not to invent social experiments and vivisection, the outcome of which is always more than doubtful.

That is how we understand the seizure of power in the socialist revolution. Applying this point of view to Russian reality we must admit that we by no means believe in the early possibility of a socialist government in Russia.

Narodnaya Volya considers the contemporary "relation of political and economic factors on Russian soil" particularly "advantageous" to the socialists. We agree that it is more advantageous for them in Russia than in India, Persia or Egypt, but it cannot be compared, of course, with the social relations in Western Europe. And if Narodnaya Volya arrives at its convictions by comparing our system not with the Egyptian or the Persian, but with the French or the English system, then it has made a very big mistake. The contemporary "relation" of social factors "on Russian soil" is the cause of the ignorance and indifference of the popular masses; when were such qualities advantageous for their emancipation? Narodnaya Volya apparently presumes that this indifference has already begun to disappear because among the people "there is growing hatred of the privileged ruling estates and persistent striving for a radical change in economic relations". But what comes of that striving? "Hatred of the privileged estates" proves nothing at all; it is often not accompanied by a single ray of political consciousness. Furthermore, at the present time we must clearly distinguish between *estate* consciousness and *class* consciousness, for the old division into estates no longer corresponds to the economic relations in Russia and is preparing to give place to formal equality of citizens in a "legal state" If Narodnaya Volya considers the contemporary outlook of our peasantry from the standpoint of the development of their *class* and *political* consciousness, it will hardly persist in saying that the relation between our social factors is advantageous to the cause of the social revolution. For it certainly cannot consider "advantageous" to that cause the rumours, for instance, circulating among the peasantry about their own struggle against the government. No matter how strongly "hatred of the ruling classes" is shown in these rumours, the fact that the revolutionary movement itself is attributed by the peasants to scheming by the serfdom-minded nobility and the officials is evidence that the "provisional revolutionary government" will be in great danger when the people begins "winning economic equality from those who have been exploiting and oppressing it for centuries". Then the relation between the factors now interesting us will perhaps display rather disadvantageous qualities for the temporarily victorious conspirators. And then, what is meant by "winning economic equality"?

Is it enough for that to expropriate the big landowners, capitalists and businessmen? Does it not require production itself to be organized in a definite manner? If so, are Russia's present economic relations favourable to such organization? In other words, does the "economic factor" offer us much chance of success? We do not think so, and for the following reason. Any organization presupposes in what is to be organised certain qualities determined by the purpose and character of the organization. The socialist organization of production implies such a character of the economic relations as will make that organization the logical conclusion of the entire previous development of the country and is therefore distinguished by an extremely significant definiteness. In other words socialist organization, like any other, requires the appropriate basis. But that basis does not exist in Russia. The old foundations of national life are too narrow, heterogeneous and one-sided, and moreover too shaky, and new ones are as yet only being formed. The objective social conditions of production necessary for socialist organization have not yet matured, and that is why the producers themselves have not yet either the striving or the ability for such organization: our peasantry can yet neither understand nor fulfil this task. Therefore, the "provisional government" will have not to "sanction", but to *carry out* "the economic revolution", granted that it is not swept away by a wave of the popular movement, granted that the producers are obedient enough.

You cannot create by decrees conditions which are alien to the very character of the existing economic relations. The "provisional government" will have to reconcile itself to what exists, to take as the basis of its reforming activity what it is given by present Russian reality. And on that narrow and shaky foundation the edifice of socialist organization will be built by a government which will include: first, town workers, as yet little prepared for such a difficult task; second, representatives of our revolutionary youth, who have always kept aloof from practical life; third, the "officer corps", whose knowledge of economics is certainly subject to doubt. We do not want to make the quite probable supposition that, besides all these elements, liberals will also find their way into the provisional government, and they will not sympathise with, but hinder the social-revolutionary "setting of the party tasks". We suggest that the reader merely weigh up the circumstances we have just enumerated and then ask himself: has an "economic revolution" which begins in such circumstances much chance of success? Is it true that the present "relation of political and economic factors on Russian soil" is favourable to the cause of the socialist revolution? Is not the confidence that this relation is advantageous one of the fictions borrowed from the old anarchist and rebel outlook and carried to impossible extremes in the programme of the new *political* party? Yet it is this fiction that determines the most "immediate tasks" of the party and underlies the desire for the immediate "seizure of power" a striving that terrifies our society and makes the entire activity of our revolutionaries onesided!

Perhaps it will be objected that Narodnaya Volya does not even think of undertaking the socialist organization of society immediately after seizing power, that the "economic revolution" it plans is intended only to educate the people for a future socialist revolution. Let us see whether this supposition is possible, and if so, what conclusions follow from it.

The leading article of No. 8-9 of *Narodnaya Volya* speaks of the economic equality which will be "won" by the people itself, or, if the people lacks initiative, created by the provisional government. We have already said that so-called economic equality is possible only with a socialist organization of production. But let us assume that *Narodnaya Volya* considers it possible under other circumstances too, that economic equality, in its opinion, will be sufficiently guaranteed by the transfer of the land and the instruments of production to the ownership of the working people. Such an opinion would be nothing but a return to the old Narodnik ideals of Zemlya i Volya, and from the economic standpoint it would show the same weaknesses that characterized those ideals. The mutual relations of individual village communes, the conversion of the product of the commune members' labour into commodities and the capitalist accumulation connected with it would threaten to make that "equality" extremely precarious! With the independence of the *mir* "as an economic and administrative unit", with "broad territorial self-government guaranteed by the electivity of all offices", and "the ownership of the land by the people" which the Executive Committee's programme demands, the central government *would not be able* to take steps to consolidate that equality, even if we assume that it would devise measures to abrogate not only the written laws of the Russian Empire, but the laws of commodity production itself. And anyhow, it would be reluctant to take such measures, for it would consist of representatives of the "economically and politically emancipated people" whose ideals would be expressed, at the best, by the words "Land and Freedom" and would leave no room for any organization of national (let alone *international)* production.

Let us suppose that in view of this danger Narodnaya Volya's "provisional government" will not hand over the power it has seized to the representatives of the people but will become a permanent government. Then it will be faced with the following alternative: either it will have to remain an indifferent spectator of the slow decay of the "economic equality" it has established, or it will be obliged to *organize* national production. It will have to fulfil this difficult task either in the spirit of modern socialism, in which it will be hindered by its own unpracticality as well as by the present stage of development of national labour and the workers' own habits; or it will have to seek salvation in the ideals of patriarchal and authoritarian communism", only modifying those ideals so that national production is managed not by the Peruvian "sons of the sun" and their officials but by a socialist caste. But even now the Russian people is too far developed for anybody to flatter himself with the hope that such experiments on it could be successful. Moreover, there is no doubt that under such a guardianship the people, far from being educated for socialism, would even lose all capacity for further progress or would retain that capacity only thanks to the appearance of the very economic inequality which it would be the revolutionary government's immediate aim to abolish. Not to mention the influence of international relations or the impossibility of Peruvian communism even in Eastern Europe in the 19th or the 20th century.

Anyhow, why speak so much of the *results* of the seizure of power by our revolutionaries? Is that seizure itself probable or even possible? In our opinion the probability is very small, so small that the seizure of power may be considered as absolutely impossible. Our "thinking proletariat" has already done much for the emancipation of its motherland. It has shaken absolutism, aroused political interest among society, sown the seed of socialist propaganda among our working class. It is intermediary between the higher classes of society and the lower, having the education of the former and the democratic instincts of the latter. This position has eased for it the diversified work of propaganda and agitation. But this same position gives it very little hope of success in a conspiracy to seize power. For such a conspiracy talent, energy and education are not enough: the conspirators need connections, wealth and an influential position in society. And that is what our revolutionary intelligentsia lacks. It can make good these deficiencies only by allying itself with other dissatisfied elements of Russian society. Let us suppose that its plans actually meet with the sympathy of those elements, that rich landowners, capitalists, officials, staff and senior officers join in the conspiracy. There will then be more probability of the conspiracy being a success, although that probability will still be very small—just remember the outcome of most of the famous conspiracies in history. But the main danger to the *socialist* conspiracy will come not from the existing government, but from the members of the conspiracy itself. The influential and high-placed personages who have joined it may be sincere socialists only by a "fortunate coincidence". But as regards the majority of them, there can be no guarantee that they will not wish to use the power they have seized for purposes having nothing in common with the interests of the working class. And once the conspirators deviate from the socialist aim of the conspiracy it can be considered not only useless but even harmful for the social development of the country; for hatred of absolutism does not warrant sympathy for the successes of the "most modern Seyans", as Stepnyak puts it in his well-known book, who would wish to use the conspiracy in their own interests. Thus, the more sympathy a conspiracy of the socialist intelligentsia to seize power in the immediate future meets among influential spheres, i.e. the greater the probability of its outward success, the more open to doubt its results will be; contrariwise, the more such a conspiracy is confined to our socialist "intelligentsia", i.e. the less the probability of its success, the less doubt there will be about its results, as far as the conspirators' intentions are concerned. Everything leads us to think that at present a Russian socialist conspiracy would be threatened with a failure of the second kind rather than of the first.

Considering all that has been said we think that only one aim of the Russian socialists would not be fantastic now: to achieve free political institutions, on the one hand, and to create elements for the setting up of the future *workers' socialist party* of Russia, on the other. They must put forward the demand for a democratic constitution which shall guarantee the workers the "rights of citizen" as well as the "rights of man" and give them, by universal suffrage, the possibility to take an active part in the political life of the country. Without trying to scare anybody with the yet remote "red spectre", such a political programme would arouse sympathy for our revolutionary party among all those who are not systematic enemies of democracy; it could be subscribed to by very many representatives of our liberalism as well as by the socialists.[37] And whereas the seizure of power by some secret revolutionary organization will always be the work only of that organization and of those who are initiated in its plans, agitation for the programme mentioned would be a matter for the whole of Russian society, in which it would intensify the conscious striving for political emancipation. Then the interests of the liberals would indeed "force" them to "act jointly with the socialists against the government", because they would cease to meet in revolutionary publications the assurance that the overthrow of absolutism would be the signal for a social revolution in Russia. At the same time another less timid and more sober section of liberal society would no longer see revolutionaries as unpractical youths who set themselves unrealizable and fantastic plans. This view, which is disadvantageous for revolutionaries, would give place to the respect of society not only for their heroism but also for their political maturity. This sympathy would gradually grow into active support, or more probably into an independent social movement, and then the hour of absolutism's fall would strike at last. The socialist party would play an extremely honourable and beneficial role in this emancipation movement. Its glorious past, its selflessness and energy would give weight to its demands and it would at least stand chances of thus winning *for the people* the possibility of political development and education, and *for itself* the right to address its propaganda openly to the people and to organize them openly into a separate party.

But that is not enough: Or more exactly, it is unachievable without simultaneous action of another kind and in another sphere. Without might there is no right. Every constitution—according to Lassalle's splendid expression—corresponds or strives to correspond to the *"real, factual relation of forces in the country"*. That is why our socialist intelligentsia must concern itself with changing the factual relations of Russian social forces in favour of the working class even in the pre-constitutional period. Otherwise the fall of absolutism will by no means justify the hopes placed in it by the Russian socialists or even democrats. Even in a constitutional Russia, the demands of the people may be left completely unattended to or satisfied only as far as is necessary to allow them to pay more taxes which they are now almost unable to do as a result of the rapacity of the state economic management. The socialist party itself, having won for the liberal bourgeoisie freedom of speech and action, may find itself in an "exceptional" position similar to that of German Social-Democracy today. In politics, only he may count on the gratitude of his allies of yesterday, now his enemies, who has nothing more serious to count on.

Fortunately, the Russian socialists can base their hopes on a firmer foundation. They can and must place their hopes first and foremost in the working class. The strength of the working class— as of any other class—depends, among other things, on the clarity of its political consciousness, its cohesion and its degree of organization. It is these elements of its strength that must be influenced by our socialist intelligentsia. The latter must become the leader of the working class in the impending emancipation movement, explain to it its political and economic interests and also the interdependence of those interests and must prepare it to play an independent role in the social life of Russia. They must exert all their energy so that in the very opening period of the constitutional life of Russia our working class will be able to come forward as a separate party with a definite social and political programme. The detailed elaboration of that programme must, of course, be left to the workers themselves, but the intelligentsia must elucidate for them its principal points, for instance, a radical review of the present agrarian relations, the taxation system and factory legislation, state help for producers' associations, and so forth. All this can be done only by intensive work among at least the most advanced sections of the working class, by oral and printed propaganda and the organization of workers' socialist study groups. It is true that these tasks have always held a more or less prominent place in the programmes of our socialists, and *Kalendar Narodnoi Voli* can convince us that they were not forgotten even in the heat of the bitterest fight against the government (see "Preparatory Work of the Party" in Section C, *Urban Workers).* But we suggest that everybody who is acquainted with our revolutionary movement should recall and compare how much energy and money was wasted on destructive work and how much was devoted to training elements for the future *workers' socialist party.* We are not accusing anybody, but we think that the distribution of our revolutionary forces was too one-sided. Yet it would be vain for us to try to explain this by the quality of the revolutionary forces themselves or of the elements of the working class which, according to their own programme, they should have influenced. The appearance and success of such publications as *Zerno* and *Rabochaya Gazeta* show that our revolutionaries have not lost their inclination for propaganda, and our working people are not indifferent to it. Of course these publications made mistakes, at times serious ones, but only he who does nothing makes no mistakes. The main trouble is that in their publications one does not see any of the energy with which printed propaganda is conducted among "intellectual" sections of society, that when a print-shop is closed by the police a new one is not opened in its stead, that when it is impossible to publish them in Russia they are not transferred abroad, and so forth. Of all the journals from abroad—and we had a fair number of them—*Rabotnik* alone wrote for the people and that was the great merit of its publishers. But *Rabotnik* has already been closed for a long time and we have heard nothing of new attempts of this kind, with, say, a new programme, better suited to the changed views of the Russian socialists. What has been published here, in Russia, for the workers besides *Zerno* and *Rabochaya Gazeta?* Absolutely nothing. Not a single booklet, not a single pamphlet.[38] And that at a time when the revolutionary movement has centred universal attention upon itself, and the people, grasping avidly at the rumours and opinions, have been wondering anxiously: What do these people want? Can one be astonished, after this, at the absurd answers to this question with which for lack of better ones, they are sometimes satisfied? We repeat: we are not accusing *anybody,* we advise *everybody* to pay attention to this aspect of the matter so as to make up for the omission in time.[39]

Thus, the struggle for political freedom, on the one hand, and the preparation of the working class for its future independent and offensive role, on the other, such, in our opinion, is the only possible "setting of party tasks" at present. To bind together in one two so fundamentally different matters as the overthrow of absolutism and the socialist revolution, to wage revolutionary struggle in the belief that these elements of social development will *coincide* in the history of our country *means to put off the advent of both.* But it depends on us to *bring* these two elements *closer together.* We must follow the splendid example of the German Communists who, as the *Manifesto* says, fight "with the bourgeoisie whenever it acts in a revolutionary way, against the absolute monarchy", and yet "never cease, for a single instant, to instil into the working class the dearest possible recognition of the hostile antagonism between bourgeoisie and proletariat". Acting thus, the Communists wanted "the bourgeois revolution in Germany" to "be but the prelude to an immediately following proletarian revolution".

The present position of bourgeois societies and the influence of international relations on the social development of each civilized country entitle us to hope that the social emancipation of the Russian working class will follow very quickly upon the fall of absolutism. If the German bourgeoisie *"came too late",* the Russian has come still later, and its domination cannot be a long one. Only the Russian revolutionaries should not, in their rum, begin "too late" the preparation of the working class, a matter which has now become of absolute urgency.

Let us make a reservation to avoid misunderstandings. We do not hold the view, which as we have seen was ascribed to Marx's school rather than it existed in reality, and which alleges that the socialist movement cannot obtain support from our peasantry until the peasant has been turned into a landless proletarian and the village commune has disintegrated under the influence of capitalism. We think that on the whole the Russian peasantry would show great sympathy for any measure aiming at the so-called "nationalization of the land". Given the possibility of any at all free agitation among the peasants,"[40] they would also sympathize with the socialists, who naturally would not be slow in introducing into their programme the demand for a measure of that kind. But we do not exaggerate the strength of our socialists or ignore the obstacles, the opposition which they will inevitably encounter from that quarter in their work. For that reason, and *for that reason only,* we think that for the beginning they should concentrate their main attention on the industrial centres. The rural population of today, living in backward social conditions is not only less capable of conscious political *initiative* than the industrial workers, it is also less *responsive* to the movement which our revolutionary intelligentsia has begun. It has greater difficulty in mastering the socialist teachings, because its living conditions are too much unlike the conditions which gave birth to those teachings. And besides, the peasantry is now going through a difficult, critical period. The previous "ancestral foundations" of its economy are crumbling, "the ill-lated village commune itself is being discredited in its eyes", as is admitted even by such "ancestral" organs of Narodism as *Nedelya* (see No. 39, the article by Mr N.Z. *"In Our Native Parts");* and the new forms of labour and life are only in the process of formation, and this creative process is more intensive in the industrial centres. Like water which washes away the soil in one place and forms new sediments and deposits in others, the process of Russian social development is creating new social formations by destroying the age-old forms of the peasants' relation to the land and to one another. These new social formations contain the embryo of a new social movement which alone can end the exploitation of Russia's working population. The industrial workers, who are more developed and have higher requirements and a broader outlook than the peasantry, will join our revolutionary intelligentsia in its struggle against absolutism, and when they have won political freedom they will organize into a workers' socialist party whose task will be to begin systematic propaganda of socialism among the peasantry. We say *systematic propaganda* because isolated opportunities of propaganda must not be missed even at present. It is hardly necessary to add that our socialists would have to change the distribution of their forces among the people if a strong independent movement made itself felt among the peasantry.

That is the "programme" which life itself suggests to the Russian revolutionary socialist party. Will the party be able to carry out of this programme? Will it be prepared to give up its fantastic plans and notions, which, it must be admitted, have a great appeal to sentiment and imagination? It is as yet difficult to answer that question with certitude. The "Announcement of the Publication of *Vestnik Narodnoi Voli*" speaks of the political tasks of the revolutionary party only in the most general terms. *Vestnik's* editorial board describes those aims as "absolutely definite" and apparently does not consider it necessary to define them again in its announcement. That is why there is ground for fear that it will not consider it necessary either to ask itself whether the "absolutely definite conditions" of present Russian actuality correspond to the "absolutely definite aims" of the Narodnaya Volya party. In that case the new publication will leave unsatisfied the most urgent need of our revolutionary literature, the need for a critical reconsideration of obsolete programmes and traditional methods of action. But we hope that the future will dissipate our fears. We wish to hope that the new publication will take a sober view of our revolutionary party's tasks, on whose fulfilment the party's future depends. Social life will be just as pitiless to the party's present illusions as it was to those of our "rebels" and propagandists. *It is better to follow its directions now than to pay for its stern lessons later by splits and new disappointments.*

Notes

1. See the pamphlet Andrei Ivanovich Zhelyabov, p. 10.
2. See *Entwicklung des Sozialismus,* S. 18.

3. Note to the 1905 edition. Now Marxism has definitely triumphed in France; its basic propositions are acknowledged, in a more or less distorted form, even by "opportunists" of Jaures' camp.
4. See Confessions d'un te'volutionnaire. Preface, p. 4. 12
5. To what extent Aristotle was "a sceptic in matters of state" is obvious from the first chapter of the first volume of his *Politics,* in which he says that "the state is the most accomplished form of community", that its purpose is "the supreme good", and that it is therefore a phenomenon "natural in the highest sense of the word, and man is an animal predestined by his very nature to the state form of community". (Book I, Chap. 1, # I-XI of the German Sussemil edition of 1879.) The author of *Politics* is just as much a "sceptic" in questions of state as Proudhon in questions of commodity production; the former could not imagine any other, higher form of community, the latter did not suspect that products could be distributed among the members of society without taking the form of commodities.
6. See *Das Kapital,* 2. Auflage, S. 607-08.
7. Let us simply remind our reader of the objection made to Proudhon by Rittinghausen. "Power, government and all its forms," said the tireless propagandist of the theory of direct popular legislation, "are only *varieties of the species that is called: interference by society in people's relations with things and, consequently, with one another....* I call on M. Proudhon to throw into my face, as the result of his intellectual labour, the following conclusion: 'No, there must be no such interference by society in people's relations with things and, consequently, with one another!'" See *Legislation directe par le peuple et ses adversaires,* pp. 194-95. Rittinghausen thought that "to pose the question in this way means to solve it", for "M. Proudhon himself admits the *necessity for such interference".* But he did not foresee that the pupils would go much further than the teacher and that the theory of anarchy would degenerate, finally, into a theory of "social amorphism". The anarchists of today recognize no interference by society in the relations of individuals, as they have repeatedly stated in certain of their publications.
8. See M.A. Bakunin's extremely interesting and typical pamphlet *Science and the Vital Cause of the Revolution.*
9. See "Offener Brief an Herm Fr. Engels".
10. To be persuaded of this one needs but to compare the "Letter to Friedrich Engels" just referred to with Bakunin's pamphlet quoted above.

11. That is whether they appear as commodities or are directly consumed by the producer's family, his master, and finally, the state, without ever reaching the market.
12. We request that it be borne in mind that we are talking not of the editorial board of the journal *Vperyod,* but of the supporters of that publication working in Russia.
13. Note to the 1905 edition. Later, Messrs. the "critics of Marx" reproached us, the "orthodox", of revolting against every attempt to develop Marx's views further. The reader sees that I showed no tendency to such a revolt. But it goes without saying that, as a pupil of Marx who understands the great significance of his theory, I had to revolt against every attempt to replace some propositions of Marxism by old, long obsolete bourgeois "dogmas". And 1 fulfilled that obligation to the best of my ability.
14. *See Zur Kritik der politischen Oekon.,* Vorwort. S. IV-VI.
15. See Herrn Eugen Dühring's Umwalz. der Wissensch, S. 6.
16. See Essai sur 1'histoire du Tiers Etat, par. Aug. Thierry, pp. 33-34.
17. The supporters of feudalism understood full well the aims of the burghers and the connection between their political and their economic demands. "Commune is a new and detestable word," said Guibert, abbe de Nogent, "and here is what it means: those who have to pay tithes pay only once a year to their lord the rent they owe him. If they commit some offence, they are quit for the payment of a fine fixed by law, and as for the money levies usually made from serfs, they are entirely exempt from them." Laurent, La fèodalitè et 1'cglise, p. 546.
18. The Statute of Liege established the principle of the inviolability of the home in the following forceful expression: *"The poor man is king in his home. "* Laurent, ibid., p. 548.
19. Von Studnitz, *Nor damerikanische Arbeiterverhaltnisse.* S. 353.
20. We quote this from B. Melon's *Le nouveau parti,* t. I, p. 15.
21. See *Sozialdemokratische Abhandlungen.* von M. Rittinghausen, drittes Heft, "Uber die Nothwendigkeit der direkten Gesetzgebung durch das Volk", S. 3.
22. See the programmes of the German and the North American Workers' parties. The *Manifesto* of the British Democratic Federation also demands "direct voting on all important questions".
23. See Schaffle, Bau und Leben des sozialen Körpers, B.III, S. 91 Und102.
24. See *Das System der erworbenen Rechte,* Leipzig, 1880, erster Theil, Vorrede, S. VII.

25. Note to the 1905 edition. These lines were written 15 years before Bernstein came forward as a "critic" of Marx. Let the reader judge for himself whether the "critic" and his numerous fellow-thinkers are right when they reproach us, the "orthodox" with understanding the revolution of the proletariat as a simple and almost instantaneous "catastrophe".
26. Note to the 1905 edition. This will seem paradoxical, but in actual fact the theory of political non-interference of the working class was formulated by Bakunin *as a conclusion from the materialist explanation of history.* Bakunin, who was an ardent supporter of this explanation, reasoned as follows: if the political system of every given society is based on its economy, then *political* revolution is unnecessary, it will itself be the result of the *economic* revolution. This man, once a pupil of Hegel and who, it seems, should have refined his logic, just could not understand that not only every particular *ready-made* political system is a result of economics, but so is every new political movement which, springing from the given economic relations, serves in turn as a necessary *instrument* for their reconstruction. All the *most serious objections* of the *anarchists* against the *Social-Democrats* are still founded on this *misunderstanding.*
27. Note to the 1905 edition. This concerns the "theory of impoverishment" which caused such a stir at the heyday of *Bernsteinians.* On this subject, see my "Criticism of Our Critics." in Nos. 2 and 3 of *Zarya.*
28. Note to the 1905 edition, i.e. Rodbertus.
29. Note to the 1905 edition.. I again mean Rodbertus.
30. See Deutsch-Französische Jahrbücher, 1. und 2. Lieferung, S. 81-85.
31. What is said here does not apply, however, to the group which published *Narodnoye Dyelo* in Geneva, a group which repeatedly affirmed its negative attitude to the "theory of political non-interference."
32. *See the article "View of the Past and the Present of Russian Socialism", *Kalendar Narodnoi Voli, 1883,* p. 109.
33. Note to the 1905 edition. Subsequently, our "legal" N. Mikhailovsky and Bros., repeated this nonsense in all keys. It must be noted in general that in their disputes with us these gentlemen could think of nothing new in comparison with what was written against us in *illegal* literature. Let anybody who wants to convince himself of this read Tikhomirov's article "What Can We Expect from the Revolution? " in the second issue of *Vestnik Narodnoi Voli* and compare it with the arguments Beltov had to refute much later in his book. "Illegal" thought long ago outstripped "legal" thought in our country.

34. See *Kritische Geschichte der Nationaloekonomie und des Sozialismus,* dritte Auflage, S. 498.
35. "Preparatory Work of the Party", p. 129, note. Plekhanov's italics.
36. See "Letter to Alexander III", *Kalendar Narodnoi Voli,* p. 14.
37. Note to the 1905 edition. The sympathy of "society" is very important for us and we can—or more exactly we had many chances to—win it without changing one iota of our programme. But, of course, it requires tact to make the possibility a reality, and that is what we have not always got. For instance, we sometimes allow ourselves to abuse "capital" about, though, or course, not because of, its "rebellion". Marx would never have made such a gross tactical blunder. He would have considered it worthy of Karl Grun and other "true socialists".
38. Note to the 1905 edition. From this we see that the idea of a popular publication is by no means a novelty in our literature. But this did not prevent it from seeming a dangerous novelty to many comrades *no further back than on the eve of our Second Congress,* when I was almost its only supporter on the staff of *Iskra.* This idea has now been practically realized—with greater or lesser success. Better late than never. But if you could hear, reader, what amazing arguments were brought out against this idea in the not-far-off time just mentioned, you would exclaim, like Faust: Wie weh, wie weh, wie weh!
39. "This year," we read in the Supplement to Listok of N.V. No. 1 (1883, p. 61), "there was a whole series of strikes which, thanks to the workers' lack of organization, were mostly failures!"
40. Note to the 1905 edition, i.e. under a constitution.

10

Socialism and the Churches

Rosa Luxemburg

From the moment when the workers of our country and of Russia began to struggle bravely against the Czarist Government and the capitalist exploiters, we notice more and more often that the priests, in their sermons, come out against the workers who are struggling. It is with extraordinary vigour that the clergy fight against the socialists and try by all means to belittle them in the eyes of the workers. The believers who go to church on Sundays and festivals are compelled, more and more often, to listen to a violent political speech, a real indictment of Socialism, instead of hearing a sermon and obtaining religious consolation there. Instead of comforting the people, who are full of cares and wearied by their hard lives, who go to church with faith in Christianity, the priests fulminate against the workers who are on strike, and against the opponents of the government; further, they exhort them to bear poverty and oppression with humility and patience. They turn the church and the pulpit into a place of political propaganda.

The workers can easily satisfy themselves that the struggle of the clergy against the Social-Democrats is in no way provoked by the latter. The Social-Democrats have placed themselves the objective of drawing together and organizing the workers in the struggle against capital, that is to say, against the exploiters who squeeze them down to the last drop of blood, and in the struggle against the Czarist government, which holds the people to ransom. But never do the Social-Democrats drive the workers to fight against clergy, or try to interfere with religious beliefs; not at all! The Social-Democrats, those of the whole world and of our own country, regard conscience and personal opinions as being sacred. Every man may hold what faith and what opinions seem likely to him to ensure happiness. No one has the right to persecute or to attack the particular religious opinion of others. That is what the socialists think. And it is for that reason, among others, that the socialists rally all the people to fight against the Czarist regime, which is continually violating men's consciences, persecuting Catholics, Russian Catholics[1], Jews, heretics and freethinkers. It is precisely the Social-Democrats who come out most strongly in favour of freedom of conscience. Therefore it would seem as if the clergy ought to lend their to the Social-Democrats who are trying to enlighten the toiling people. If we understand properly the teachings which the socialists bring to the working class, the hatred of clergy towards them becomes still less understandable.

The Social-Democrats propose to put an end to the exploitation of the toiling people by the rich. You would have that the servants of the Church would have been the first to make this task easier for the Social-Democrats. Did Jesus Christ (whose servants the priests are) teach that "it is easier for a camel to pass through the eye of a needle than for a rich man to enter the Kingdom of Heaven?"[2] The Social-Democrats try to bring about in all countries social regimes based on the equality, liberty and fraternity of all the citizens. If the clergy really desire that the principle "Love thy neighbour as thyself" be applied in real life why do they not welcome keenly the propaganda of the Social Democrats? The Social Democrats try, by a desperate struggle, by the education and organization of the people, to draw them out of the downtrodden state in which they now are and to offer a better future to their children. Everyone should admit, that at this point, the clergy should bless the Social-Democrats, for did not he whom they serve, Jesus Christ, say "That you do for the poor you do for me"?[3]

However we see the clergy on the one hand, excommunicating and persecuting the Social-Democrats, and, on the other hand, commanding the workers to suffer in patience, that is, to let themselves patiently be exploited by the capitalists. The clergy storm against the Social Democrats, exhort the workers not to "revolt" against the overlords, but to submit obediently to the oppression of this government which kills defenceless people, which sends to the monstrous butchery of the war millions of workers, which persecutes Catholics, Russian Catholics and "Old Believers"[4]. Thus, the clergy, which makes itself the spokesman of the rich, the defender of exploitation and oppression, places itself in flagrant contradiction to the Christian doctrine. The bishops and the priests are not the propagators of Christian teaching, but the worshippers of the Golden Calf[5] and of the Knout which whips the poor and defenceless.

Again, everyone knows how the priests themselves make profit from the worker, extract money out of him on the occasion of marriage, baptism or burial. How often has it happened that the priest, called to the bedside of a sick man to administer the last sacraments, refused to go there before he had been paid his "fee"? The worker goes away in despair, to sell or pawn his last possession, so as to be able to give religious consolation to his kindred.

It is true that we do meet churchmen of another kind. There exist some who are full of goodness and pity and who do not seek gain; these are always ready to help the poor. But we must admit these are indeed uncommon and that they can be regarded in the same way as white blackbirds. The majority of priests, with beaming faces, bow and scrape to the rich and powerful, silently pardoning them for every depravity, every iniquity. With the workers the clergy behave quite otherwise: they think only of squeezing them pity; in harsh sermons they condemn the "covetess" of the workers when these latter do no more than defend themselves against the wrongs of capitalism. The glaring contradiction between the actions of the clergy and teachings of Christianity must make everyone reflect.

The workers wonder how it comes about that the working class in its struggle for emancipation, finds in the servants of the Church, enemies and not allies. How does it happen that the Church plays the role of a defence of wealth and bloody oppression, instead of being the refuge of the exploited? In order to understand this strange phenomenon, it is sufficicent to glance over the history of the Church and to examine the evolution through which it has passed in the course of the centuries.

The Social-Democrats want to bring about the state of "communism"; that is chiefly what the clergy have against them. First of all, it is striking to notice that the priests of today who fight against "Communism" condemn in reality first Christian Apostles. For these latter were nothing else than ardent communists.

The Christian religion developed, as is well known, in ancient Rome, in the period of the decline of the Empire, which was formerly rich and powerful, comprising the countries which today are Italy and Spain, part of France, part of Turkey, Palestine and other territories. The state of Rome at the time of the birth of Jesus Christ much resembled that of Czarist Russia. On one side there lived a handful of rich people in idleness, enjoying luxury and every pleasure; on the other side was an enormous mass of people rotting in poverty; above all, a despotic government, resting on violence and corruption, exerted a vile oppression. The whole Roman Empire was plunged into complete disorder, ringed round by threatening external foes; the unbridled soldiery in power practised its cruelties on the wretched populace; the countryside was deserted, the land lay waste; the cities, and especially Rome, the capital, were filled with the poverty-stricken who raised their eyes, full of hate, to the palaces of the rich; the people were without bread, without shelter, without clothing, without hope, and without the possibility of emerging from their poverty.

There is only one difference between Rome in her decadence and the Empire of the Czars; Rome knew nothing of capitalism; heavy industry did not exist there. At that time slavery was the accepted order of things in Rome. Noble families, the rich, the financiers, satisfied all their needs by putting to work the slaves with which war had supplied them. In the course of time these rich people had laid hands on nearly all the provinces of Italy by stripping the Roman peasantry of their land. As they appropriated cereals in all the conquered provinces as tribute without cost, they profited thereby to lay out on their own estates, magnificent plantations, vineyards, pastures, orchards, and rich gardens, cultivated by armies of slaves working under the whip of the overseer. The people of the countryside, robbed of land and bread, flowed from all the provinces into the capital. But there they were in no better a position to earn a livelihood, for all the trades were carried on by slaves. Thus there was formed in Rome a numerous army of those who possessed nothing—*the proletariat*[6]—having not even the possibility of selling their labour power. This proletariat, coming from the countryside, could not, therefore, be absorbed by industrial enterprises as is the case today; they became victims of hopeless poverty and were reduced to beggary. This numerous popular mass, starving without work, crowding the suburbs and open spaces and streets of Rome, conuted a permanent danger to the government and the possessing classes. Therefore, the government found itself compelled in its own interest to relieve the poverty. From time to time it distributed to the proletariat corn and other foodstuffs stored in the warehouses of the State. Further, to make the people forget their hardships it offered them free circus shows. Unlike the proletariat of our time, which maintains the whole of society by its labours, the enormous proletariat of Rome existed on charity.

It was the wretched slaves, treated like beasts, who worked for Roman society. In this chaos of poverty and degradation, the handful of Roman magnates spent their time in orgies and debauchery. There was no way out of these monstrous social conditions. The proletariat grumbled, and threatened from time to time to rise in revolt, but a class of beggars, living on crumbs thrown from the table of the lords, could not establish a new social order. Further, the slaves who maintained by their labour the whole of society were too downtrodden, too dispersed, too crushed under the yoke, treated as beasts and lived too isolated from the other classes to be able to transform society. They often revolted against their masters, tried to liberate themselves by bloody battles, every time the Roman army crushed these revolts, massacring the slaves in thousands and putting them to death on the cross.

In this crumbling society, where there existed no way out of their tragic situation for the people, no hope of a better life, the wretched turned to Heaven to seek salvation there. The Christian religion appeared to these unhappy beings as a life-belt, a consolation and an encouragement, and became, right from the beginning, the religion of the Roman proletarians. In conformity with the material position of the men belonging to this class, the first Christians put forward the demand for property in common—communism. What could be more natural? The people lacked means of subsistence and were dying of poverty. A religion which defended the people demanded that the rich should share with the poor the riches which ought to belong to all and not to a handful of privileged people; a religion which preached the equality of all men would have great success. However, this had nothing in common with the demand which the Social-Democrats put forward today with a view to making into common property the instruments of work, the means of production, in order that all humanity may work and live in harmonious unity.

We have been able to observe that the Roman proletarians did not live by working, but from the alms which the government doled out. So the demand of the Christians for collective property did not relate to the means of production, but the means of consumption. They did not demand that the land, the workshops and the instruments of work should become collective property, but only that everything should be divided up among them, houses, clothing, food and finished products most necessary to life. The Christian communists took good care not to enquire into the origin of these riches. The work of production always fell upon the slaves. The Christian people desired only that those who possessed the wealth should embrace the Christian religion and should make their riches common property, in order that all might enjoy these good things in equality and fraternity.

It was indeed in this way that the first Christian communities were organized. A contemporary wrote, "these do not believe in fortunes, but they preach collective property and no one among them possesses more than the others. He who wishes to enter their order is obliged to put his fortune into their common property. That is why there is among them neither poverty nor luxury—all possessing all in common like brothers. They do not live in a city apart, but in each they have houses for themselves. If any strangers belonging to their religion come there, they share their property with them, and they can benefit from it as if it is their own. Those people, even if previously unknown to each other, welcome one another, and their relations are very friendly. When travelling they carry nothing but a weapon for defence against robbers. In each city they have their steward, who distributes clothing and food to the travellers. Trade does not exist among them. However, if one of the members offers to another some object which he needs, he receives some other objects in exchange. But each can demand what he needs even if he can give nothing in exchange."

We read in the "Acts of the Apostles" (4:32, 34, 35) the following description of the first community at Jerusalem: "no one regarded as being his what belonged to him; everything was in common. Those who possessed lands or houses, after having sold them, brought the proceeds and laid them at the feet of the Apostles. And to each was distributed according to his needs."

In 1780, the German historian Vogel wrote nearly the same about the first Christians: "According to the rule, every Christian had the right to the property of all the members of the community; in case of want, he could demand that the richer members should divide their fortune with him according to his needs. Every Christian could make use of the property of his brothers; the Christians who possessed anything had not the right to refuse that their brothers should use it. Thus, the

Christian who had no house could demand from him who had two or three to take him in; the owner kept only his own house to himself. But because of the community of enjoyment of goods, housing accommodation had to be given to him who had none."

Money was placed in a common chest and a member of the society, specially appointed for this purpose, divided the collective fortune among all. But this was not all. Among the early Christians, communism was pressed so far that they took their meals in common (see the "Acts of the Apostles"). Their family life was therefore done away with; all the Christian families in one city lived together, like one single large family.

To finish, let us add that certain priests attack the Social Democrats on the ground that we are for the community of women. Obviously, this is simply a huge lie, arising from the ignorance or the anger of the clergy. The Social-Democrats consider that as a shameful and bestial distortion of marriage. And yet this practice was usual among the first Christians.[7]

Thus the Christians of the First and Second Centuries were fervent supporters of communism. But this communism was based on the consumption of finished products and not on work, and proved itself incapable of reforming society, of putting an end to the inequality between men and throwing down the barrier which separated rich from poor. For, exactly as before, the riches created by labour came back to a restricted group of possessors, because the means of production (especially the land) remained individual property, because the labour—for the whole society—was furnished by the slaves. The people, deprived of means of subsistence, only received only alms, according to the good pleasure of the rich.

While some, a handful (in proportion to the mass of the people), possess exclusively for their own use all the arable lands, forests and pastures, farm animals and farm buildings, all the workshops, tools and materials of production, and others, the immense majority, possess nothing at all that is indispensable in production, there can be no question whatever of equality between men. In such conditions society evidently finds itself divided into two classes, the rich and the poor, those of luxury and poverty. Suppose, for example, that the rich proprietors, influenced by the Christian doctrine, offered to share up between the people all the riches which they possessed in the form of money, cereals, fruit, clothing and animals, what would the result be? Poverty would disappear for several weeks and during this the time the populace would be able to feed and clothe themselves. But the finished products are quickly used up. After a short lapse of time, the people, having consumed the distributed riches, would once again have empty hands. The proprietors of the land and the instruments of production could produce more, thanks to the labour power provided by the slaves, so nothing would be changed. Well, here is why the Social-Democrats consider these things differently from the Christian communists. They say, "We do not want the rich to share with the poor: we do not want either charity or alms; neither being able to prevent the recurrence of inequality between men. It is by no means a sharing out between the rich and the poor which we demand, but the complete suppression of rich and poor". This is possible on the condition that the source of all wealth, the land, in common with all other means of production and instruments of work, shall become the collective property of the working people which will produce for itself, according to the needs of each. The early Christians believed that they could remedy the poverty of the proletariat by means of the riches offered by the possessors. That would be to draw water in a sieve! Christian communism was not only incapable of changing or of improving the economic situation, and it did not last.

At the beginning, when the followers of the new Saviour constituted only a small group in Roman society, the sharing of the common stock, the meals in common and the living under the same roof were practicable. But as the number of Christians spread over the territory of the Empire, this communal life of its adherents became more difficult. Soon there disappeared the custom of common meals and the division of goods took on a different aspect. The Christians no longer lived like one family; each took charge of his own property, and they no longer offered the whole of their goods to the community, but only the superfluity. The gifts of the richer of them to the general body, losing their character of participation in a common life, soon became simple *almsgiving,* since the rich Christians no longer made any use of the common property, and put at the service of the others only a part of what they had, while this part might be greater or smaller according to the good will of the donor. Thus in the very heart of Christian communism appeared the difference between the rich and the poor, a difference analogous to that which reigned in the Roman Empire and against which the early Christians had fought. Soon it was only the poor Christians—and the proletarian ones— who took part in the communal meals; the rich having offered a part of their plenty, held themselves apart. The poor lived from the alms tossed to them by the rich, and society again became what it had been. The Christians had changed nothing.

The Fathers of the Church struggled for a long time, yet, with burning words, against this penetration of social inequality into the Christian community, scourging the rich and exhorting them to return to the communism of the early Apostles.

Saint Basil, in the 4th century after Christ, preached thus against the rich:

> "Wretches, how will you justify yourselves before the Heavenly Judge? You say to me, 'What is our fault, when we keep what belongs to us?' I ask you, 'How did you get that which you called your property? How do the possessors become rich, if not by taking possession of things belong to all? If everyone took only what he strictly needed leaving the rest to others, there would be neither rich nor poor'".

It was St. John Chrysostom, patriarch of Constantinople, (born at Antioch in 347, died in exile in Armenia in 407), who preached most ardently to the Christians the return to the first communism of the Apostles. This celebrated preacher, in his 11th Homily on the "Acts of the Apostles", said:

> "And there was a great charity among them (the Apostles): none was poor among them. None considered as being as

> being his what belonged to him, all their riches were in common ... a great charity was in all of them. This charity consisted in that there were no poor among them, so much did those who had possessions hasten to strip themselves of them. They not divide their fortunes into two parts, giving one and keeping the other back: they gave what they had. So there was no inequality between them; they all lived in great abundance. Everything was done with the greatest reverence. What they gave was not passed from the hand of the giver to that of the recipient; their gifts were without ostentation; they brought their goods to the feet of the apostles who became the controllers and masters of them and who used them from then on as the goods of the community and no longer as the property of individuals. By that means they cut short any attempt to get vain glory. Ah! Why have these traditions been lost? Rich and poor, we should all profit from these pious usages and we should both feel the same pleasure from conforming to them. The rich would not impoverish themselves when laying down their possessions, and the poor would be enriched ... But let us try to give an exact idea of what should be done...

"Now, let us suppose—and neither rich nor poor need be alarmed, for I am just supposing—let us suppose that we sell all that belongs to us to put the proceeds into a common pool. What sums of gold would be piled up! I cannot say exactly how much that would make: but if all among us, without distinction between the sexes were to bring here their treasures, if they were to sell their fields, their properties, their houses—I do not speak of slaves for there were none in the Christian community, and those who were there became free—perhaps, I say if everyone did the same, we would reach hundreds of thousands of pounds of gold, millions, enormous values.

"Well! How many people do you think there are living in this city? How many Christians? Would you agree that there are a hundred thousand? The rest being made up of Jews and Gentiles. How many should we not unite together? Now, if you count up the poor, what do you find? Fifty thousand needy people at the most. What would be needed to feed them each day? I estimate that the expense would not be excessive, if the supply and the eating of the food were organized in common.

"You will say, perhaps, 'But what will become of us when these goods are used up?' So what! Would that ever happen? Would not the grace of God be a thousand times abundant? Would we not be making a heaven on earth?

If formerly this community of goods existed among three to five thousand faithful and had such good results and did away with poverty amidst them, what would not result in such a great multitude as this? And among the pagans themselves who would not hasten to increase the common treasure? Wealth which is owned by a number of people is much more easily and quickly spent; the diffusion of ownership is the cause of poverty. Let us take as an example a household composed of a husband, a wife and ten children, the wife being occupied in weaving wool, the husband in bringing in the wages of his work outside; tell me in which case this family would spend more; if they live together in common, or lived separately. Obviously, if they lived separately. Ten houses, ten tables, ten servants, and ten special allowances would be needed for the children if they were separated. What do you do, indeed if you have many slaves? Is it not true, that, in order to keep expenses down, you feed them at a common table? The division is a cause of impoverishment; concord and the unity of wills is a cause of riches.

In the monasteries, they still live as in the early Church. And who dies of hunger there? Who has not found enough to eat there? Yet the men of our times fear living that way more than they fear falling into the sea! Why have we not tried it? We would fear it less. What a good act that would be! If a few of the faithful, hardly eight thousand dared in the face of a whole world, where they have nothing but enemies, to make a courageous attempt to live in common, without any outside help, how much more could we do it today, now that there are Christians throughout the whole world? Would there remain one single Gentile? Not one. I believe. We would attract them all and win them to us."[8]

These ardent sermons of St. John Chrysostom were in vain. Men no longer tried to establish communism either at Constantinople or anywhere else. At the same time as Christianity expanded and became, at Rome after the 4th century, the dominant religion, the faithful went further and further away from the example of the first Apostles. Even within the Christian community itself, the inequality of goods between the faithful increased.

Again, in the 6th century, Gregory the Great said: "It is by no means enough not to steal the property of others; you are in error if you keep to yourself the wealth which God has created for all. He who does not give to others what he possesses is a murderer, a killer; when he keeps for his own use what would provide for the poor, one can say that he is slaying all those who could have lived from his plenty; when we share with those who are suffering, we do not give what belongs to us, but what belongs to them. This is not an act of pity, but the payment of a debt."

These appeals remained fruitless. But the fault was by no means with the Christians of those days, who were indeed, more responsive to the words of the Fathers of the Church than are the Christians of today. This was not the first time in the history of humanity that economic conditions have shown themselves to be stronger than fine speeches.

The communism, this community of the consumption of goods, which the early Christians proclaimed, could not be brought into existence without the communal labour of the whole population, on the land, as common property, as well as in the communal workshops. At the period of the early Christians, it was impossible to inaugurate communal labour (with communal means of production) because as we have already stated, the labour rested, not upon free men, but upon the slaves, who lived on the edge of society. Christianity did not undertake to abolish the inequality between the labour of different men, nor between their property. And that is why its efforts to suppress the unequal distribution of consumption goods did not work. The voices of the Fathers of the Church proclaiming Communism found no echo: Besides, these voices soon became less and less frequent and finally fell silent altogether. The Fathers of the Church ceased to preach the community, and the dividing up of goods, because the growth of the Christian community, produced fundamental changes within the Church itself.

In the beginning, when the number of Christians was small, the clergy did not exist in the proper sense of the word. The faithful, who formed an independent religious community, united together in each city. They elected a member responsible for conducting the service of God and carrying out the religious rites. Every Christian could become the bishop or prelate. These functions were elective, subject to recall, honorary and carried no power other than that which the community gave of its own free will.[9] In proportion as the number of the faithful increased and the communities became more numerous and richer, to run the business of the community and to hold office became an occupation which demanded a great deal of time and full concentration. As the office-bearers could not carry out these tasks at the same time as following their private employment, the custom grew up of electing from among the members of the community, an ecclesiastic who was exclusively entrusted with these functions. Therefore, these employees of the community had to be paid for their exclusive devotion to its affairs. Thus there formed within the Church a new order of employees of the Church, which separated itself from the main body of the faithful, the clergy. Parallel with the inequality between rich and poor, there arose another inequality, that between the clergy and the people. The ecclesiastics, at first elected among equals with a view to performing a temporary function raised themselves to form a caste which ruled over the people.

The more numerous the Christian communities became in the cities of the enormous Roman Empire, the more the Christians, persecuted by the government, felt the need to unite to gain strength. The communities, scattered over all the territory of the Empire, therefore organized themselves into one single Church. This unification was already a unification of the clergy and not of the people. From the 4th century, the ecclesiastics of the communities met together in Councils. The first council took place at Nicaea in 325. In this way there was formed the clergy, an order apart and separated from the people. The bishops of the stronger and richer communities took the lead at the Councils. That is why the Bishop of Rome soon placed himself at the head of the whole of Christianity and became the Pope. Thus an abyss separated the clergy, divided up in the hierarchy, from the people.

At the same time, the economic relations between the people and the clergy underwent a great change. Before the formation of this order, all that the rich members of the Church offered to the common property belonged to the poor people. Afterwards, a great part of the funds was spent on paying the clergy and running the Church. When, in the 4th century, Christianity was protected by the government and was recognized at Rome as being the dominant religion, the persecutions of the Christians ended, and the services were no longer carried on in catacombs, or in modest halls, but in Churches which began to be more and more magnificently built. These expenses thus reduced the funds intended for the poor. Already, in the 5th century, the revenues of the Church were divided into four parts; the first for the bishop, the second for the minor clergy, the third for the upkeep of the Church, and it was only the fourth part which was distributed among the needy. The poor Christian population received therefore a sum equal to what the Bishop received for himself alone.

In course of time the habit was lost of giving to the poor a sum determined in advance. Moreover, as the higher clergy gained in importance, the faithful no longer had contol over the property of the Church. The Bishops gave to the poor according to their good pleasure. The people received alms from their own clergy. But that is not all. At the beginning of Christianity, the faithful made goodwill offerings to the common stock. As soon as the Christian religion became a State religion, the clergy demanded that gifts must be brought by the poor as well as by the rich. From the 6th century, the clergy imposed a special tax, the tithe (tenth part of the crops), which had to be paid to the Church. This tax crushed the people like a heavy burden; in the course of the Middle Ages it became a real scourge to the peasants oppressed by serfdom. The tithe was levied on every piece of land, on every property. But it was always the serf who paid it by his labour. Thus the poor people not only lost the help and support of the Church, but they saw the priests ally themselves with their other exploiters: princes, nobles, moneylenders. In the Middle Ages, while the working people sank into poverty through serfdom, the Church grew richer and richer. Beside the tithe and other taxes, the Church benefited at this period from great donations, legacies made by rich debauchees of both sexes who wished to make up, at the last moment, for their life of sin. They gave and made over to the Church, money, houses, entire villages with their serfs, and often ground-rents or customary labour dues (corvees).

In this way the Church acquired enormous wealth. At the same time, the clergy ceased to be the "administrator" of the wealth which the Church had entrusted it. It openly declared in the 12th century, by formulating a law which it said came from Holy Scripture, that the wealth of the Church belongs not to the faithful but is the individual property of the clergy and of its chief the Pope, above all. Ecclesiastical positions therefore offered the best opportunities to obtain large revenue. Each ecclesiastic disposed of the property of the Church as if it were his own and largely endowed from it his relatives, sons and grandsons. By this means the goods of the Church were pillaged and disappeared into the hands of the families of the clergy. For that reason, the Popes declared themselves to be the sovereign proprietors of the fortunes of the Church and ordained the celibacy of the clergy, in order to keep it intact and to prevent their patrimony from being dispersed. Celibacy was decreed in the 11th century, but it was not put into practice until the 13th century, in view of the opposition of the clergy. Further to prevent the dispersal of the Church's wealth, in 1297 Pope Boniface VIII forbade ecclesiastics to make a present of their incomes to laymen, without permission of the Pope. Thus the Church accumulated enormous wealth, especially in arable lands, and the clergy of all Christian countries became the most important landed proprietor. It often possessed a third, or more than a third of all the lands of the country!

The peasant people paid not only the labour dues (corvee) but the tithe as well and that not only on the lands of the princes and the nobles but on enormous tracts where they worked directly for the bishops, archbishops, parsons and convents. Among all the mighty lords of feudal times the Church appeared as the greatest exploiter of all. In France for example at the end of the 18th century before the Great Revolution the clergy possessed the fifth part of all the territory of the country with an annual income of about 100 million francs. The tithes paid by the proprietors amounted to 23 million. This sum went to fatten 2,800 prelates and bishops, 5,600 superiors and priors, 60,000 parsons and curates, and 24,000 monks and 26,000 nuns who filled the cloisters.

This army of priests was freed from taxation and from the requirement to perform military service. In times of "calamity"—war, bad harvest, epidemics—the Church paid to the State Treasury a "voluntary" tax which never exceeded 16 million francs.

The clergy, thus privileged, formed, with the nobility, a class living on the blood and sweat of the serfs. The high posts in the Church, and those which paid best, were distributed only to the nobles and remained within the hands of the nobility. Consequently, in the period of serfdom, the clergy was the faithful ally of the nobility, giving it support and helping it to oppress the people, to whom it offered nothing but sermons, according to which they should remain humble and resign themselves to their lot. When the country and town proletariat rose up against oppression and serfdom, it found in the clergy a ferocious opponent. It is also true even within the Church itself there existed two classes: the higher clergy who engulfed all the wealth and the great mass of the country parsons whose modest livings brought in no more than 500 francs to 2,000 francs a year. Therefore this unprivileged class revolted against the superior clergy and in 1789, during the Great Revolution, it joined up with the people to fight against the power of the lay and ecclesiastical nobility.

Thus were the relations between the Church and the people modified with the passage of time. Christianity began as a message of consolation to the disinherited and the wretched. It brought a doctrine which combated social inequality and the antagonism between rich and poor; it taught the community of riches. Soon this temple of equality and fraternity became a new source of social antagonisms. Having given up the struggle against individual property which was formerly carried on by the early Apostles, the clergy itself gathered riches together, it allied itself with the possessing classes who lived by exploiting the labour of the toiling class. In feudal times the Church belonged to the nobility, the ruling class, and fiercely defended the power of the latter against revolution. At the end of the 18th century and the beginning of the 19th century, the people of Central Europe swept away serfdom and the privileges of the nobility. At that time, the Church allied itself afresh with the dominant classes—with the industrial and commercial bourgeoisie. Today, the situation has changed and the clergy no longer possess great estates, but they own capital which they try to make productive by the exploitation of the people through commerce and industry, as do the capitalists.

The Catholic Church in Austria possessed, according to its own statistics, a capital of more than 813 million crowns,[10] of which 300 million were in arable lands and in property, 387 million of debentures, and, further, it lent at interest the sum of 70 million to factory owners and businessmen. And that is how the Church, adapting itself to modern times, changed itself into an industrial and commercial capitalist from being a feudal overlord. As formerly, it continues to collaborate with the class which enriches itself at the expense of the rural proletariat.

This change is even more striking in the organization of convents. In certain countries, such as Germany and Russia, the Catholic cloisters have been suppressed for a long time. But where they still exist, in France, Italy and Spain, all evidence points how enormous is the part played by the Church in the capitalist regime.

In the Middle Ages the convents were the refuge of the people. It was there that they sought shelter from the severity of lords and princes; it was there that they found food and protection in case of extreme poverty. The cloisters did not refuse bread and nourishment to the hungry. Let us not forget, especially, that the Middle Ages knew nothing of the commerce such as is usual in our days. Every farm, every convent produced in abundance for itself, thanks to the labour of the serfs and the craftsmen. Often the provisions in reserve found no outlet. When they had produced more corn, more vegetables, more wood than was needed for the consumption of the monks, the excess had no value. There was no buyer for it and not all products could be preserved. In these conditions, the convents freely looked after their poor, in any case offering them only a small part of what has been extracted from their serfs. (This was the usual custom in this period and nearly every farm belonging to the nobility acted similarly.) In fact the cloisters profited considerably from this benevolence; having the reputation of opening their doors to the poor, they received large gifts and legacies from the rich and powerful. With the appearance of capitalism and production for exchange, every object acquired a price and became exchangeable. At this moment the convents, the houses of the lords, and the ecclesiastics ceased their benefactions. The people found no refuge anywhere. Here is one reason, among others, why at the beginning of capitalism, in the 18th century, when the workers were not yet organised to defend their interests, there appeared poverty so appalling that humanity seemed to have gone back to the days of the decades of the Roman Empire. But while the Catholic Church in former times undertook to bring help to the Roman proletariat by the preaching of communism, equality and fraternity, in the capitalist period it acted in a wholly different fashion. It sought above all to profit from the poverty of the people; to put cheap labour to work. The convents became literally hells of capitalist exploitation, all the worse because they took in the labour of women and children. The law case against the Convent of the Good Shepherd in France in 1903 gave a resounding example of these abuses. Little girls, 12, 10 and 9 years old were compelled to work in abominable conditions, without rest, ruining their eyes and their health, and were badly nourished and subjected to prison discipline.

At present the convents are almost entirely suppressed in France and the Church loses the opportunity of direct capitalist exploitation. The tithe, the scourge of the serfs, has likewise long since been abolished. This does not stop the clergy from extorting money from the working class by other methods and particularly through masses, marriages, burials and baptisms. And the governments which support the clergy compel the people to pay their tribute. Further, in all countries, except the USA and Switzerland, where religion is a personal matter, the Church draws from the State enormous sums which obviously come from the hard labour of the people. For instance, in France the expenditure of the clergy amounts to 40 million francs a year.[11]

To sum up, it is the labour of millions of exploited people, which assures the existence of the Church, the government, and the capitalist class. The statistics concerning the revenue of the Church in Austria give an idea of the considerable wealth of the Church, which was formerly the refuge of the poor. Five years ago (that is, in 1900) its annual revenues amounted to 60 million crowns, and its expenditure did not exceed 35 million. Thus, in the course of a single year, it "put aside" 25 million—at the cost of the sweat and blood shed by the workers. Here are a few details about that sum:

The Archbishopric of Vienna, with an annual revenue of 300,000 crowns and the expenses of which were not more than half of that sum, made 150,000 crowns of "savings" a year; the fixed capital of the Archbishopric amounts to about 7 million crowns. The Archbishopric of Prague enjoys an income of over half a million and has about 300,000 in expenses; its capital reaches nearly 11 million crowns. The Archbishopric of Olomouc (Olmutz) has over half a million in revenue and about 400,000 in expenses; its fortune exceeds 14 million. The subordinate clergy which so often pleads poverty exploits the population no less. The annual incomes of the parish priests of Austria reach more than 35 million crowns, the expenses 21 million only, with the result that the "savings" of the parsons yearly reach 14 million. The parish properties make up over 450 million. Finally, the convents of five years ago possessed, with all expenses deducted, a "net revenue" of 5 million a year. These riches grew every year, while the poverty of the toilers exploited by capitalism and by the state grew from year to year. In our country and everywhere else, the state of things is exactly as in Austria.

After having briefly reviewed the history of the Church, we cannot be surprised that the clergy supports the Czarist government and the capitalists against the revolutionary workers who fight for a better future. The class-conscious workers organized in the Social-Democratic Party, fight to bring into reality the idea of social equality and of fraternity among men, the object which was formerly that of the Christian Church.

Nonetheless, equality cannot be realised either in a society based on slavery nor in a society based on serfdom; it becomes capable of being realised in our present period, that is, the regime of industrial capitalism. What the Christian Apostles could not accomplish by their ardent discourses against the egoism of the rich, the modern proletarians, workers conscious of their class-position, can start working in the near future, by the conquest of political power in all countries by tearing the factories, the land, and all the means of production from the capitalists to make them the communal property of the workers. The communism which the Social-Democrats have in view does not consist of the dividing up, between beggars and rich and lazy, of the wealth produced by slaves and serfs, but in honest, common, united work and the honest enjoyment of the common fruits of that work. Socialism does not consist of generous gifts made by the rich to the poor, but in the total abolition of the very difference between rich and poor, by compelling all alike to work according to their capacity by the suppression of the exploitation of man by man.

For the purpose of establishing the Socialist order, the workers organize themselves in the workers' Social-Democratic Party which pursues this aim. And that is why the Social-Democracy and the workers' movement meets with the ferocious hatred of the possessing classes which live at the expense of the workers.

The enormous riches piled up by the Church without any effort on its part, come from the exploitation and the poverty of the labouring people. The wealth of the archbishops and bishops, the convents and the parishes, the wealth of the factory-owners and the traders and the landed proprietors are bought at the price of the inhuman exertions of the workers of town and country. For what can be the only origin of the gifts and legacies which the very rich lords make to the Church? Obviously not the labour of their hands and the sweat of their brows, but the exploitation of the workers who toil for them; serfs yesterday and wage-workers today. Further, the allowance which the governments today make to the clergy come from the State Treasury, made up in the greater part from the taxes wrung from the popular masses. The clergy, no less than the capitalist class, lives on the backs of the people, profits from the degradation, the ignorance and the oppression of the people. The clergy and the parasitic capitalists hate the organized working-class, conscious of its rights, which fights for the conquest of its liberties. For the abolition of capitalist mix-rule and the establishment of equality between men would strike a mortal blow especially at the clergy which exists only thanks to exploitation and poverty. But above all, Socialism aims at assuring to humanity an honest and solid happiness here below, to give to the people the greatest possible education and the first place in society. It is precisely this happiness here on earth which the servants of the Church fear like the plague.

The capitalists have shaped with hammer blows the bodies of the people in chains of poverty and slavery. Parallel to this the clergy, helping the capitalists and serving their own needs enchain the mind of the people, hold it down in crass ignorance, for they well understand that education would put an end to their power. Well, the clergy falsifying the early teaching of Christianity, which had as its object the earthly happiness of the lowly, tries today to persuade the toilers that the suffering and the degradation which they endure come not from a defective social structure, but from heaven, from the will of "Providence". Thus the Church kills in the workers the strength, the hope, and the will for a better future, kills their faith in themselves and their self-respect. The priests of today, with their false and poisonous teachings, continually maintain the ignorance and degradation of the people. Here are some irrefutable proofs.

In the countries where the Catholic clergy enjoys great power over the minds of the people, in Spain and in Italy for instance, the people are held down in complete ignorance. Drunkenness and crime flourish there. For example, let us compare two provinces of Germany, Bavaria and Saxony. Bavaria is an agricultural state where the population is preponderantly under the influence of the Catholic clergy. Saxony is an industrialised state where the Social-Democrats play a large part in the life of the workers. They win the Parliamentary elections in nearly all the constituencies, a reason why the bourgeoisie shows its hatred for this "Red" Social-Democrat Province. And what do we see? The official statistics show that the number of crimes committed in ultra-Catholic Bavaria is relatively much higher than that in "Red Saxony". We see that in 1898, out of every 100,000 inhabitants there were:

	Bavaria	Saxony
Robbery with Violence	204	185
Assault and Battery	296	72
Perjury	4	1

A wholly similar situation is found when we compare the record of crime in priest-dominated Possen with that in Berlin, where the influence of Social-Democracy is greater. In the course of the year, we see for every 100,000 inhabitants in Possen, 232 cases of assault and battery, and in Berlin 172 only.

In the Papal City, in Rome during one single month of the year 1869 (the last year but one of the temporal power of the Popes), there were condemned: 279 for murder, 728 for assault and battery, 297 for robbery and 21 for arson. These are the results of clerical domination over the poverty-stricken people.

This does not mean to say that the clergy directly incite people to crime. Quite the contrary, in their sermons the priests often condemn theft, robbery, and drunkenness. But men do not steal, rob, or get drunk at all because they like to do so or insist upon it. It is poverty and ignorance that are the causes of it. Therefore, he who keeps alive the ignorance and poverty of the people, he who kills their will and energy to act out of this situation, he who puts all sorts of obstacles in the way of those who try to educate the proletariat, he is responsible for these crimes just as if he were an accomplice.

The situation in the mining areas of Catholic Belgium was similar until recently. The Social-Democrats went there. Their vigorous appeal to the unhappy and degraded workers sounded through the country: "Worker, lift yourself up! Do not rob, do not get drunk, do not lower your head in despair! Read, teach yourself! Join up with your class brothers in the organization, fight against the exploiters who maltreat you! You will emerge from poverty, you will become a man!"

Thus the Social-Democrats everywhere lift up the people and strengthen those who lose hope, rally the weak into a powerful organization. They open the eyes of the ignorant and show them the way of equality, of liberty and of love for our neighbours.

On the other hand, the servants of the Church bring to the people only words of humiliation and discouragement. And, if Christ were to appear on earth today, he would surely attack the priests, the bishops and archbishops who defend the rich and live by exploiting the unfortunate, as formerly he attacked the merchants whom he drove from the temple so that their ignoble presence should not defile the House of God.

That is why there has broken out a desperate struggle between the clergy, the supporters of oppression and the

Social-Democrats, the spokesmen of liberation. Is this fight not to be compared with that of the dark night and the rising sun? Because the priests are not capable of combating socialism by means of intelligence or truth, they have recourse to violence and wickedness. Their Judas-talk calumniates those who rouse class-consciousness. By means of lies and slander, they try to besmirch all those who give up their lives for the workers' cause. These servants and worshippers of the Golden Calf support and applaud the crimes of the Czarist Government and defend the throne of this latest despot who oppresses the people like Nero.

But it is in vain that you put yourselves about, you degenerate servants of Christianity who have become the servants of Nero. It is in vain that you help our murderers and our killers, in vain that you protect the exploiters of the proletariat under the sign of the cross. Your cruelties and your calumnies in former times could not prevent the victory of the Christian idea, the idea which you have sacrificed to the Golden Calf; today your efforts will raise no obstacle to the coming of Socialism. Today it is you, in your lies and your teachings, who are pagans, and it is we who bring to the poor, to the exploited the tidings of fraternity and equality. It is we who are marching to the conquest of the world as he did formerly who proclaimed that it is easier for a camel to pass through the eye of a needle than for a rich man to enter the kingdom of heaven.

A few final words.

The clergy has at its disposal two means to fight Social Democracy. Where the working class movement is beginning to win recognition, as is the case in our country (Poland), where the possessing classes still hope to crush it, the clergy tights the socialists by threatening sermons, slandering them and condemning the "covetousness" of the workers. But in the countries where political liberties are established and the workers' party is powerful, as for example in Germany, France and Holland, there the clergy seeks other means. It hides its real purpose and does not face the workers any more as an open enemy, but as a false friend. Thus you will see the priests organizing the workers and launching "Christian" Trade Unions. In this way they try to catch the fish in their net, to attract the workers into the trap of these false trade unions, where they teach humility, unlike the organizations of the Social-Democracy which have in view struggle and defence against mal-treatment.

When the Czarist Government finally falls under the blows of the revolutionary proletariat of Poland and Russia, and when political liberty exists in our country, then we shall see the same Archbishop Popiel and the same ecclesiastics who today thunder against the militants, suddenly beginning to organize the workers into "Christian" and "National" associations in order to mislead them. Already we are at the beginning of this underground activity of the "National Democracy" which assures the future collaboration with the priests and today helps them to slander the Social-Democrats.

The workers must, therefore, be warned of the danger so that they will not let themselves be taken in, on the morrow of the victory of the revolution, by the honeyed words of those who today from the heights of the pulpit, dare to defend the Czarist Government, which kills the workers, and the repressive apparatus of capital, which is the principal cause of the poverty of the proletariat.

In order to defend themselves against the antagonism of the clergy at the present time, during the revolution, and against their false friendship tomorrow, after the revolution, it is necessary for the workers to organize themselves in the Social-Democratic Party.

And here is the answer to all the attacks of the clergy: the Social-Democracy in no way fights against religious beliefs. On the contrary, it demands complete freedom of conscience for every individual and the widest possible toleration for every faith and every opinion. But, from the moment when the priests use the pulpit as a means of political struggle against the working classes, the workers must fight against the enemies of their rights and their liberation. For he who defends the exploiters and who helps to prolong this present regime of misery, he is the mortal enemy of the proletariat, whether he be in a cassock or in the uniform of the police.

First published in pamphlet form by the Polish Social Democratic Party in 1905. A Russian edition appeared in Moscow in 1920. A French edition was issued by the French Socialist Party in 1937. First English Edition published by *Socialist Review*, Birmingham and was translated from the French by Juan Punto. The text here is reproduced from the 1979 Colombo edition.

Notes

1. Orthodox Christians who recognize the supremacy of the Pope.
2. Mark 10:25; Luke 18:25; Matthew 19:25
3. Matthew 25:40
4. Otherwise known as "Raskilniki" (Splitters), a Russian religious sect which regarded as contrary to the true faith the revision of the texts of the Bible and the reform of the liturgy by Patriarch Nikon in 1654.
5. See Exodus 32:1-8
6. "*Proles* is the Latin for children, for offspring. Proletarians, therefore, constituted that class of citizens who owned nothing but the arms of their body and the children of their loins." *Communist Journal*, No. 1, September 1847 (London)

   "The Roman proletariat lived at the expense of society, whereas modern society lives at the expense of the proletariat." Sismondi quoted by Karl Marx in *The Eighteenth Brumaire.*

   See also: Engels: *Principles or Communism* (question 2)
7. But see Tertullian (c. 160-230): "We are brethren in our property, which with you mostly dissolves brotherhood. We therefore, who are united in mind and soul, doubt not about having possessions in common. With us all things are shared promiscuously, except the wives. In that alone do we part fellowship, in which alone others (Greeks and Roman pagans) exercise it" Acts 1:39
8. Abbe Barcille: *Jean Chrycostome*, Paris 1869, Vol. 7, pp. 599-603
9. Assuredly however the local ministries, as they appear in St. Paul's Epistles and the Acts, appear as being under authority (I am inclined to use a vulgarism and say) "with a vengeance". However they were elected, and this was often probably by the nomination

of local prophets, the Apostles, Paul and Barnabas appointed them. In view of the evidence of Acts 6 and the pastoral Epistles, I think, with Harnock, that we cannot reasonably doubt that the appointment was by prayer with the laying-on of hands, and ranked as "Sacramental". And when they were appointed during St. Paul's life, they were certainly controlled from above." Gore: *Dr. Streeter and the Primitive Church*, pp. 12 and 13.

10. In 1900, a crown was worth about the same as a franc or 10d (pence).
11. It must not be forgotten that this was written in 1905. Since then France has shaken off the yoke of the Church, and the State no longer appoints the clergy, except in the departments of Haut-Rhin, Bas-Rhin and Moselle, where Republican France perpetuates, for some unknown reason, the traditions of Imperial Germany and the French Second Empire.

11
Socialism and Religion

V.I. Lenin

Present-day society is wholly based on the exploitation of the vast masses of the working class by a tiny minority of the population, the class of the landowners and that of the capitalists. It is a slave society, since the "free" workers, who all their life work for the capitalists, are "entitled" only to such means of subsistence as are essential for the maintenance of slaves who produce profit, for the safeguarding and perpetuation of capitalist slavery.

The economic oppression of the workers inevitably calls forth and engenders every kind of political oppression and social humiliation, the coarsening and darkening of the spiritual and moral life of the masses. The workers may secure a greater or lesser degree of political liberty to fight for their economic emancipation, but no amount of liberty will rid them of poverty, unemployment, and oppression until the power of capital is overthrown. Religion is one of the forms of spiritual oppression which everywhere weighs down heavily upon the masses of the people, over burdened by their perpetual work for others, by want and isolation. Impotence of the exploited classes in their struggle against the exploiters just as inevitably gives rise to the belief in a better life after death as impotence of the savage in his battle with nature gives rise to belief in gods, devils, miracles, and the like. Those who toil and live in want all their lives are taught by religion to be submissive and patient while here on earth, and to take comfort in the hope of a heavenly reward. But those who live by the labor of others are taught by religion to practice charity while on earth, thus offering them a very cheap way of justifying their entire existence as exploiters and selling them at a moderate price tickets to well-being in heaven. Religion is opium for the people. Religion is a sort of spiritual booze, in which the slaves of capital drown their human image, their demand for a life more or less worthy of man.

But a slave who has become conscious of his slavery and has risen to struggle for his emancipation has already half ceased to be a slave. The modern class-conscious worker, reared by large-scale factory industry and enlightened by urban life, contemptuously casts aside religious prejudices, leaves heaven to the priests and bourgeois bigots, and tries to win a better life for himself here on earth. The proletariat of today takes the side of socialism, which enlists science in the battle against the fog of religion, and frees the workers from their belief in life after death by welding them together to fight in the present for a better life on earth.

Religion must be declared a private affair. In these words socialists usually express their attitude towards religion. But the meaning of these words should be accurately defined to prevent any misunderstanding. We demand that religion be held a private affair so far as the state is concerned. But by no means can we consider religion a private affair so far as our Party is concerned. Religion must be of no concern to the state, and religious societies must have no connection with governmental authority. Everyone must be absolutely free to profess any religion he pleases, or no religion whatever, i.e. to be an atheist, which every socialist is, as a rule. Discrimination among citizens on account of their religious convictions is wholly intolerable. Even the bare mention of a citizen's religion in official documents should unquestionably be eliminated. No subsidies should be granted to the established church nor state allowances made to ecclesiastical and religious societies. These should become absolutely free associations of like minded citizens, associations independent of the state. Only the complete fulfilment of these demands can put an end to the shameful and accursed past when the church lived in feudal dependence on the state, and Russian citizens lived in feudal dependence on the established church, when medieval, inquisitorial laws (to this day remaining in our criminal codes and on our statute-books) were in existence and were applied, persecuting men for their belief or disbelief, violating men's consciences, and linking cosy government jobs and government-derived incomes with the dispenzation of this or that dope by the established church. Complete separation of Church and State is what the socialist proletariat demands of the modern state and the modern church.

The Russian Revolution must put this demand into effect as a necessary component of political freedom. In this respect, the Russian revolution is in a particularly favorable position, since the revolting officialism of the police-ridden feudal autocracy has called forth discontent, unrest and indignation even among the clergy. However abject, however ignorant Russian Orthodox clergymen may have been, even they have now been awakened by the thunder of the downfall of the old, medieval order in Russia. Even they are joining in the demand for freedom, are protesting against bureaucratic practices and officialism, against the spying for the police imposed on the "servants of God". We socialists must lend this movement our support, carrying the demands of honest and sincere members of the clergy to their conclusion, making them stick to their words about freedom, demanding that they should resolutely break all ties between religion and the police. Either you are sincere, in which case you must stand for the complete separation of Church and State and of School and Church, for religion to be declared wholly and absolutely a private affair. Or you do not accept these consistent demands for freedom, in which case you evidently are still held captive by the traditions of the inquisition, in which case you evidently still cling to your cosy government jobs and government-derived incomes, in which case you evidently do not believe in the spiritual power of your weapon and continue to take bribes from the state. And in that case the class-conscious workers of all Russia declare merciless war on you.

So far as the party of the socialist proletariat is concerned, religion is not a private affair. Our Party is an association of class-conscious, advanced fighters for the emancipation of the working class. Such an association cannot and must not be indifferent to lack of class-consciousness, ignorance or obscurantism in the shape of religious beliefs. We demand complete disestablishment of the Church so as to be able to combat the religious fog with purely ideological and solely ideological weapons, by means of our press and by word of mouth. But we founded our association, the Russian Social-Democratic Labour Party, precisely for such a struggle against every religious bamboozling of the workers. And to us the ideological struggle is not a private affair, but the affair of the whole Party, of the whole proletariat.

If that is so, why do we not declare in our Programme that we are atheists'? Why do we not forbid Christians and other believers in God to join our Party?

The answer to this question will serve to explain the very important difference in the way the question of religion is presented by the bourgeois democrats and the Social-Democrats.

Our Programme is based entirely on the scientific, and moreover the materialist, world-outlook. An explanation of our Programme, therefore, necessarily includes an explanation of the true historical and economic roots of the religious fog. Our propaganda necessarily includes the propaganda of atheism; the publication of the appropriate scientific literature, which the autocratic feudal government has hitherto strictly forbidden and persecuted, must now form one of the fields of our Party work. We shall now probably have to follow the advice Engels once gave to the German Socialists: to translate and widely disseminate the literature of the eighteenth-century French Enlighteners and atheists.

But under no circumstances ought we to fall into the error of posing the religious question in an abstract, idealistic fashion, as an "intellectual" question unconnected with the class struggle, as is not infrequently done by the radical-democrats from among the bourgeoisie. It would be stupid to think that, in a society based on the endless oppression and coarsening of the worker masses, religions prejudices could be dispelled by purely propaganda methods. It would be bourgeois narrow-mindedness to forget that the yoke of religion that weighs upon mankind is merely a product and reflection of the economic yoke within society. No number of pamphlets and no amount of preaching can enlighten the proletariat, if it is not enlightened by its own struggle against the dark forces of capitalism.

Unity in this really revolutionary struggle of the oppressed class for the creation of a paradise on earth is more important to us than unity of proletarian opinion on paradise in heaven.

That is the reason why we do not and should not set forth our atheism in our Programme; that is why we do not and should not prohibit proletarians who still retain vestiges of their old prejudices from associating themselves with our Party. We shall always preach the scientific world-outlook, and it is essential for us to combat the inconsistency of various "Christians". But that does not mean in the least that the religious question ought to be advanced to first place, where it does not belong at all; nor does it mean that we should allow the forces of the really revolutionary economic and political struggle to be split up on account of third rate opinions or senseless ideas, rapidly losing all political importance, rapidly being swept out as rubbish by the very course of economic development.

Everywhere the reactionary bourgeoisie has concerned itself, and is now beginning to concern itself in Russia, with the fomenting of religious strife—in order thereby to divert the attention of the masses from the really important and fundamental economic and political problems, now being solved in practice by the all-Russian proletariat uniting in revolutionary struggle. This reactionary policy of splitting up the proletarian forces, which today manifests itself mainly in Black-Hundred pogroms, may tomorrow conceive some more subtle forms. We, at any rate, shall oppose it by calmly, consistently and patiently preaching proletarian solidarity and the scientific world-outlook—a preaching alien to any stirring up of secondary differences.

The revolutionary proletariat will succeed in making religion a really private affair, so far as the state is concerned. And in this political system, cleansed of medieval mildew, the proletariat will wage a broad and open struggle for the elimination of economic slavery, the true source of the religious humbugging of mankind.